D1709648

Life of Fred®

Pre-Algebra 2 with Economics

Life of Fred®

Pre-Algebra 2 with Economics

Stanley F. Schmidt, Ph.D.

Polka Dot Publishing

ISBN: 978-0-9791072-3-8

Library of Congress Catalog Number: 2010926892
Printed and bound in the United States of America

Polka Dot Publishing   Reno, Nevada

To order copies of books in the Life of Fred series,

visit our website PolkaDotPublishing.com

Questions or comments? Email the author at lifeoffred@yahoo.com

Fifth Printing

Life of Fred: Pre-Algebra 2 with Economics was illustrated by the author with additional clip art
furnished under license from Nova Development Corporation, which holds the copyright to that art.

for Goodness' sake

or as J.S. Bach—who was
never noted for his plain
English—often expressed it:

Ad Majorem Dei Gloriam
(to the greater glory of God)

About This Book

THE FONTS OF TYPE

There are three fonts that are used in the book. The text of the book is written in this font. It is called Times New Roman.

When Fred is thinking, I will put his thoughts in this font.

When you, the reader, want to interject your thoughts, **you express yourself in this font.** Yes. You get to talk. You'll start two pages from now.

THE *Your Turn to Play*

At the end of each chapter there is an opportunity to play with the ideas in that chapter. The questions are not the:

☹ 40 questions that are all alike

☹ drill-and-kill and

☹ boring questions

that you find in most math books.

I had fun writing the questions. In the first *Your Turn to Play*: "Let's play with the paint-mixing function. . . ." In a later *Your Turn to Play*, we look at how would you find something to eat if you were the only person on Earth.

In Chapter 26 we talk about opportunity cost. In the *Your Turn to Play*, you are to invent economic reasons involving opportunity costs for why you might turn down an $80/hour job at Terry's Taffy & Taco.

The complete solutions are provided right after the questions—all worked out in detail. <u>Don't just read the questions and look at the</u>

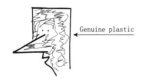

Genuine plastic

<u>answers.</u> You won't learn much if you take that shortcut. Take out a piece of paper and write out your answers before you peek at mine. Put something over my answers if you are tempted to cheat. One reader suggested that I sell plastic Fred Heads to cover the answers.

THE BRIDGES

After every six or seven chapters, you will encounter **The Bridge**.

> Small note to parents: The Life of Fred series is intended to be self-teaching. Learning how to learn by reading is an essential skill.
>
> Your kids are old enough now. If you teach/tutor/help your kids, two things happen:
> ① They love it since they don't have to work so hard.
> ② They will not do as well in college because they won't have the practice of learning by reading.
>
> Your opportunity to be involved is when they take their weekly Bridge exam. It's all explained right after Chapter 7.

After the last chapter in the book is **The Final Bridge**.

Of course, **The Bridges** are not just quizzes like the ones you might find in any other pre-algebra/economics book. You will learn a lot about Joe, Darlene, and her mom. Even if you pass a **Bridge** on the first try, you will probably want to read (or even do!) the other tries.

CALCULATORS?

You've done the arithmetic part of your education. You know your addition and multiplication tables. If you can tell me instantly that seven times eight is equal to fifty-six, then feel free to use your calculator.

TYPOS AND ERRORS

I am human. My proofreaders are also. I've done every problem in this book twice. If you happen to spot an error, it would be a lovely gift to please let me know with an email to: lifeoffred@yahoo.com

SPECIAL OFFER

As a thank you, I'll email you a list of all the corrections that other readers have reported.

ECONOMICS

Economics is only useful if there are other people around.

You will probably use your knowledge of economics much more than balancing chemical equations, computing inertia in physics, or counting your chromosomes in biology.

Economics is much more than shopping (despite the subliminal message on this page). Even life itself is about much more than shopping. (**Horrors! Nobody ever told me that!**)

You are going to learn a lot of important things in these pages:

»→ A sure-fire way to create 100% employment.
   One simple law will do it.
»→ The difference between socialism and communism.
   Most adults can't tell you the difference.
»→ The difference between freedom and liberty.
   The word on our coins is "Liberty"—not "Freedom."
»→ The most surprising fact that *Each person in the world has a job that he or she can do at a comparative advantage to all other people.*
   David Ricardo's Law of Comparative Advantage.
»→ The proof of Ricardo's Law of Comparative Advantage.
   I know of no other economics book that proves this law.

And you'll also learn:

»→ How to do word problems, which is often the hardest part of beginning algebra.
»→ How to solve algebraic equations.
»→ How to run a successful hot dog business.
»→ What a real $100,000 bill looks like.

There is so much. Let's just get started.

Okay. I, your reader, am ready.

Contents

13

Chapter One
Summertime

Bittersweet.

The last day of the spring semester.

Fred had given his last final exam.

He had turned in the grades for his students.

He had picked up his monthly paycheck.

And all of endless summer lay ahead of him.

He walked back to his office in the warm Kansas sunshine thinking about the coming days. He stopped at his office door and took down his spring schedule.

Fred Gauss
—room 314—
Spring Schedule
8–9 Beginning Algebra
9–10 Advanced Algebra
10–11 Geometry
11–noon Trigonometry
noon–1 Calculus
1–2 Statistics
2–3 Linear Algebra
3–3:05 Break
3:05–5 Seminar in Biology, Economics,
    Physics, Set Theory, Topology,
    and Metamathematics.

There was now a nine-hour hole in his day that needed filling. He entered his office and put his grade book on a shelf with the other nine grade books.

Fred thought to himself: Ten semesters of teaching at KITTENS University. They have passed so quickly. Sometimes life seems so evanescent.*

---

* ev-a-NES-ent Like a vapor that grows less and less until it disappears. Although Fred is only five years old, he has read many good books and his large vocabulary reflects his wide reading.

Fred looked out his office window and saw his students heading off in a hundred directions. He sat at his desk and looked at the books on his desktop. He had bookmarks in a dozen books that he was reading. For several years now, he had been working on reading Dante's *Divine Comedy* in Italian (*Divina Commedia*). Besides learning Italian, he had the pleasure of reading poetry in its original language. Poetry often loses a lot in translation.

He loved reading history. On his desk was *Caesar's Gallic War* which begins with the famous words: *Omnis Gallia est divisa in tres partes.**

Fred enjoyed biographies, science, math (of course), the sermons of Peter Marshall, books on the history of art, and all of the great literature of Western civilization listed in Clifton Fadiman's *The Lifetime Reading Plan* (third edition).

Today Fred turned to Christina Rossetti's poetry.** He opened the book at random and began to read "A Daughter of Eve":

> *A fool I was to sleep at noon . . .*
> *Oh it was summer when I slept,*
> *It's winter now I waken. . . .*
> *No more to laugh, no more to sing,*
> *I sit alone with sorrow.*

Fred became a little teary-eyed. He shut the book. He could hear the hum of the vending machines in the hallway. He didn't know what to do with himself.

At least Fred thought to himself I don't have to worry about money. He took his paycheck out of his pocket and looked at it. For his nine hours of teaching each day, KITTENS University paid him $500 per month.

The KITTENS pay schedule is very simple. It is a function of how old you are. When Fred was three years old, they paid him $300 per

---

* "All Gaul is divided into three parts." Even though it wasn't poetry, Fred was reading it in the original Latin.

** She is often considered the most important woman poet in England before the twentieth century.

month. When he was four, his salary was $400 per month. Now that he was five, he was making $500 per month.

He pictured writing on a blackboard:

Let x = my age.
Then 100x = my monthly salary.
My salary is a function of my age.
You tell me my age, and I'll tell you my salary.

Then Fred realized that he wasn't teaching right now. He was alone in his office. The semester was over.

Intermission

The whole idea of **function** is wrapped up in the last sentence Fred wrote on his mental blackboard: *You tell me this, and I'll tell you that.*

★ If you tell me where you live, I can tell you your ZIP code.
★ If you tell me how old you are, I can tell you whether you are older than Fred.
★ If you tell me what paint colors you mixed together, I can tell you your final color.

Your Turn to Play

1. Let's play with the paint-mixing function.

    If you tell me red + blue, I will say purple.

    This could be written as red + blue → purple.

Now it's your turn.

        blue + yellow → ?

        black + white → ?

        red + white → ?

2. Do functions always involve numbers? Give a reason for your answer.

3. In an office down the hall from Fred's is a man that KITTENS hired this semester to teach about the music of ancient Greece. His specialty is the popular tunes of that period. His paycheck is $6,700. How old is he?

4. Eight percent of our music teacher's $6,700 salary is taken out for Social Security. How much is that deduction?

5. Every Monday when walks down the hall, he is singing Plato's Waltz. Every Tuesday, he sings Aristotle's Tango. Every Wednesday, he sings Pythagorus's Melody in Blue, etc.

If you tell me the day of the week, I can tell you what is singing.

      The **domain** of this function is the days of the week.

      The **codomain** is the set of all ancient Greek songs.

What is the domain of the function that Fred wrote on his mental blackboard (on the top of the previous page)?

6. Each month spends $134 of his salary on Greek sheet music. What percent of his salary is that? ($134 is what percent of $6,700?)

. . . . COMPLETE SOLUTIONS . . . .

1.   blue + yellow → green

                black + white → gray

                red + white → pink

2. In the previous question, we looked at a function involving paint colors. There were no numbers mentioned. Functions do not have to involve numbers.

3. We know that at KITTENS University if x = your age, then 100x = your monthly salary. Since he receives $6,700, he must be 67 years old.

4. 8% of 6,700 = ?   8% → 8.% → 0.08

We know both sides of the *of*, so we multiply.

$0.08 \times 6,700 = \$536$.

5. In the KITTENS salary function, you tell me the age of the teacher, and I will tell you his monthly salary. The domain is the set of all possible ages of teachers.

6. 134 = ?% of 6,700. We don't know both sides of the *of* so we divide the number closest to the *of* into the other number.

$$\frac{0.02}{6700 \overline{)134.00}} = 2\%$$

Chapter Two
Getting Paid in Nickels

Fred kept thinking about the line from Rossetti's poem, *Oh it was summer when I slept.* He hopped off his chair[*] and headed out the door, down the hallway past the vending machines, down two flights of stairs, and out of the Math building.

I'm going to do something this summer he resolved. *I'm not going to just sleep away the summer.*

He noticed that he had his paycheck in his hand. *I guess my first stop should be the bank.* He started jogging toward the bank. *I don't want to waste a minute of my summer.*

Jogging was nothing new to Fred. Every morning he liked to go out jogging—a time to think, a time to enjoy the dawn. This morning he had already done his usual four-mile jog. It was now 9:30 a.m. *This will be my "dessert jog."* He giggled.

I wonder what it would be like if I didn't just deposit my check in the bank but changed it all into nickels. How much would that weigh? Could I even carry $500 worth of nickels?

First, he needed to convert dollars into nickels. Since there are 20 nickels in a dollar, the **conversion factor** will be either

$$\frac{20 \text{ nickels}}{1 \text{ dollar}} \quad \text{or it will be} \quad \frac{1 \text{ dollar}}{20 \text{ nickels}}$$

depending on which fraction allowed the dollars to be canceled away.

$$\frac{500 \text{ dollars}}{1} \times \frac{20 \text{ nickels}}{1 \text{ dollar}} = 10{,}000 \text{ nickels}$$

Next, he needed to convert nickels into weight. In chemistry classes, if they use balance scales, it is commonly taught that if you don't have a 5-gram weight, a worn nickel is almost exactly 5 grams.

---

[*] If you are only three-feet tall, your feet do not touch the floor when you are sitting in an adult-sized chair.

So the conversion factor will be either

$$\frac{1 \text{ nickel}}{5 \text{ grams}} \quad \text{or it will be} \quad \frac{5 \text{ grams}}{1 \text{ nickel}}$$

depending on which fraction allows the nickels to be canceled away.

$$\frac{10,000 \text{ nickels}}{1} \times \frac{5 \text{ grams}}{1 \text{ nickel}} = 50,000 \text{ grams}$$

In the metric system, 1000 grams = 1 kilogram, so the conversion factor will be either $\frac{1000 \text{ grams}}{1 \text{ kilogram}}$ or it will be $\frac{1 \text{ kilogram}}{1000 \text{ grams}}$

depending on which fraction allows the grams to be canceled away.

$$\frac{50,000 \text{ grams}}{1} \times \frac{1 \text{ kilogram}}{1000 \text{ grams}} = 50 \text{ kilograms}$$

Fred knew that one kilogram was roughly 2.2 pounds, so the conversion factor will be either $\frac{1 \text{ kilogram}}{2.2 \text{ lbs.}}$ or it will be $\frac{2.2 \text{ lbs.}}{1 \text{ kilogram}}$

depending on which fraction allows the kilograms to be canceled away.

$$\frac{50 \text{ kilograms}}{1} \times \frac{2.2 \text{ lbs.}}{1 \text{ kilogram}} = 110 \text{ lbs.}$$

Geep! I could never carry 110 pounds. I only weigh 37 pounds. I had better just deposit my check instead of getting it in nickels.

And that is what he did. Actually, since Fred is pretty good in arithmetic (an understatement), he did all the conversions in one step in order to go from dollars to pounds:

$$\frac{500 \text{ dollars}}{1} \times \frac{20 \text{ nickels}}{1 \text{ dollar}} \times \frac{5 \text{ g}}{1 \text{ nickel}} \times \frac{1 \text{ kg}}{1000 \text{ g}} \times \frac{2.2 \text{ lbs.}}{1 \text{ kg}} = 110 \text{ lbs.}$$

Your Turn to Play

1. As Fred jogged, each of his breaths took in 0.8 liters of air. Each liter of air weighs 0.02 grams. What is the weight of the air he inhaled in 7 breaths?

2. In Fred's pocket was six-sevenths of a tuna sandwich. It weighed five-eighths of a pound. How much would a whole tuna sandwich weigh?

(The English is always a lot harder than the math. If we translate the problem it might read: Convert a whole tuna sandwich into pounds.)

3. In the old days, trading baseball cards was fashionable. On the KITTENS University campus, Culture Cards™ are now all the rage.

You could trade 6 cards for 5 cards.

Joseph Lister

George Eliot

Or you could trade 2 Lister cards for 3 cards.

Dante Alighieri

(Joseph Lister was the founder of modern antiseptic surgery. George Eliot was the pen name of Mary Ann Evans. She wrote great novels. Dante Alighieri, whom everyone calls Dante, wrote *The Divine Comedy*.)

If you had 20 Eliot cards, how many Dante cards would that be worth?

. . . .**COMPLETE SOLUTIONS**. . . . . . .

1. $\dfrac{7 \text{ breaths}}{1} \times \dfrac{0.8 \text{ liters}}{1 \text{ breath}} \times \dfrac{0.02 \text{ grams}}{1 \text{ liter}} = 0.112 \text{ grams}$

2. $\dfrac{1 \text{ whole } \cancel{\text{tuna sandwich}}}{1} \times \dfrac{5/8 \text{ pounds}}{6/7 \text{ of a } \cancel{\text{tuna sandwich}}} = \dfrac{5}{8} \div \dfrac{6}{7} =$

$\dfrac{5}{8} \times \dfrac{7}{6} = \dfrac{35}{48}$ pounds.

3. $\dfrac{20 \cancel{\text{Eliots}}}{1} \times \dfrac{6 \cancel{\text{Listers}}}{5 \cancel{\text{Eliots}}} \times \dfrac{3 \text{ Dantes}}{2 \cancel{\text{Listers}}} = 36$ Dantes

I, your reader, have a small question. Why in the world did Mary Ann Evans choose George Eliot as her pen name? Isn't that a bit masculine?

Mary Ann Evans lived in the 1800s, and in those days the common expectation was that women wrote cookbooks and domestic moral tales.

In order to get around that prejudice and make sure her works were taken seriously, she wrote under the pen name of George Eliot.

Her most famous works are *Middlemarch, Adam Bede, The Mill on the Floss,* and *Silas Marner.* (These are all available free online.)

She was no dummy.* Only one of her novels does *not* require the use of a Greek typeface in order to be printed.

Here are all 24 Greek letters in lowercase and capitals:

alpha αA, beta βB, gamma γΓ, delta δΔ, epsilon εE, zeta ζZ, eta ηH, theta θΘ, iota ιI, kappa κK, lambda λΛ, mu μM, nu νN, xi ξΞ, omicron oO, pi πΠ, rho ρP, sigma σΣ, tau τT, upsilon υY, phi φΦ, chi χX, psi ψΨ, and omega ωΩ.

Blackwood's Magazine (in 1883) declared, "*Middlemarch* gives George Eliot the chiefest claim to stand by the side of Shakespeare."

---

* An example of litotes. Litotes = "the negative of the opposite." Instead of saying that Tokyo is the largest city in the world (its population is around 35,000,000), you could use litotes and say that Tokyo *is not a small town.*

Chapter Three
Finding a Job

F red jogged through the crowds of students. Some were heading off to the dorms to pack up their stuff and then head home. Some were sitting by the Fred Falls at the center of the KITTENS campus. (Originally, the university president named this water display the Leucreius M. Malestrom, Jr. Memorial Pond and Falls. Malestrom was the president's uncle. The students renamed it after their favorite professor.)

Fred jogged very carefully near the wet stones. He was afraid of what the campus newspaper's headline would be if he tripped.*

But he was a ~~man~~ boy with a purpose. I know exactly what I'm going to do after I deposit my salary check. I'm going to.... Then Fred realized that he really didn't know what he was going to do with his summer.

Fred arrived at the bank and deposited his check in the ATM. Now was the time to decide what to do for the rest of his summer. I know! I could be a teller in the bank. I'm pretty good with numbers. I wonder if the salary as a teller is as much as I make teaching at KITTENS?

He did a quick mental calculation using conversion factors:

$$\frac{\$500}{\text{one month of teaching}} \times \frac{\text{one month of teaching}}{22 \text{ school days}} \times \frac{1 \text{ school day}}{9 \text{ hours in class}}$$

$$\doteq \frac{\$2.53}{\text{hour of teaching}} \text{ !!!!}$$

And this doesn't even include the time I spend preparing to teach each class. I bet the tellers make more than that.

---

* Fred Falls at Fred Falls

Fred walked into the bank. He was sure they would hire him as a teller. He knew that being short wouldn't disqualify him because he could stand on a stool so that the customers could see him. He hadn't been inside a bank in a long time and was shocked to see the "new look" in tellers.

Hi! I'm Jan.   Hi! I'm Jean.   Hi! I'm Kim.

Robots! But Fred was willing to try to be employed. He could still picture himself as one of the tellers.

Hi! I'm Fred

Fred knocked on the door marked **President of KITTENS Bank** and walked into his office.

The president took off his reading glasses and asked, "What are you selling, boy? If it's candy, circus tickets, magazine subscriptions, cookies, barbell sets, raffle tickets, condo timeshares, spark plug repair kits, stock options on bankrupt companies, or doughnuts, I don't want any."

Fred thought for a moment* and replied, "I am not selling candy, circus tickets, magazine subscriptions, cookies, barbell sets, raffle tickets, condo timeshares, spark plug repair kits, stock options on bankrupt companies, or doughnuts, but I am selling something—my labor. Would you care to buy some?"

"How much do you cost?" the president asked.

---

* Which for Fred is 0.00058 seconds.

This was the first key point of economics: *Your labor is something you sell. It has a price.*

Fred was hoping that the president of KITTENS Bank would buy his labor.

The president of KITTENS Bank is a consumer. One of his jobs is to buy labor. Like every buyer, he wants to buy the best product at the lowest cost. That is why his first question to Fred was, "How much do you cost?"

Fred answered, "My salary is negotiable, but I think I should receive at least $2.53 an hour for my labor."

The president laughed a little and said, "Jan, Jean, and Kim cost a lot less. Each of them only costs 10¢ an hour, which is the price of the electricity it takes to operate them."

Fred knew that the second key point of economics is: *Consumers are concerned about both the price and the quality of the product.*

Since he couldn't offer his labor as cheaply as the robots, he would try to show that his labor was better than the robots' labor.

Fred: I'm never late for work.

President: My robots never go home. I just turn them off at night.

Fred: I won't require any extra benefits like health insurance, dental insurance, sick leave, extra holidays, bathroom breaks, or office parties.

President: Do you think that Jan needs dental insurance or that Jean needs bathroom breaks?

Fred: I'm good at . . . He was going to say "Arithmetic," but then realized that any hand calculator could multiply 9867 by 5482 faster than he could.

Fred thanked the president for his time and headed back into the lobby of the bank. As he walked past the tellers, he heard, "Hi! I'm Jan. Hi! I'm Jean. Hi! I'm Kim." Since Fred was always polite, even to robots, he answered, "Hi! I'm Fred."

In the middle of the lobby was a huge bottle on a table.

Kim said to Fred, "You missed our big contest. It was our Jug of Dimes contest. We filled the jug with 497 dimes and threw in some silver dimes." Kim handed Fred the advertisement:

> ## Jug of Dimes Contest
>
> There are 497 dimes in this jug plus some silver dimes.
> Silver dimes are worth 37¢ each.
> All the dimes are worth $59.32.
> Guess how many silver dimes are in the jug.
>
> Contest ends May 3.

Fred had all kinds of questions as he read the contest advertisement.

Q #1: What are silver dimes?

Answer: In the old days (before 1965), dimes used to have real silver in them. Since that date, the government stopped putting silver in the dimes.

Q #2: Are silver dimes always worth 37¢?

Answer: No. It depends on the price of silver.

Q #3: How can I get silver dimes?

Answer: You will probably never find them in the change you receive at the store. When the value of the silver dimes exceeded 10¢, everyone looked at their change and pulled the silver dimes out of circulation. Nowadays you can buy silver dimes at coin stores.

Q #4: This seems like such an easy contest. Anyone who knows algebra can figure out that there are 26 silver dimes mixed in with the 497 regular dimes. Who won that contest?

Answer: All of your students in your Beginning Algebra class.

Hey! I, your reader, also have a question. How did those students figure out there were 26 silver dimes in the jug?

This is called a **word problem**. For many students, it is the hardest part of algebra. And the hardest part of word problems is getting from the English to the equation. Once you have the equation, things generally get easier.

In the next chapter, I'll show you how to get from the English to the equation. The equation will be $37n + 4970 = 5932$. For now, let's review* solving equations.

Original equation	$37n + 4970 = 5932$
Subtract 4970 from both sides	$37n = 5932 - 4970$
Combine like terms	$37n = 962$
Divide both sides by 37	$n = 26$

Your Turn to Play

1. Solve $5x + 17 = 2x + 56$
2. Solve $385 = 7x$
3. Solve $2x + 9x + 42 = 7x + 306$
4. Solve $32 + 6w + 2w = 24w$
5. Solve $44 = 3x - 4$
6. If Kim can do 5 bank transactions in 8 minutes, how long would it take Kim to do 18 bank transactions? (Use a conversion factor.)
7. $\frac{2}{3} + \frac{1}{5} = ?$
8. Fill in one word in the sentence: The central idea of _____ is: *If you tell me this, I'll tell you that.*

★ We did this in Chapters 25–26 in *Life of Fred: Pre-Algebra 1 with Biology.*

.... COMPLETE SOLUTIONS ....

1. Solve $\qquad\qquad$ $5x + 17 = 2x + 56$

    Subtract 17 from both sides $\qquad$ $5x = 2x + 39$

    Subtract 2x from both sides $\qquad$ $3x = 39$

    Divide both sides by 3 $\qquad\qquad$ $x = 13$

2. Solve $\qquad\qquad\qquad$ $385 = 7x$

    Divide both sides by 7 $\qquad$ $55 = x$

3. Solve $\qquad\qquad$ $2x + 9x + 42 = 7x + 306$

    Combine like terms $\qquad$ $11x + 42 = 7x + 306$

    Subtract 7x from both sides $\qquad$ $4x + 42 = 306$

    Subtract 42 from both sides $\qquad$ $4x = 264$

    Divide both sides by 4 $\qquad\qquad$ $x = 66$

4. Solve $\qquad\qquad$ $32 + 6w + 2w = 24w$

    Combine like terms $\qquad$ $32 + 8w = 24w$

    Subtract 8w from both sides $\qquad$ $32 = 16w$

    Divide both sides by 16 $\qquad$ $2 = w$

5. Solve $\qquad\qquad\qquad$ $44 = 3x - 4$

    Add 4 to both sides $\qquad$ $48 = 3x$

    Divide both sides by 3 $\qquad$ $16 = x$

6. $\dfrac{18 \text{ bank transactions}}{1} \times \dfrac{8 \text{ minutes}}{5 \text{ bank transactions}} = 28.8 \text{ minutes}$

7. $\dfrac{2}{3} + \dfrac{1}{5} = \dfrac{2(5)}{3(5)} + \dfrac{1(3)}{5(3)} = \dfrac{10}{15} + \dfrac{3}{15} = \dfrac{13}{15}$

8. The central idea of function is: *If you tell me this, I'll tell you that.*

Chapter Four
From English to Equations

F red had all kinds of questions about silver dimes, but didn't have questions about going from the word problem to the equation.

First: Read the problem. Read it so that you can almost recite it by heart. Draw pictures if that helps.

Second: Write on a piece of paper: *Let x* = the thing you are trying to find out.

Third: Look at the *Let x* = statement that you have just written down. Look at the problem. You will then be able to write: *Then XXX = YYYY* where *XXX* is some expression involving x and *YYYY* is something in English.

Applying this to the Jug of Dimes Contest . . .
First: Really read the problem.

Draw a picture if it helps.

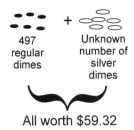

Jug of Dimes Contest

There are 497 dimes in this jug plus some silver dimes.

Silver dimes are worth 37¢ each.

All the dimes are worth $59.32.

Guess how many silver dimes are in the jug.

Second: If you have really read the problem, you know that what they want to find out is how many silver dimes are in the jug. So you write:

<u>Let n = number of silver dimes in the jug.</u>

(You could have written Let x = number of silver dimes in the jug, or you could have written Let w = number of silver dimes in the jug. Use any letter you like.)

Third: You write: "Then *XXX = YYYY*" statement(s).

The starting place for those "Then" statements is the "Let n =" statement you just wrote.

We start with Let n = number of silver dimes in the jug.

We read the problem again. *Each silver dime is worth 37¢.*

If we have 1 silver dime, it would be worth 37¢.

If we have 2 silver dimes, they would be worth (2)(37) = 74¢.

If we have 10 silver dimes, they would be worth (10)(37) = 370¢.

How many silver dimes do we have? We have n silver dimes. (That's the "Let" statement you wrote down.)

If we have n silver dimes, they would be worth 37n.

That is our "Then statement."

Then 37n = the worth of the n silver dimes.

From the first sentence in the problem (There are 497 regular dimes in the jug . . .), we have:

Then 4970¢ = the worth of the regular (non-silver) dimes.

From the third sentence in the problem, we know that the total value of all the dimes is 5932¢. (I'm working in cents to avoid decimals.)

So   37n + 4970 = 5932.

Intermission

The first time you see English turned into an equation, it can be confusing, especially if you tried to read these two pages at the same speed you read stories. It's not unusual to take 40 minutes to read these two pages.

The first time you drive a car, you may have the same feeling: There is so much to remember.

The good news is that driving a car and solving coin problems both become much easier with practice.

First, really read the problem. Maybe, draw pictures.

Second, Let x = the thing you want to find out.

Third, write: Then *XXX = YYYY* statements.

Your Turn to Play

1. If we have x nickels, how much are they worth?

2. If we have y $10 bills, how much are they worth?

3. Joe liked to keep his change in a piggy bank.
To pay for a pizza, Joe handed Stanthony (the
owner of PieOne Pizza) his piggy bank. There
were a bunch of quarters in it plus $7.67 in other
coins. The contents of his piggy bank exactly paid
for the $11.42 pizza. How many quarters were in
his piggy bank?

4. Darlene liked to collect scissors. The good scissors were worth 80¢
each. The broken scissors weren't worth much at all.

 All the broken scissors together
were worth only 17¢.

Darlene's whole collection of
scissors was worth $13.77. How
many good scissors were in that collection?

5. $\frac{3}{8} \times \frac{4}{7}$

6. Solve $7w + 2w + 231 = 19w - 6$

.......**COMPLETE SOLUTIONS**.......

1. If you have 3 nickels, they are worth (3)(5) = 15¢.

   If you have 7 nickels, they are worth (7)(5) = 35¢.

   If you have x nickels, they are worth 5x¢.

2. If you have 2 $10 bills, they are worth (2)(10) = $20.

   If you have y $10 bills, they are worth $10y.

3. After you have read the problem, your second step is to write on a piece
of paper: Let x = the number of quarters in his piggy bank.

The third step is to write: "Then *XXX* = *YYYY*" statements.

Then 25x = the worth of the quarters in his piggy bank.

Then 767¢ = the worth of the other coins.

(I work in cents to avoid decimals.)

Then 1142¢ = the worth of all the coins.

$$25x + 767 = 1142$$

Subtract 767 from both sides $\qquad 25x = 375$

Divide both sides by 25 $\qquad x = 15$

Joe had 15 quarters in his piggy bank.

4. Let x = the number of good scissors in Darlene's collection.

Then 80x = the worth of the good scissors.

Then 17¢ = the worth of all the broken scissors.

Then 1377¢ = the worth of the whole collection.

$$80x + 17 = 1377$$

Subtract 17 from both sides $\qquad 80x = 1360$

Divide both sides by 80 $\qquad x = 17$

Darlene had 17 good scissors in her collection.

5. $\frac{3}{8} \times \frac{4}{7} = \frac{12}{56}$ which reduces to $\frac{3}{14}$

6. Solve $\qquad\qquad 7w + 2w + 231 = 19w - 6$

   Combine like terms $\qquad\qquad 9w + 231 = 19w - 6$

   Subtract 9w from both sides $\qquad\qquad 231 = 10w - 6$

   Add 6 to both sides $\qquad\qquad 237 = 10w$

   Divide both sides by 10 $\qquad\qquad 23.7 = w$

Chapter Five
Tools

Fred waved goodbye to Jan, Jean, and Kim. They waved and said, "Bye!" He headed out into the Kansas sunshine. It felt good on his face.

Wait a minute! I, your reader, can't figure this out.

What's bothering you?

Fred didn't get hired at KITTENS Bank, right?

That's right.

If the bank didn't own those stupid robots, he would have gotten hired, right?

Fred is cheerful. He is always on time. He would have no problem doing the arithmetic that a teller's job requires. And there are few people who would work for $2.53 an hour.

I would guess that he would probably have gotten the job if the bank didn't own those robots.

Grrrrr! I don't like those robots. Why isn't Fred angry?

Because Fred understands economics. He sees the big picture.

I want to turn those robots into a pile of junk. Then Fred can have a job as a teller.

It is a matter of looking at the big picture. Take this small quiz.

Small Quiz

1. Would it be nice if Fred got a job as a teller? ☒yes ☐no

2. Would it be wonderful if everyone were engaged in productive work? ☒yes ☐no

3. Is there a way to pass a law that makes sure that virtually everybody would have work? ☒yes ☐no

Hey! This sounds great! I would vote for such a law. What would the law be?

Outlaw All Farm Machines

Kansas State Law §349.3 subparagraph F: It is hereby enacted that effective immediately all farm equipment including, but not limited to, tractors, trucks, harvesters, plows, irrigation systems, and wheelbarrows are to be turned over to the State Commissioner for destruction. Shovels, hoes, and buckets will still be permitted.

This "wonderful" law will create full employment. Half of our population will have to head out to the

fields to plant the crops and harvest them. Hundreds of people will do the work that one farmer used to do with his tractor. Isn't that neat?

No. I don't want to work out there in the middle of the summer heat. And the price of food would be much higher.

Now you are seeing the big picture. Take away the farmers' tools and things get worse for the community.

Take away computers. Then the banks would have to hire lots of people to work with adding machines all day long. Take away adding machines and they would have to hire even more people to do the arithmetic that banks have to do. And bank customers would have to pay a lot more to use the services that banks offer.

The computers, the adding machines, and the teller-robots are all tools that banks use.

The third key point of economics is: *Our goal is not to have everybody working 60 hours a week, but to have abundant, cheap things.*

The mechanic who has a full set of tools can fix your car quicker and more cheaply than the one who has only a screwdriver.

Several generations ago, making dinner for the family took most of every afternoon. The cakes made in wood-burning stoves were often either burned or soggy—and smelled a little like ashes. The convection oven and the microwave are tools for the cook.

Tools make the difference.

And one of the most important tools is education.

Your Turn to Play

1. Multiple-choice question.
Who gets paid more?

    A) The 60-year-old doctor

    B) The 20-year-old junior in college

2. Multiple-choice question.
Who is physically stronger?

    A) The 60-year-old doctor

    B) The 20-year-old junior in college

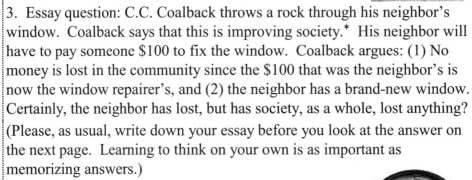

3. Essay question: C.C. Coalback throws a rock through his neighbor's window. Coalback says that this is improving society.* His neighbor will have to pay someone $100 to fix the window. Coalback argues: (1) No money is lost in the community since the $100 that was the neighbor's is now the window repairer's, and (2) the neighbor has a brand-new window. Certainly, the neighbor has lost, but has society, as a whole, lost anything?

(Please, as usual, write down your essay before you look at the answer on the next page. Learning to think on your own is as important as memorizing answers.)

4. This is a Mercury dime. It and the Roosevelt dime pictured on page 28 are 90% silver. Fred had asked if silver dimes are always worth 37¢. He was told that it depends on the price of silver, which varies a great deal. On November 27, 2009, it was $18.24 per ounce. Silver dimes weigh 2.5 grams.   One gram is 0.032

∗ S-o-c-i-e-t-y   What ever happened to "I before E except after C"?

ounces. Using conversion factors, find the value of the silver in a pre-1965 silver dime.

. . . . COMPLETE SOLUTIONS . . . .

1. You know the answer. (The doctor gets paid more because of his education and experience.)

2. You know the answer. (Put them both in the field harvesting strawberries, and the 20-year-old would probably harvest more strawberries than the doctor.)

3. You know in your heart that Coalback's argument is flawed. Otherwise, we would all go around vandalizing other people's property.

So, where's the flaw?

The fourth key point of economics is: *You have to look at the whole picture—especially the consequences that are not immediately obvious.*

It's obvious that the amount of money in the community will stay the same: The neighbor loses $100, and the window repairer gains $100.

It's obvious that the neighbor will have a new window.

What isn't obvious is that both natural resources and human effort were wasted. Because Coalback threw the rock, there is one fewer good window in existence.

Because Coalback threw the rock, hours of time were wasted by the neighbor, the window repairer, and all the people who made the glass. After all the work, things were no better than before Coalback threw the rock. That time could have been spent in productive work or in leisure—both of which are good things.

4. $\dfrac{1 \text{ dime}}{1} \times \dfrac{2.5 \text{ grams}}{1 \text{ dime}} \times \dfrac{90 \text{ grams silver}}{100 \text{ grams of dime}} \times \dfrac{0.032 \text{ ounces}}{1 \text{ gram}} \times \dfrac{\$18.24}{\text{ounce}}$

$\doteq \$1.31$ ($\doteq$ means *equals after rounding*)

Wow. $1.31 for a dime. And that's just for the silver content of a silver dime. The Mercury dimes (1916–1945) are worth a bit more than the Roosevelt dimes (1946–now) because coin collectors like the older, rarer coins.

Chapter Six
Which Job?

Fred thought of the words of George Eliot: "It is never too late to be what you might have been." At the age of 5, Fred's life was not quite over.* Even summer was not quite over yet, since Fred's summer vacation just began about an hour ago.

Fred wondered what kind of jobs he would be best suited for. *I like books. What about being a librarian? No. That wouldn't work. You have to be at least four feet tall to put books on the top shelf. I'm only 36 inches tall and that's less than four feet.* (36" < 4')

What about being a football player? That would be fun. I could hear all the people cheering when I made a touchdown. Then he realized that he didn't weigh much more than a football.

Footballs must weigh 397–425 grams. Fred weighs 37 pounds. Since 1 lb. ≐ 454 grams, Fred's weight in grams is

$$\frac{37 \text{ lbs.}}{1} \times \frac{454 \text{ grams}}{1 \text{ lb.}} = 16{,}798 \text{ grams}$$

Fred weighed more than a football: 16,798 > 425

But he was still small enough that he might be mistaken for a football and be kicked.

Fred wasn't meant to play football.

---

* Remember *litotes*? Fred has a long life ahead of him. He is only 5 and doesn't have any of the habits that bring death more quickly (smoking, heavy drinking, worrying, hang gliding). He goes out jogging almost every morning. Litotes (LIE-teh-tease) is a special kind of understatement. You say the opposite of what you mean and put a "not" in front of it.

For example, *Fred doesn't have big eyes.*
Or, *Elvis won't be doing a lot of concerts this year.*

I need a job where my size will be an advantage. I could be a jockey and ride racehorses. It's better for jockeys to be light than to be big and fat.

The only thing Fred knew about jockeys is that they wear special hats and light, shiny clothes.

Fred turned around and headed back into KITTENS Bank. He walked past the tellers and heard, "Hi! I'm Jan. Hi! I'm Jean. Hi! I'm Kim." He walked into the office of the president of KITTENS Bank's office and asked if he could use his computer.

In a moment's time, Fred went online and ordered a bunch of jockey hats and $17 worth of silk pajamas. The order came to $1,753. The jockey hats were $56 each. How many hats did Fred order?

First: Read the problem and draw a picture if that helps.

x jockey hats   +   Silk pajamas $17   = $1753

Second: Write on a piece of paper: *Let x* = the thing you are trying to find out.

<u>Let x = the number of jockey hats Fred purchased.</u>

Third: Look at the *Let x* = statement that you have just written down. Look at the problem. You will then be able to write: *Then XXX = YYYY* where *XXX* is some expression involving x and *YYYY* is something in English.

<u>Then 56x = the value of the jockey hats.</u>

Since the value of the jockey hats plus the value of the pajamas ($17) is equal to $1,753, the equation is:

$$56x + 17 = 1753$$

1. Solve $56x + 17 = 1753$

2. If a football weighs 400 grams, what is its weight in pounds?
(1 lb. $\doteq$ 454 grams) ($\doteq$ means equal after rounding)

3. Four percent of all jockeys weigh more than 120 pounds. If there are 500 jockeys, how many of them weigh more than 120 pounds?

4. $\dfrac{1}{4} + \dfrac{1}{6} = ?$

. . . . COMPLETE SOLUTIONS . . . .

1. Solve

    Subtract 17 from both sides

    Divide both sides by 56

    $$56x + 17 = 1753$$
    $$56x = 1736$$
    $$x = 31$$

Fred bought 31 jockey hats.

2. The conversion factor will either be

$$\frac{1 \text{ lb.}}{454 \text{ g}} \quad \text{or it will be} \quad \frac{454 \text{ g}}{1 \text{ lb.}}$$

depending on which fraction allows the grams to be canceled away.

$$\frac{400 \cancel{g}}{1} \times \frac{1 \text{ lb.}}{454 \cancel{g}} \doteq 0.88 \text{ lbs.}$$

3. We are looking for 4% of 500. Since we know both sides of the *of*, we multiply. To change 4% into a decimal do this:

    4% → 4.% → .04   (To change a percent into a decimal you move the decimal two places to the left. As my elementary school teacher used to say to me, "When the percent has left, you move the decimal to the left.")

    $$0.04 \times 500 = 20$$

Twenty jockeys weigh more than 120 pounds.

4. $\dfrac{1}{4} + \dfrac{1}{6} = \dfrac{1(\mathbf{3})}{4(\mathbf{3})} + \dfrac{1(\mathbf{2})}{6(\mathbf{2})} = \dfrac{3}{12} + \dfrac{2}{12} = \dfrac{5}{12}$

Chapter Seven
Fred's Career as a Jockey

Fred had never ridden a horse, so he figured he should get a little horse-riding experience before he applied for a job as a jockey. He looked in the phone book, but couldn't find any listings under "Jockey Schools."

He turned to "Horses" and found:

Horse Rentals for Everybody
from Beginners to Jockeys

Perfect! thought Fred. I don't have my jockey outfit yet, but I won't need it until I start racing professionally. Fred jogged over to the stables.

When he got to the stables, the KITTENS mailman was waiting for him.* He handed Fred a large package with all of Fred's jockey hats and silk pajamas in it.

Fred opened the package and put on one of his 31 jockey hats. He was now ready to rent a horse and learn how to ride.

Fred wasn't sure how you were supposed to act when you are renting a horse. He stood up tall (36") and walked in the horse rental place. He greeted the woman behind the counter with, "Howdy!" He had heard that expression in a cowboy movie. Nobody had told Fred that jockeys and cowboys are not quite the same thing. (litotes)

The woman behind the counter said, "What are you selling, boy? If it's candy, circus tickets, magazine subscriptions, cookies, barbell sets,

---

* The mail service at KITTENS is a little better (understatement) than your average mail service. They find you, wherever you are, and deliver almost as fast as email.

raffle tickets, condo timeshares, spark plug repair kits, stock options on bankrupt companies, or doughnuts, I don't want any."

Those words sounded familiar to Fred. There must be a lot of kids running around selling things he thought to himself.

"No, ma'am," Fred answered. "I come to these parts to rent me a horse." (Fred was really trying to sound like a cowboy.)

"What kind of horse would you like to rent?" she asked.

Fred didn't know how to answer that. The possible answers that came to his mind were:

> a race horse
>
> a plow horse
>
> a thoroughbred
>
> a regular horse.

He decided to play it safe and said, "I'd like a brown horse."

When the woman went in back to get a horse, Fred pictured himself as a jockey winning races.

The woman brought Fred the smallest and sweetest brown horse she could find.

When she saw that Fred had to reach up to touch the stirrup, she lifted him up and put him on the horse. "Be back by sunset," she told him.

Fred said to the horse, "Go." Nothing happened.

He said, "It's time we git on down the trail." Nothing happened.

He pulled Prof. Eldwood's *Guide to Riding Horses,* 1844, out of his back pocket and read: In order to signal to the horse that you wish it to proceed in a forward direction, one should indicate that to the horse by kicking it in the flanks using one's heels.

Fred gently kicked. Nothing happened.

Fred tried harder. Nothing happened.

Fred kicked as hard as he could. Nothing happened. He then realized that the horse couldn't feel anything because Fred was so small that his heels were hitting the saddle instead of the horse.

After several minutes, the horse got tired and wandered back to his stall. He took Fred with him.

The woman gently lifted Fred off of the horse.

"How much do I owe you?" Fred asked.

She smiled and said, "We don't charge for four-minute horse rides."

Fred left the stables with his 31 jockey hats and his silk pajamas. As he passed a thrift store, he put them all in the donations box.

If I may, I, your reader, have a couple of silly questions. First of all, why didn't Fred keep the pajamas?

Fred had ordered the extra-extra small size, but they were much too large for him.

And second, I have been wondering why in the world Fred ordered 31 jockey hats. That seems like a funny number.

In the fall when Fred told his students about his jockey adventures, he was asked that same question. He said that he wanted one hat for each day of the month so that the horses wouldn't get bored with him for wearing the same hat all the time.

Fred had it all figured out.

If it was the first day of the month, he would wear the red hat.

If it was the second day, he would wear the orange hat.

$3^{rd} \rightarrow$ the yellow hat with the green stripes.

$4^{th} \rightarrow$ the hat with a duck on it.

$5^{th} \rightarrow$ the hat with the feather.

. . .

$29^{th} \rightarrow$ the smoky gray hat.

$30^{th} \rightarrow$ the hat with $\sqrt{49} = 7$ on it.

$31^{st} \rightarrow$ the polka dot hat.

4th day duck hat

This, of course, is a function. In this case, it is a rule that associates to each day of the month one of Fred's jockey hats. The domain is the days of the month.

Here's the new part: A function is **one-to-one** (also written as 1-1) if no two elements of the domain have the same **image** in the codomain. (The image of 31ˢᵗ is the polka dot hat.)

Your Turn to Play

1. Here is a function. (That means that every element in the domain has exactly one image in the codomain.)

   Is this function 1-1?

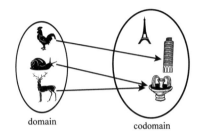

domain   codomain

2. Is this a function?

$$✁ \rightarrow A$$
$$✾ \rightarrow C$$
$$✁ \rightarrow M$$
$$✐ \rightarrow R$$

3. Is this a function?

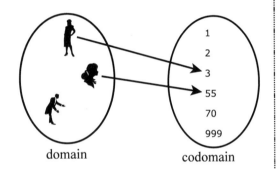

domain   codomain

4. Here is the official definition of **function**: *Given two sets, a function is a rule which assigns to each element of the first set exactly one element of the second set.*

   The first set is called the domain, and the second set is called the codomain.

   Is this a function? *Let the first set be the set of all people in Kansas who are alive. Let the second set be {0, 1, 2, 3, 4, 5}. Let the rule be that you assign to each person the number of children that they have given birth to.*

5. Which of these are true?

$$\frac{2}{3} > 0.6 \qquad \frac{1}{2} + \frac{1}{3} > 0.8 \qquad 50\% < \frac{5}{8} \qquad 0.17 < \frac{1}{6}$$

·······COMPLETE SOLUTIONS·······

1. A function is 1-1 if no two elements in the domain are assigned the same image. Since both 🐌 and 🦌 are assigned to 🏆, this function is not 1-1.

2. The most important phrase in the definition of function is *exactly one*. A function is a rule that assigns to each element of the domain *exactly one* element of the codomain. Since ✂ is assigned to both A and M, this is not a function.

3. The second most important phrase in the definition of function is *each element of the first set*. A function is a rule that assigns to *each element of the first set*, exactly one element of the second set.

This fellow 🏃 doesn't have an image in the second set. Therefore, this is not a function.

4. All the men in Kansas will be assigned to 0, since men don't give birth to children. But there are women in Kansas who have been blessed with more than five kids. Those women are like the 🏃 in the previous question. They don't have an image in the codomain. Therefore, this is not a function.

5. In *Life of Fred: Decimals and Percents,* there were Nine Conversions that you memorized. In *Life of Fred: Pre-Algebra 1 with Biology*, we added the final two to the list ($\frac{1}{6}$ and $\frac{5}{6}$).

Here are the **Eleven Conversions** that you memorized:

$$\frac{1}{2} = 50\% \qquad \frac{1}{4} = 25\% \qquad \frac{3}{8} = 37\frac{1}{2}\% \qquad \frac{1}{6} = 16\frac{2}{3}\%$$

$$\frac{1}{3} = 33\frac{1}{3}\% \qquad \frac{3}{4} = 75\% \qquad \frac{5}{8} = 62\frac{1}{2}\% \qquad \frac{5}{6} = 83\frac{1}{3}\%$$

$$\frac{2}{3} = 66\frac{2}{3}\% \qquad \frac{1}{8} = 12\frac{1}{2}\% \qquad \frac{7}{8} = 87\frac{1}{2}\%$$

The original problem was

$$\frac{2}{3} > 0.6 \qquad \frac{1}{2} + \frac{1}{3} > 0.8 \qquad 50\% < \frac{5}{8} \qquad 0.17 < \frac{1}{6}$$

With the Eleven Conversions they instantly become

$0.66\frac{2}{3} > 0.6$	$0.5 + 0.33\frac{1}{3} > 0.8$	$0.5 < 0.625$	$0.17 < 0.16\frac{2}{3}$
true	true	true	false

The Bridge

For those of you who have read *Life of Fred: Fractions*, *Life of Fred: Decimals and Percents*, or *Life of Fred: Pre-Algebra 1 with Biology* you can skip the rest of this page. You can take out a piece of paper and turn to the next page right now.

For the rest of you . . .

We are at **The Bridge**.

After every six or seven chapters, we give you the chance to show that you haven't forgotten what you have learned. **The Bridge** consists of ten questions from the beginning of the book up to the present moment.

It also gives you the chance to show that you actually worked the problems in the *Your Turn to Play*.

If you get 90% or more right, you have crossed the Bridge and have earned the right to go on to the next chapter. You are permitted to look back at earlier material in the book and use a calculator while you take this quiz.

After you have finished all ten problems, you and your parent (or guardian or teacher or jailer or superintendent or whoever is your supervisor) may compare your answers with those in the back of this book to see if you have crossed the Bridge.

Good luck.

The Bridge

from Chapter 1 to Chapter 7

first try

Goal: Get 9 or more right and you cross the bridge.

1. Joe had just learned a new word in Fred's class. When Darlene came over to visit Joe, he told her, "Life is effervescent." Darlene agreed that life was bubbling and sparkling.

Joe frowned. "That's not what Fred said it was. He said that effervescent means "like a vapor that grows less and less until it disappears."

Darlene corrected Joe, "No. The word Fred used was *evanescent*."

Joe said, "Oh." Then, in order to appear a little smarter, he said, "I just thought of a function. Take each word and assign to it its one meaning."

Is this a function? If it is, explain why it is. If it isn't, show why it isn't.

2. Joe bought a dictionary so he wouldn't confuse *effervescent* with *evanescent*. It cost $16. The sales tax was 7%. How much sales tax did Joe pay?

3. He looked up the word *go* in his dictionary. There were 84 definitions (*Random House Webster's College Dictionary*) including (1) to move, (27) to die, and (38) to urinate. Joe was fascinated. He decided to read the whole dictionary—one page each day. There are about 1500 pages in that dictionary. Using conversion factors (one month = 30 days, reading one page per day), find how many months it will take Joe to finish the dictionary.

4. Solve $3x + 5x + 23 = 4x + 375$

5. If a dictionary cost $16, how much would x dictionaries cost?

6. At the bookstore the German–English dictionaries were on sale. They were $11 each. Joe bought a bunch of them to give to his friends and he bought $14 worth of candy for himself. The total bill was $487. How many German–English dictionaries did he buy?

7. $\frac{3}{7} \times \frac{3}{8}$

8. $\dfrac{1}{5} + \dfrac{2}{3}$

9. Is this a function?

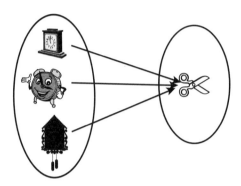

10. Is the following function 1-1? *The domain is the set of all women in Kansas. The codomain is {0, 1, 2, . . . }. Assign to each woman the number of children she has given birth to.*

Intermission
{0, 1, 2, . . . } is called the set of **whole numbers**. The three dots indicate that the listing in the set goes on forever. {0, 1, 2, . . . } means the same thing as {0, 1, 2, 3, 4, 5, . . . }.

After you have written the answers to all ten problems, and after you have checked your work as much as you want to, it will be time to find out whether you have crossed the bridge. If you got nine or ten correct, you are ready to go on to Chapter 8.

If not, then you probably have been reading too fast. You may earn the right to another try (on the next page) by first correcting all the errors you made.

 # The Bridge
from Chapter 1 to Chapter 7

second try

1. Darlene often thought about Joe. She wondered why he always seemed to be thinking about food and fishing. She knew there were other things in life that were just as important—for example, fingernail polish.

Just today, she received 2.1 kilograms of Polish fingernail polish in the mail. How many quarts was that? (1 kilogram = 1000 grams and 1 gram of polish = 0.012 cups and 4 cups = 1 quart.)

2. Darlene tore open the package and set the bottles on her kitchen table.

Ruby red, Blood red, Heart red, Lip red, Righteous red, Pale red, Pretty pink, Placid pink, Super pink, Lady pink, Sky pink, Melon orange, Toenail orange, Lasting orange....

Every week Darlene ordered nail polish. When she had so many bottles that they wouldn't all fit in her bathroom, she stored them in different parts of her apartment. She put all the red polishes in the bathroom, the pink ones in the living room, the orange ones in her bedroom, etc. This is a function. Its domain is the bottles of nail polish she owned. The codomain is the places in her apartment. Is this function one-to-one?

3. Which of these are true?

$$\frac{3}{4} < 72\% \qquad \frac{7}{8} > 0.8 \qquad \frac{1}{8} = 0.125 \qquad \frac{5}{6} > 82\%$$

4. Darlene giggled when she read "Polish polish" on the bottle's label. She thought to herself, "The word *polish* changes its pronunciation when you capitalize it. I wonder if there are other words like that?"

She took the Sky pink bottle and used three-fourths of it painting her toenails. The bottle originally contained $\frac{2}{3}$ of an ounce of Sky pink. How many ounces did she use painting her toenails?

5. While they were drying, she phoned Joe. She liked to hear his voice.

"Just a moment," Joe said. "Hold it. . . .Wow! That was some nice touchdown."

Darlene knew what was happening. Joe was watching football on his television. She waited until after the extra point, and then Joe could talk on the telephone. Joe continued, "Hi. Who is it?"

"It's me, Darlene," she answered. She knew that she had exactly two minutes to talk to him, because the commercials before the next kickoff were two minutes long.

Joe was all excited, "That was so nice. You should have seen it."

Darlene suddenly realized that one of the words Joe had just used was a word that changes pronunciation when you capitalize it. (Only one reader in a thousand will be able to spot that word. I'll put it in the answer key.)

Joe continued, "There have been eight touchdowns in this game so far, and three of them have been really nice."

Your question: What percentage of the touchdowns were really nice?

6. Darlene paid $124 for the shipment from Poland. It contained $16 worth of nail files and 27 bottles of nail polish. The nail polish bottles were all the same price. How much was each bottle?

7. Is it possible to invent a function whose domain is the whole numbers ($\{0, 1, 2, 3, 4, \ldots\}$) and whose codomain is Joe?

8. $\frac{1}{3} + \frac{1}{4} + \frac{1}{6}$

Please obey the four
General Rules for Fractions
(from *Life of Fred: Fractions*)

1. Reduce fractions in your answers as much as possible.

2. Fractions like $\frac{0}{4}$ are equal to 0.

3. Fractions like $\frac{4}{4}$ are equal to 1.

4. Division by zero doesn't make sense.

9. Suppose the domain is Darlene and the codomain is the 26 capital letters $\{A, B, C, D, E, \ldots, X, Y, Z\}$. Assign Darlene to the letter J. Is this a function?

10. Solve $18 + 5y + 17 = 90$

If you got nine or ten correct, you are ready to go on to Chapter 8. Otherwise, correct your errors, and you have earned the right to a third try.

 # The Bridge
from Chapter 1 to Chapter 7

third try

1. Darlene wanted to go over to Joe's apartment and sit next to him while he watched his football game. She knew that he would like it if she brought over a snack for him to eat while he watched football.

She looked through her *Mastering the Art of Football Cooking* and found the perfect recipe: "End Zone Smashes."

Start with $\frac{1}{12}$ cup of cinnamon.

Darlene was stuck. She had the normal assortment of measuring cups:
1 cup, $\frac{1}{2}$ cup, $\frac{1}{3}$ cup, and $\frac{1}{4}$ cup, but no $\frac{1}{12}$ cup.

 Darlene phoned her mother. Her mother was also watching football on television. During one of the commercial breaks she told Darlene, "Listen Little Lamby. All you gotta do is fill the $\frac{1}{3}$ cup with cinnamon and then pour that into the $\frac{1}{4}$ cup. What's left over in the $\frac{1}{3}$ cup is $\frac{1}{12}$ cup."

Was Darlene's mother right?

2. The next line of the End Zone Smashes recipe said:

Stir in $\frac{1}{6}$ cup of salt.

Without calling her mother, Darlene figured out how to do that.

How did she do it with her four measuring cups?

3. The cinnamon and salt mixture was how many cups? Remember the four General Rules for fractions, which were listed on the previous page.

4. The recipe continued: Then take a bag of marshmallows and discard the 15% of them that are not perfectly shaped. How many are left? (A bag of marshmallows has 160 marshmallows.)

5. The recipe continued: Take the remaining marshmallows, stir in the cinnamon-salt mixture and heat and stir until it is a gooey mess. Smear it between two cookies that you bought at the store, and you have End Zone Smashes that will delight anyone who watches football on television.

Darlene decided to test the Smashes on her mother before she took the rest of them over to Joe's.

She packed the 24 Smashes into a box. The whole thing weighed 78 ounces. The box itself weighed 18 ounces. How much did each Smash weigh?

6. Darlene knocked on her mom's door. (She lived next door.) Darlene had to wait until the next commercial break before her mother answered the door. Her mother said, "Hi, Little Lamby," and without another word they both headed back to the couch to watch the game. Over the next hour, Darlene ate 5 of the Smashes, and her mother ate 17 of them. What percent of the original two dozen Smashes were left for Joe?

7. Darlene's mother's cat ate the last two Smashes. Let the domain be the set of all 24 Smashes that Darlene made, and the codomain be the set {Darlene, her mom, her mom's cat}. Assign to each Smash the stomach it entered. Is this a function? Is it one-to-one?

8. The cat died. (At the autopsy the veterinarian said it died of a "stuck throat.") Neither Darlene nor her mom had stuck throats since they each had consumed a liter of Sluice. How many ounces are 2 liters of Sluice? (1 liter ≐ 1.06 quarts and 1 quart = 32 ounces.)

9. Solve $2x = 9x - 119$

10. $\dfrac{1}{10} \times \dfrac{1}{100}$

The Bridge

from Chapter 1 to Chapter 7

fourth try

1. "Little Lamby, would you look at that!" Darlene's mother exclaimed. "Whoever said that television isn't educational?" She was looking at a commercial announcing Dairy Month.

June is Dairy Month

She raced into the kitchen and got some whipping cream, poured it into a bowl, and used her mixer to turn it into a pile of whipped cream. She brought it out and gave it to Darlene. Three-eighths of a cup of whipping cream had produced 3 cups of whipped cream.

"You should make some for yourself," Darlene suggested. Her mom poured $\frac{5}{8}$ of a cup of whipping cream into a bowl. How much whipped cream could she expect?

2. As mother and daughter sat in front of the television set, the power

went out. Instead of  all they saw was

"You didn't?" Darlene asked.

"Yes, I didn't," her mom replied.

They both knew that mom had not paid her electric bill . . . again. Many times Darlene had gone over her mom's budget with her. She worked part-time as a sign waver and her income was $500 per month. She spent 20% of her income on nail polish. (That's how Darlene had gotten into that habit also.) She spent 40% on shoes and three-eighths of her income on rent. What percent was left?

3. (Continuing the previous problem) How many dollars were left after Darlene's Mom spent money on nail polish, shoes, and rent?

4. Mother and daughter left their unfinished bowls of whipped cream and headed next door to Darlene's apartment. Darlene turned on her television while her mom headed into her bathroom to look at Darlene's collection of red nail polish bottles.

 # The Bridge
from Chapter 1 to Chapter 7

"Wow. Lamby, can I use some of your Heart red polish? That's one color I don't have."

Before Darlene could say yes, her mom had applied Heart red to all of her toes and 6 of her fingers. What percent of the job had she done? (Assume she was going to paint all of her toenails and fingernails.)

5. After she finished her toenails and fingernails, she came back into the living room and sat down next to her daughter. "You know, Lamby, that doing your own nails is so much cheaper than having them done at the beauty shop. There they charge you x dollars for every finger they do. Last year I treated myself and got my fingernails done. I also gave a $3 tip to the manicurist."

Darlene asked, "And how much did it cost?"

"$16.50 including the tip."

How much did the manicurist charge for each nail?

6. Is it possible for a function whose domain is $\{ ☎, ✈, ✉ \}$ and whose codomain is $\{\pi, \theta\}$ to be 1-1?

7. Since they didn't get a chance to finish their bowls of whipped cream, they were still a bit hungry. During one of the two-minute commercial breaks, they headed into Darlene's kitchen to see how they might honor June Is Dairy Month. In her refrigerator were several dozen bottles of green nail polish, a cube of butter, and some Swiss cheese.

"Oh, it's been so long since you made the thing for Dad," Darlene told her mother. "Could you make that?"

Her mother laughed and said, "You remember that was the treat I used to give your father before he died?" She took $\frac{3}{5}$ of a cup of butter and $\frac{1}{3}$ cup of Swiss cheese and melted them together in a pot on the stove.

What is the volume of that mixture?

8. Solve $100 - 2x = 18x$

9. Which of these are true?

$\frac{1}{4} > 22\%$ $\qquad \frac{3}{8} < 0.37$ $\qquad \frac{5}{6} = 83\frac{1}{3}\%$

10. $\frac{5}{7} \times \frac{3}{8}$

 # The Bridge
from Chapter 1 to Chapter 7

fifth try

1. Darlene's mother took the $\frac{14}{15}$ cups of melted Swiss cheese and butter and poured $\frac{2}{3}$ cup of it into a glass for Darlene to drink. The rest she kept for herself in the pot so she wouldn't dirty another glass. (Do you know how hard it is to wash a glass that has had melted Swiss cheese and butter in it?) How much did she leave in the pot?

2. Everyone who has ever had melted Swiss cheese and butter knows that the proper way to consume this is with a straw. Darlene headed to the kitchen and got out her box of Colored Straws.™ Each of the ten straws in the box was a different color. One was red, one was blue, one was black, etc. She picked out one straw for herself and one for her mother. Would this be a function?: *Let the domain be* {Darlene, her mom} *and the codomain be* {all the ten straws}, *and assign to each woman the straw that Darlene picked out.*

3. Suppose the first set is {A, B} and the second set is {L, M}. Is it possible to invent a function from the first set to the second set that is *not* one-to-one?

4. "This melted Swiss cheese and butter tastes so good," Darlene said as they watched the third quarter of the game begin. "I know that Dad liked it a lot.*"

"He sure did. Six nights a week when we watched football together, I would serve it."

Assuming he had 400 grams per serving of the melted Swiss and butter, how many grams of that did he have in 7 weeks? Use conversion factors.

5. Darlene's Mom reminisced, "Those were hard days for us financially. After the bills came in from his first heart attack, we had to watch our spending. Instead of spending $90 each week on nail polish, I went on a

---

✷ There is no such word as alot.

The Bridge

budget and spent 20% less on nail polish. But you can be sure I loved your father. I served him our wonderful melted Swiss cheese and butter six days a week and whipped cream on Sundays until the day he died."

How much did her mother spend on nail polish each week after she went on her budget?

6. Which of these are true?

$$12\% > \frac{1}{8} \qquad 62\frac{1}{2}\% < \frac{5}{8} \qquad \frac{1}{6} > 0.16$$

7. A box of 10 Colored Straws™ plus 40¢ worth of cheese cost $2. How much does each straw cost? (Hint: First change $2 to cents.)

8. If the electricity cost 4¢ per minute to operate a television set, how much would it cost to watch a 3-hour football game? (Use conversion factors.)

9. During a 3-hour football game, there are 54 minutes of commercials. What percent of the 3 hours is commercials? (Hint: First change everything to minutes.)

10. Every once in a while, Darlene's fingernails start to feel heavy because of all the coats of polish she's put on them. If it takes her x minutes to clean off a nail, how long would it take her to clean off all ten nails?

Chapter Eight
In Business

The three months of summer vacation were fading fast. Fred knew that he had already used up 90 minutes of it.[*] He had found out that he couldn't get a job as a teller at KITTENS Bank. He couldn't be employed as a jockey.

---

[*] Perhaps more important than learning mathematics is learning how to read. It is a skill that you will use increasingly through college. After your college years, reading will be the major way you learn important things for the next 40 years of your life—not by hearing lectures, not by listening to the radio or by watching television.

Being able to read well means more than just knowing the meaning of all the words you read. Many third-graders think that all there is to reading is understanding what the words mean.

But authors sometimes mean something different than what their naked words mean. It's hard to find a major work of literature in which the author doesn't use exaggeration, understatement, or irony.

Exaggeration need not be considered lying—if your reader knows you are doing that. The Valley of Echoes in Wyoming is reported to be large. The novice writer might write, "The Valley of Echoes is big." And his readers would fall asleep.

Instead, you could describe that valley as so large that it takes eight hours to hear your echo come back. You might tell about the camper who shouted "Wake up!" just before he went to bed.

Understatement need not be considered lying—if your reader knows you are doing that. "We were so poor that we would break pennies into small pieces and spend parts of them." That's much more memorable than writing, "We were poor."

Irony is what you experienced in the first two sentences of this chapter. Unless the reader is completely asleep, the fact that those two sentences couldn't both be true is obvious. Writers use irony to express something different from—or even opposite to—what the words literally mean.

Children's books rarely use irony. Their readers wouldn't understand it. They read everything literally.

But much of great literature will contain irony because it conveys meaning much better than any literal wording. If a poor writer such as Prof. Eldwood had started this chapter, he might have written, "Ninety minutes have passed since Fred stopped his teaching. Even though 90 minutes are a small part of Fred's entire summer vacation, Fred felt a sense of urgency in determining what his summer endeavors should be." Prolix and soporific. (Wordy and sleep-inducing.)

He briefly thought of becoming an astronaut. Since I'm so light it will take less rocket fuel to send me into outer space but once they strap me in I won't be able to reach the steering wheel.

Then Fred thought of working as a teacher in a pre-school. I could teach them how to read and do math. Then he realized that half the kids in the pre-school would be bigger than he is, and things just wouldn't work out.

I know! I could be a movie star! Think of the different roles I could play.

Shakespeare

E = mc²

Sigmund
Fred

I could play Napoleon. Then he thought of the one big drawback of being a movie star. They couldn't find other actors who were so short.

The only part he could play would be a Munchkin in *The Wizard of Oz*, but that movie has already been filmed.

Stop! I, your reader, have a small question. Looking at the title of this book, I've been waiting for Fred to start a business. When is he going into business for himself?

And I hee hee have been waiting for you ho ho to spring that question. I wondered how many jobs ha ha that I would have to write about before hee hee you asked one of the central questions ho ho of economics.

And what, may I ask, is so funny? Did I say something funny?

You asked, "When is he going into business for himself?"

Yes, I did. And I meant it.

The truth of the matter is that Fred has always been in business for himself. The fifth key point of economics is:

Everyone is in business.

Everyone.

This is going to take some explaining.

I'm all ears. Start explaining.

Whenever anyone thinks of someone in business, Stanthony, the owner of PieOne Pizza, is the first person that comes to mind. He is world famous (at least near the KITTENS University campus). He cooks his famous pizza sauce with its 18 special herbs. He spoons it over his triple-wheat crust and adds some toppings: pepperoni, mushrooms, sausage, green peppers, onion, and six kinds of cheese. For a meaty pizza he includes: pieces of bacon, beef, chicken, chorizo, duck, honey-cured ham, meatballs, pepperoni, salami, sausage, turkey, venison, American bison, steak, veal, yak, hare, rabbit, kangaroo, opossum, goat, ibex, pork, reindeer, moose, antelope, giraffe, squirrel, whale, bear, dove, quail, mutton, ostrich, pheasant, grouse, partridge, pigeon, woodcock, goose, frog, anchovy, cod, eel, halibut, shark, abalone, clam, conch, oyster, scallop, crayfish, lobster, prawn, salmon, shrimp, squid, and tuna, and he doesn't skimp on the veggies: alfalfa sprouts, artichoke hearts, avocado, baby leeks, broccoli, capers, capicolla, carrots, cherry tomatoes, eggplant, green peppers, olives, lettuce, mushrooms, onions, peas, both porcini and portobello mushrooms, red onions, red peppers, roasted cauliflower, roasted garlic, scallions, shallots, snow peas, spinach, sun-dried tomatoes, sweet corn, watercress, yellow peppers, yellow squash, and zucchini.

Then he tops it with some herbs: basil, bay leaf, chili powder, chives, dill, garlic, jalapeno peppers, laurel, marjoram, fenugreek, oregano, parsley, pepper, rosemary, and cardamon.

He bakes it. Customers from miles around smell it and come in and trade their dollars for Stanthony's pizzas.

Stanthony makes stuff and exchanges it—usually for money.

To be in business is to make stuff and exchange it.

All of us are in business. The only difference is with whom we trade. Usually, we make things and trade for money, but not always.

Hungry.
Will work
for food.

Stanthony trades his work for money with the people who like pizza. A baby will trade smiles and giggles (a baby's work) with his parents. The president of KITTENS Bank will trade his work (mostly decision making) with the board of directors of the bank who hired him.

All of us are in business. All of us have customers—the people with whom we trade.

Some of us have few customers. If Fred had been hired as a jockey, his customer would have been the person who owned the horse.

___Who Is an Employee?___

All of us are employees.

We all have someone who pays us, someone who decides whether we will get money (or other goods) for our labor.

Even Stanthony is an employee. If no one liked his pizza, then he would have no income.

I hate the stuff.

(Not everyone will pay you, even if you are Stanthony.)

All of us are in business for ourselves.

We each decide what business we will engage in. We each decide how hard we will work. We each look for customers who will buy what we have to offer.

Even if you are a cashier in a grocery store, you are in business for yourself. You are selling your cashier skills and labor to the store.

Then Fred saw a sign on the street corner. It seemed to be the perfect answer.

Picture This

Your New Career!
We'll help you find it.
123 Main Street

Fred started jogging toward 123 Main Street. (He was jogging at 500 feet per minute.) After a while, he got so excited he broke into a run and ran the last 1000 feet to get to the New Career Center.

The total trip was 10,000 feet. How many minutes did he jog before he broke into a run?

Word problems are probably the hardest part of beginning algebra. You know the steps by now: First, you read the problem until you can almost tell it to someone else without looking at it. You draw a picture if that helps.

Second, you write on a piece of paper: *Let x = the thing you are trying to find out.*

Third, you write: *Then XXX = YYYY* where *XXX* is some expression involving x, and *YYYY* is something in English.

We want to know how many minutes Fred jogged before he broke into a run. So . . .

Let x = the number of minutes Fred jogged.

We can draw a diagram:

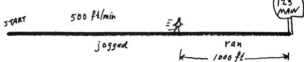

If we know he jogged for x minutes, and we know that he jogs at the rate of 500 ft/min, we can write . . .

Then 500x = the distance he jogged.

Two Ways to See
500x = the distance he jogged

Using *d = rt*

This is probably the most famous formula from algebra: d = rt. "Distance equals rate times time."

In everyday life people use this formula without thinking about it. If you tell someone you drove 3 hours at 60 mph, they will say you went 180 miles.

In the same way, if Fred went x minutes at 500 ft/min, he would have traveled 500x feet.

Using *dimensional analysis*

If you went 3 hours at 60 mph, we compute

$$\frac{3 \text{ hours}}{1} \times \frac{60 \text{ miles}}{\text{hour}} = 180 \text{ miles}$$

Similarly, if Fred went x minutes at 500 ft/min, we compute

$$\frac{x \text{ minutes}}{1} \times \frac{500 \text{ ft}}{\text{min}} = 500x \text{ ft}$$

Dimensional analysis is also called **unit analysis**.

So far, we have:

      Let x = the number of minutes Fred jogged.

      Then 500x = the distance he jogged.

Reading the problem, we can also write

      Then 500x + 1000 = the total distance he covered.

Reading the problem, we see that the total distance he covered was 10,000 feet, so the equation is   500x + 1000 = 10,000.

Solving the equation is usually the easier part.

$$500x + 1000 = 10,000$$
$$500x = 9,000 \quad \text{Subtract 1000 from both sides}$$
$$x = 18 \quad \text{Divide both sides by 500}$$

He jogged for 18 minutes.

Your Turn to Play

1. In Chapter 3, we had coin problems. (The Jug of Dimes Contest.) We just played with a distance-rate-time problem. Let's go back and look at another coin problem.

    Suppose your mother gave you your weekly allowance. It was a whole fistful of these things and $1000 in quarters.

As you headed out the door to spend your allowance, you counted up how much she gave you. It was $10,000. How many $500 bills did she give you?

2. If it's been a while since you've seen a $500 bill, it may be because they pulled them out of circulation in 1969.

    Suppose your father gave you your allowance in the form of three credit cards instead of all that dirty old cash. The first had a credit limit of $1,000. The second had a credit limit of $8,000.50 and the third, $500.75.

    How much was your allowance?

.......**COMPLETE SOLUTIONS**.......

1. You let x equal the thing you are trying to find out.

   Let x = the number of $500 bills she gave you.

   Then 500x = the value of those $500 bills.

   Then 500x + 1000 = your allowance.

Reading the problem, we see that your total allowance was $10,000, so

$$500x + 1000 = 10,000$$
$$500x = 9,000 \qquad \text{Subtract 1000 from both sides}$$
$$x = 18 \qquad \text{Divide both sides by 500.}$$

Your mother gave you 18 $500 bills.

   Wait a minute! This is the exact same problem as the Fred-jogging-and-running problem. In coin problems you are often given the number of coins, and you compute their value. In d = rt problems, you are often given a rate and time, and you compute a distance.

2.   1000.

        8000.50   To add numbers with decimals, you line up

        <u>500.75</u>   the decimals.

        9501.25

Your dad gave you $9,501.25 as your allowance.

Eye catching, isn't it.

It is real.

It isn't fake like:

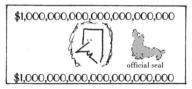

Chapter Nine
Career Guidance

Fred knew he was at the right spot. It was the correct address and it even had a sign saying the center specialized in helping people find out what career they should choose.

The man behind the counter told Fred that for $500 they would give him a "massive amount of scientific testing" and would analyze the results using "both computers and trained psychometricians." They even showed him their guarantee:

Iron-Clad Guarantee
We will give you our
opinion of what you should do.
CC Coalback, owner

How can I miss? Fred thought. All that testing and they are even going to have psychometricians—whatever they are—look at it. And it comes with a guarantee.

Fred handed over most of his life savings, and the man behind the counter took Fred into a small back room. He cleared off a table and put Fred in a seat. Fred noticed that the table was very dusty.

"Here are your psychometric evaluative forms," the man said. He put a 14-inch stack of papers in front of Fred. Wow. I'm sure going to get my money's worth Fred thought.

Fred asked, "Do you want me to use a pencil or a pen? Or would you prefer I use my fountain pen?"

in the small back room

62

"Our psychometricians would be happy with any of those," the salesclerk told Fred as he left the room and shut the door.

The salesclerk rushed into C.C. Coalback's office and exclaimed, "Someone actually came in for career counseling! I can't believe it. And he forked over the $500. What a patsy!"

Coalback gave the clerk his cut of the money ($15) and pocketed the rest. He said, "We've never had anybody complete that 14-inch stack of test questions. They all quit halfway through. Then they think it's their fault and never file a complaint."

The first sheet on the top of the pile was marked **Personal Information**. Here is how Fred filled it out.

Name: *Fred Gauss*

Age: *5½*

Address: *KITTENS University, Math building, room 314, Kansas*

List all your credit card numbers: *I don't have any credit cards.*

List all the valuable things you own (> $100) and where they are kept: *I don't have any right now.*

Intermission

Just make a tiny guess why Coalback would want to know people's credit card numbers and where they kept their valuable things.

Hint: The Eighth Commandment says that you are not to take other people's things.

The second sheet of paper was **Your Knowledge of Civics**.

Essay Question: What is the Bill of Rights?

It is the first Ten Amendments to the United States Constitution.

Some people think that the Bill of Rights are rights that are given to us by the government. That's silly. The Declaration of Independence says that everyone is "endowed by their Creator with certain unalienable Rights. . . ." The government can't give me rights that I already have.

The real purpose of the Bill of Rights is to prevent the government from taking away our rights. The First Amendment, for example, says that Congress can't interfere with our practice of religion, with our speech, with the press, or with our right to peaceable gatherings.

The Second Amendment says that the government can't even infringe on our right to own and bear weapons.

The Tenth Amendment is my favorite. It says that if the Constitution doesn't specifically give a right to the United States government, it does not have that right.* That means that if Congress passes a law and the Constitution hasn't given Congress that power, then that law is unconstitutional.

The powers of Congress are laid out in Article One, Section 8. There aren't that many powers. They can tax, borrow money, regulate commerce between the states, say how to become a citizen, deal with bankruptcies, coin money, determine weights and measures, establish a postal service, establish copyrights and patents, set up a court system, punish pirates, establish armies, navies, and militia and declare war, and set up a place for the seat of government (District of Columbia). The only other power granted to Congress is in the 16th Amendment that allows for an income tax.

Any sixth-grader can read the Tenth Amendment and the Article One, Section 8 and understand them. The words were meant to be plain and understandable. The members of Congress have each sworn to uphold the Constitution, and yet they pass laws that are clearly prohibited by the Constitution. Congress doesn't have the authority to pass a law just because it is nice and promotes the general welfare.

Article One, Section 8 doesn't give Congress the right to build a museum in Texas or fund research for bees or pay a doctor. Congress has thrown the Constitution in the garbage can.

---

* "The powers not delegated to the United States by the Constitution, nor prohibited by it to the States, are reserved to the States respectively, or to the people."

Fred was mildly sweating after he wrote that. He turned to the next page in the stack of test questions.

Astronomy.

Explain the Schwarzschild Radius. Fred relaxed. This would be much easier than explaining the Bill of Rights. *In 1916 Karl Schwarzschild figured this out. If you want to make a black hole, all you have to do is stuff enough matter inside a ball with a given radius.*

Either you need a lot of matter or you have to do a lot of compressing.

Lot of matter: If you have a ball of water that is 150,000,000 (one hundred fifty million) times the mass of the Sun, then it is automatically inside its Schwarzschild radius and a black hole will form.

Lot of compressing: If you have something small, like the Earth, you would have to compress it down to a ball with radius 9mm (3/8") in order to get it to turn into a black hole.

The formula is
$$r = \frac{1.48m}{1,000,000,000,000,000,000,000,000,000}$$

where r is in meters and m is in kilograms.

English

When should you use quotation marks? *You put them around direct quotes, and around titles of short stories, short poems, songs, speeches, and lectures.*

You don't use them for emphasis.

Wrong: You "really" need to come on time.

Right: You *really* need to come on time.   *(use italics)*

Right: You <u>really</u> need to come on time.   *(use underline)*

Right: You **really** need to come on time.   *(use boldface)*

Fred has read widely over his lifetime. He knew a lot about many things, but there were areas where he knew little.

Child's Games

Explain the rules of hopscotch. *You throw stuff and hop around.*

Your Turn to Play

1. The clerk received \$15 out of the \$500 that Fred had paid. What percent is that?

2. Using **exponents** can make life easier. 2^5 means $2\times2\times2\times2\times2 = 32$. 5 is the exponent on the 2.

Instead of writing 1,000,000, you could write $10\times10\times10\times10\times10\times10$ or 10^6.

Simplify the denominator in the Schwarzschild Radius formula:

$$r = \frac{1.48m}{1{,}000{,}000{,}000{,}000{,}000{,}000{,}000{,}000{,}000}$$

3. A ream of paper is 500 sheets. A ream is approximately 2-inches thick. Using a conversion factor, approximately how many pages are in that 14-inch stack of test papers?

4. Fred was going through that 14-inch stack of papers at the rate of 1.25 inches per hour. How far would he get in 3.5 hours? (Using a calculator, this would be super easy. You would just multiply 1.25 times 3.5. Do your computation using fractions instead of decimals.)

. . . . COMPLETE SOLUTIONS . . . .

1. 15 is ?% of 500. We don't know both sides of the *of*, so we divide the number closest to the *of* into the other number.

$$500\overline{)15.00} \quad \begin{array}{c} 0.03 \\ \end{array} \quad 0.03 = 3\%$$

2. $r = \dfrac{1.48m}{10^{27}}$ (Isn't this a lot nicer?)

3. $\dfrac{14\ \text{inches}}{1} \times \dfrac{500\ \text{sheets}}{2\ \text{inches}} = 3500$ sheets

4. 1.25 is the same as 1 plus 0.25, which is the same as $1 + \dfrac{1}{4}$ which is $\dfrac{5}{4}$

3.5 is the same as $3 + \dfrac{1}{2}$ which is $\dfrac{7}{2}$

$$\dfrac{5}{4} \times \dfrac{7}{2} = \dfrac{35}{8} = 4\dfrac{3}{8} \text{ inches.}$$

$$\begin{array}{r} 4\frac{3}{8} \\ 8\overline{)35} \\ -32 \\ \hline 3 \end{array}$$

Chapter Ten
Money

Fred was really enjoying himself. He liked to play the game of Questions.* The 14-inch stack of test questions he was working on was just like playing Questions, except that he would write his answers.

Economics
What is money? *Exchanging things is at the heart of economics. If Joe raises mice and Stanthony makes pizzas, then they might decide to exchange. Joe might give Stanthony 40 mice, and Stanthony might give Joe a medium combo pizza.*

✶ The game of **Questions** is only played in a car. The driver will say something like, "Question number one: What does a red curb mean?" The youngest kid always gets first shot at the answer. If the youngest can't answer it, the question is passed on to the next youngest. "It means you can't park there."

Then "Question number two: Name the green stuff in plants."

"Question three: Name two constellations in the sky."

"Question four: Who was the first president of the United States?"

"Question five: How many pairs of animals did Moses bring into the ark?" (Answer is "None. Noah did it.")

"Question six: Trees that lose their leaves in winter are called what?" (Deciduous.)

Name the five vowels. Name a composer whose name starts with B. How many days in a fortnight? What's the third planet from the sun? Name four spices. Name a number that if you square it, you would get the same answer as multiplying it by two. (Both zero and two are correct answers.) Where on your body are your incisors?

On a trip to the grocery store, you can get in 20 or 30 questions. Kids absolutely love it. About a third of the questions get repeated the next time you play. It doesn't take long before they know that the green stuff in plants is called chlorophyll.

Kids love to learn "stuff." It doesn't matter whether it's music, medicine, or meteorology. Many times, when the family gets in the car, the kids will shout, "Let's play Questions." Those same kids never seem to say, "It's Saturday, and I don't get to go to school. I can hardly wait till Monday." Does this say something about a natural education (the game of Questions) and the school system?

The problem is that Stanthony might not want mice. He might trade the 40 mice for a pair of size 9 shoes. But Stanthony has size 13 feet, so he might trade those size 9 shoes for 23 boxes of peppermint toothpaste. But he doesn't like peppermint, so he trades it for. . . . This gets crazy.

In almost every society money gets "invented." In prison camps during World War II, cigarettes were used. Even people who didn't smoke would accept them in trade, because they knew that they could "spend" them with others who did.

Nobody likes a cow that smokes.

In some societies, cows are used as money. We use little pieces of gray-green paper.

Anything can be used as money, but a good choice of money is one that is:

✱ Durable. Don't use bananas. They rot too quickly.

✱ Portable. Don't use sheets of plywood. Too hard to get into your wallet.

✱ Limited. Don't use air.

✱ Fungible. That means that the units of money are alike. One dollar bill is the same value as any other dollar bill. Pieces of art are not fungible. (Fungible rhymes with sponge-able.)

✱ Divisible. Don't use 12 carat diamonds that are each worth a year's wages. You can't make change.

In many societies, gold and silver have been the best choice for money. They are durable, portable, in limited supply, fungible, and divisible.

If tomorrow, nobody wanted dollar bills, they would be worth . . . nothing. They would just be dirty little pieces of gray-green paper.

Fred was lost in the work as the hours flew by. Outside the storeroom where they had stuck Fred, the clerk and Coalback had their lunches. When they closed up the store at 6 p.m., they had totally forgotten about Fred.

🐞 🐞 🐞

When they opened the store the next morning, the clerk went into the storeroom to get a mop. Fred was just completing the last page of the stack of test papers.

"Hi!" Fred said to the clerk. "That was fun. Are there any more tests to do?"

"No. This will be enough." The clerk took the stack and left the room. He headed into Coalback's office and put the stack on his desk.

"What's this?" Coalback growled.

"That kid from yesterday. He stayed here all night and finished the pile."

Coalback took the stack and dropped it into the garbage. "Never had that happen before. Take the kid and put him in the waiting room, and we'll figure out what to do with him."

The clerk went back to Fred and told him that the psychometricians were using their computers to analyze his tests. He took Fred to the waiting room, which had a television and a bunch of old magazines. The clerk left. A roller derby contest was blaring on the TV. Fred turned it off.

"What are we going to do, boss?" the clerk asked Coalback.

"We'll just let him sit there till he gets so bored or hungry that he will leave. Then we'll close the store."

Little did they realize who Fred was. It would probably be weeks until Fred started to feel any hunger. And Fred has so much to think about, he never gets bored.

🍒   🍒   🍒

The next morning(!) Fred was still in the waiting room. He was thinking about how sad the story of *The Romance of Tristan and Iseult* was. He especially liked, ". . . for most men are unaware that what is in the power of magicians to accomplish, that the heart also can accomplish by dint of love and bravery."*

As Coalback walked in, Fred was straightening the magazines. Coalback began, "Young man, our staff has spent innumerable hours evaluating every page of your submission. We appreciate the thoroughness

_____

* *The Romance of Tristan and Iseult* as retold by Joseph Bédier from the first complete English edition, translated from the French by Hilaire Belloc and Paul Rosenfeld, p. 40.

with which you have done your work. Given the depth and complexity of many of your answers, we have had to hire extra, specially trained individuals to analyze your answers."

Fred was thinking to himself Yes, yes. I can hardly wait to find out the results.

Coalback could sense Fred's eagerness. He continued, "Indeed, our costs have exceeded the nominal* fee we have asked from you."

Before Coalback could go on, Fred interjected, "Oh. I am so sorry. Is there anything I can do?"

Coalback's eyes brightened. "If you could find it in your heart, any additional contribution would be a lot of help to us."

"All I have left in my checking account is $84.27."

"That would be fine."

Fred wrote out:

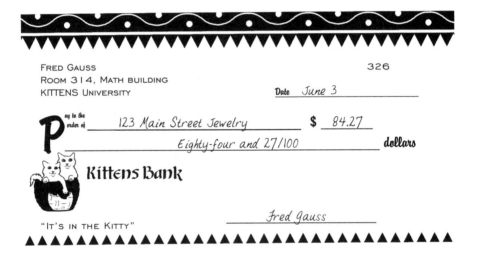

Fred had never been taught by his parents how to correctly write a check. When Coalback saw this check he immediately thought of altering it. You don't leave all that space to the left of the numbers.

---

* *Nominal* prices or fees are those that are trivial compared with the value received.

Here's how Coalback could have changed Fred's check:

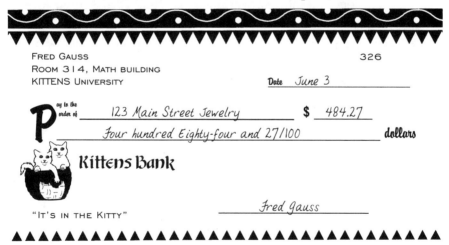

The only reason he didn't alter Fred's check was that he knew that Fred was telling the truth when he said that he only had $84.27 left in his account.

Then Fred added, "You can be sure that my $84.27 check won't bounce. I have overdraft protection on my account. If I overdraw my account by four hundred dollars, they will still honor the check."

Coalback altered Fred's check before he deposited it.

FRED GAUSS   326
ROOM 3 I 4, MATH BUILDING
KITTENS UNIVERSITY   Date   *June 3*

Pay to the order of   *123 Main Street Jewelry* $ *484.27*
      Four hundred Eighty-four and 27/100   dollars

Kittens Bank

                 Fred Gauss
"IT'S IN THE KITTY"

"Now, as I was saying," Coalback continued, "we have come to a definite and unanimous conclusion. There is a unique direction your career path should take." Coalback paused. He thought, "What in blazes am I going to tell this kid? I don't have the foggiest idea which way he should head."

He looked at the magazine that was on top of the pile that Fred had carefully arranged.

Coalback said, "You, young man, should go into hot dog sales. It is the one clear occupation for which you are uniquely suited."

"How can I ever thank you enough for all the work you have done," Fred exclaimed. Fred extended his little hand and shook the meaty paw of Coalback—the paw that didn't have Fred's check in it.

Fred headed out into the warm Kansas sun. Fred's mind was racing: I sell hot dogs. I'm in the business of marketing hot dogs. Everyone likes hot dogs. I could sell long hot dogs for people who are hungry and short hot dogs for people who are dieting. This is perfect. Why didn't I ever think of it? This is so obvious. I must write a letter to Mr. Coalback, thanking him for all the work he and his psychometricians have done.

Your Turn to Play

1. Money systems have five desirable properties, which we listed four pages ago. Without looking back, how many of those five properties can you name?

2. When Coalback wasn't selling career counseling, he was selling diamond rings. He put an ad in the paper: "Five carat diamond rings—only $60 each."

When he opened the store at 6 a.m., he and his clerk were selling the rings over the counter at the rate of 3 per minute. During the sale they also sold 13 rings over the Internet. The sale ended when the last of their 913 rings was sold. How long did they sell those fake diamond rings?

3. To the nearest percent, what percent of the 913 rings were sold over the Internet?

. . . . COMPLETE SOLUTIONS . . . .

1. The five properties of a desirable money system are: ☐1 Durable, ☐2 Portable, ☐3 Limited Supply, ☐4 Fungible, and ☐5 Divisible.

2. After you have read the problem, the first step is to let x equal the thing that you are trying to find out.

Let x = the number of minutes that they were selling rings.

The second step is to write *Then* statements based on the *Let x =* line that you just wrote.

If I know that the sale lasted x minutes, and that they were selling rings at the rate of 3 per minute . . .

Then 3x = the number of rings they sold over the counter.

Then 3x + 13 = the total number of rings they sold.

Now, writing the equation becomes straightforward:

$$3x + 13 = 913$$
$$3x = 900 \qquad \text{Subtract 13 from both sides}$$
$$x = 300 \qquad \text{Divide both sides by 3}$$

The sale lasted 300 minutes.

One little word of caution: Some readers might have avoided the procedure of writing *Let x =* and *Then 3x =* and, instead, just figured out the answer in their heads. The whole point of these word problems is *not* to find the answer. It is to learn how to use the procedures of algebra. It won't be long before the word problems will be too hard to solve by just messing with them in your head. Algebra was invented to solve those too-tough-to-solve-in-your-head problems. Now is the time to learn the procedures of algebra.

3. 13 is ?% of 913. $913\overline{)13.000}^{\,0.014} = 1.4\%$

1.4% is closer to 1% than it is to 2%.

Chapter Eleven
Borrowing Money

The first thought that Fred had was Who are my customers? He knew that "Everyone is in business"—that was the fifth key point of economics. It's important to pay attention to whom you are trading with—who your customers are.

If my customers are going to be the rich and famous, then I'm going to have to make super hot dogs. I could call them Gourmet Gauss Dogs.* I'm going to have to charge a lot since there won't be that many customers to serve.

If I deliver hot dogs to people's houses like some pizza stores deliver pizzas, then it will take a long time between customers. Each driver would only be able to visit four to seven houses per hour.

An outdoor possibility

What about operating a hot dog stand on a sidewalk? Then I could have a lot more customers than a delivery service would have, but when it rained I would get wet.

Fred had the right idea: *If you want a successful business, you need to find a significant need that others don't see.* (That's the sixth key point of economics.)

Fred thought over the alternatives: There may be a need for gourmet hot dogs for the rich and famous, but there wouldn't be enough sales.

There may be a need for home delivery of hot dogs, but delivering four to seven hot dog orders per hour would mean that I would have to charge a lot and if I charge too much, then there wouldn't be any demand.

There are already tons of hot dog stands on the streets near KITTENS University selling traditional hot dogs, so this isn't a need "that others don't see."

Fred put a lot of thought into the possibilities for hot dog sales.

✳ Gauss is Fred's last name.

• He thought of having a restaurant. He might call it Fred's Dog House.

• He imagined being a hot dog producer and selling his hot dogs to various grocery stores. But there are others who have seen and filled that need.

• Dogs are meat eaters. You don't often see them munching on carrots. He pictured selling hot dogs that are made especially for dogs. He could call it Going to the Dogs. The motto of the company could be "It's a dog-eat-dog world."

Fred put all those thoughts aside for a moment. He would let his subconscious work on it. Often he solved tough math problems by "letting it cook on the back burner" of his mind for a day or two.

I have no money in my checking account, he thought to himself. But Fred was wrong. He didn't have $0 in his checking account. After Coalback had altered Fred's check and cashed it, Fred's account was overdrawn by $400. In algebra, we could say he had –$400 in his account. Minus 400 is a negative number. On the number line, it would be to the left of zero.

If someone put $400 cash into Fred's checking account, his balance would come back up to $0.

If someone put $500 into his account, his balance would be $100.

If someone put $100 into his account, his balance would be –$300.

In symbols: $-400 + 400 = 0$
$$-400 + 500 = 100$$
$$-400 + 100 = -300$$

In any event, Fred knew that he would need some money to start up his business. If he waited until his July paycheck from KITTENS University, then a third of his summer would be gone. He thought about borrowing the start-up money.

Throughout all the (five) years of his life, Fred had never borrowed money. This was going to be something new. He didn't know where to start. He had seen that sign on the street, which led him to his career counseling.

Fred looked up and down the street. He was happy to see that there weren't any signs advertising hot dog sales. He knew that if he was going to be successful in hot dog sales, he needed to be supplying a need that others didn't see.

But there was a sign that got Fred's attention. And it was right next door to Mr. Coalback's career counseling center.*

Fred didn't know what a pawn shop was, but if they were in the business of lending money, he knew that he needed to investigate.

When Fred walked in, he had a surprise. "Mr. Coalback!" Fred exclaimed. "Do you also own this store?"

Coalback held out his paw so that Fred could shake it again. He knew that Fred liked doing that. He smirked** and said, "How nice of you to say that. I don't own either piece of real estate. I just rent." And in his head he silently completed that sentence: I just rent *so that I can make a quicker getaway when the cops come after me.*

"Could you please tell me how a pawn shop works?" Fred asked.

"I would be delighted. You bring in something you own, and I put it in safekeeping. I lend you money, and later when you pay me back, I

---

* 125 Main Street is right next door to 123 Main Street. Almost always, the odd-numbered addresses are on one side of the street and the even-numbered addresses are on the other side of the street. Here are some **consecutive numbers**: 7, 8, 9, 10, 11. Here are some **consecutive odd numbers**: 123, 125, 127, 129, 131.

** To smirk is to smile with a feeling of superiority and offensive familiarity. For many adults who know a lot more about the nature of evil than Fred does, when they see Coalback smirk, they want to throw up.

give you the thing you brought in. What do you own that you would like to pawn? Jewelry, guns, home theater sound systems, gold watches. . . ."

"I don't have a watch," Fred said. "At KITTENS University they have clocks on all the walls, so I've never needed a watch."

"Well, what other things do you own?"

Fred thought for a moment. His desk was owned by the university. Then he remembered, "I have Kingie. I own Kingie."

"And, please tell me what Kingie is?" Coalback said.

"Kingie is the name of my doll. When I was less than a week old, I got it for free when my parents and I went to King of French Fries to eat. Kingie is really cute."

Coalback knew he had some explaining to do to Fred. "Pawn shops accept items that are valuable so that if you don't pay back the loan, then we can sell the items and get our money that way. I know that Kingie is valuable to you, but a free prize toy that you got five years ago at a fast food place isn't very valuable to me.*

Kingie

"Do you have anything that is valuable—something that would be worth a lot of money if you sold it?"

Fred shook his head and said, "I'm afraid not."

Silently, Coalback almost gently pushed Fred out the door.

Your Turn to Play

1. Almost secretly, in this chapter we have mentioned the first two stages in starting a successful business. Can you guess what those two steps are (before you look at the answer on the next page)?

2. List the five even consecutive numbers that come after 16.

3. $-10 + 30 = ?$

   $-10 + 10 = ?$

   $-10 + 7 = ?$

---

* English lesson: When you have two paragraphs of quotation from the same person, you don't put closing quotation marks at the end of the first paragraph, but you do put opening quotation marks at the beginning of each paragraph.

. . . . COMPLETE SOLUTIONS . . . .

1. The first step in creating a successful business is to find a significant need that others don't see. If everyone is

  building bowling alleys,

  opening video rental stores,

  selling plastic kitchen gadgets, or

  buying tulips,

  then those might not be the things for you to do.

The second step in creating a successful business is to avoid being **undercapitalized**—not having enough money. Studies have shown that one major cause of failure for new businesses is undercapitalization. (That word is too big. Instead, call it Lack Of Loot. If you show your business plan to someone who knows about starting a business, and you have a Lack Of Loot, they may write on your plan: LOL.)

The first years of your business are often the lean years. You have all the expenses of starting the business, and you have few customers.

2. 18, 20, 22, 24, 26

3. $-10 + 30 = 20$
   $-10 + 10 = 0$
   $-10 + 7 = -3$

TiMe oUt FoR TuLiPS!

In the answer to question 1 was the fad of buying tulips.

Question: Who ever heard of the fad of buying tulips?
Answer: Everyone who has ever studied economics.

The story: If you are a member of the human race, you need to know that whole groups of people occasionally go nuts. They go crazy about housing prices, about dueling, about some movie star, about seances, about alchemy, about witches, about when the world will end, about racoon coats, and about . . . tulips.

78

It is called the tulip mania, and it happened in the early 1600s in Holland. The tulip mania is perhaps the best-known financial bubble in economic history.

It started out simple enough. For some reason, tulip prices seemed to be increasing—not a whole lot, but enough that people started to notice the increase.

a tulip

The conversations were something like:

"I'll buy a couple more this year to avoid the higher prices next year."

"Did you hear how much tulips are?"

"I think I'll get a bunch now."

"Hey! There seems to be a shortage of the good bulbs."

"They'll never be cheaper than they are now."

"If you've got some extra cash, there probably is no safer investment than tulips."

"Panic! Have you seen how much they've gone up? I'll buy some and get super rich when someone buys them from me."

And by 1636, tulips were being traded in many Dutch cities the way stocks are traded today. Prices were skyrocketing. People went nuts.

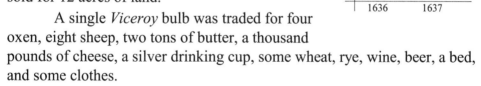

One of two existing *Semper Augustus* bulbs sold for 12 acres of land.

A single *Viceroy* bulb was traded for four oxen, eight sheep, two tons of butter, a thousand pounds of cheese, a silver drinking cup, some wheat, rye, wine, beer, a bed, and some clothes.

Wanna buy a tulip? You can get rich.

And then, as with all manias, it came to an end.

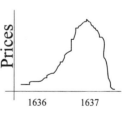

If you would like to read about the history of how people have gone crazy over the years, the book to read is *Extraordinary Popular Delusions and the Madness of Crowds* by Charles Mackay.

Type Extraordinary Popular Delusions and the Madness of Crowds pdf into any search engine on the Web. The book is free.

Chapter Twelve
Ownership

One of the most valuable things that Fred owned was his education. He knew a lot about many things. It was his education that landed him his teaching position at KITTENS University. But you can't pawn your education.

Then he remembered that he owned the books in his office, but he was certain that he didn't want to pack them all up and haul them to the pawn shop.

What does it mean to own something? To *really* own it? Fred owns the books in his office. He can do with them whatever he wants. He can sell them. He can rent them out to other people. He can give them away.

In other words, he has total control over them. No one else has a claim on them.

Does this mean that he can dump all his books on the desk of the man down the hall that teaches the popular tunes of ancient Greece? No, because that man owns his desk space. Fred's ownership of his books doesn't give him the right to violate the **ownership rights** of others.

You own your fists. I own my nose. Your ownership rights to your fists end before they get to the skin of my nose.

Of course, since Fred owns his nose, he can voluntarily give up his right not to be hit. For example, if he were to take up boxing, he would be giving up part of his ownership of his nose.

Your neighbor next door owns a set of drums. If he stays on his property, can he do whatever he likes with his drums? Can he beat them at 3 a.m.? No, because you own the right to the "peaceable enjoyment" of your property. (That's a legal phrase.) Who decides who owns what in this situation is usually determined by law. For example, the law might read: "No loud noises after 10 p.m."

WHO OWNS WHAT? is the **central question of politics**. You might think that this was a stupid question with an obvious answer, but it isn't. People disagree about this all the time.

I, your reader, think this Who Owns What question is really silly. Fred owns his books, and he can do whatever he wants with them, except stack them on someone else's desk.

When Fred gets a hot dog business, it's his business. He owns it. Right?

It depends.

Depends on what? He owns his books and his hot dog business. That's obvious.

It is not obvious. It depends on what political system Fred is living under. There are three main possibilities of WHO OWNS WHAT?

POSSIBILITY #1	Fred owns both his books and his hot dog business. No one else has a claim on them. He may do as he wishes with his books or his business—as long as he doesn't interfere with the ownership rights that other people have with their things.

This political system is called **capitalism**.

POSSIBILITY #2	Fred owns his books and other personal things, but he doesn't own his business. In this second political system, all hot dog businesses, all auto factories, all "the means of production" are owned by the state, or the government, or the collective. The state will issue a license (permission) for Fred to operate a hot dog business. The state will tell him where his business can be located, what hours it may be open, and exactly how he will run it. And the state will take all the profits that Fred makes.

This political system is called **socialism**.

If you think socialism is bad, you should hear about the third possibility.

POSSIBILITY
#3

Fred owns . . . nothing. The state (or government or collective) owns everything. Fred's business belongs to the state. His books belong to the state. Even Kingie belongs to the state.

This political system is called **communism**.

It gets worse than this.

I, your reader, can't believe this. How in blazes could it get worse than communism?

In the dictionary *communism* is defined as "a system of social organization based on holding all property in common, actual ownership by the community or state."

But *Communism* (with a capital C) goes one step further. Under Communism, besides individuals owning nothing, there is the objective of violently overthrowing capitalism wherever it exists. Wherever it exists—not just in your own country, but in any other country.

So it all boils down to WHO OWNS WHAT?

Those who sing the praises of socialism or communism are very clever singers. Marx, who sang of Communism, promised a workers' paradise. But everywhere Communism has been tried, it has become a workers' hell.

Charles Dickens painted a horrible picture of factory life in the early days of the Industrial Revolution in England: workers, including children, toiling for long hours in dangerous jobs. But Dickens failed to remember the fourth key point of economics: *You have to look at the whole picture.*

The whole picture: Before the Industrial Revolution in the 1700s, you ate black bread, gruel, and acorns. (Pizza Hut didn't deliver.) Kids often had one set of clothes and got baths once a year. If you had five children, four of them, on the average, died before the age of eight. Before the Industrial Revolution there was no choice. You lived and died in medieval socialism in which the nobles owned the means of production— land, farm tools, etc.

When the factories came into existence, you had a choice. Sure, it was bad in those factories, but it was heaven in comparison to the medieval socialism that proceeded it.

Hey, you forgot one political system. What about the Nazis? Isn't Nazism different from socialism? Once I heard that socialists are on the "right" and Nazis are on the "left"—whatever that means?

Nazism was the party under Hitler (1933–1945) that controlled Germany. In German, *Nazi* is short for *Nationalsozialist,* which translates as National Socialist. If you were in Germany during the Nazi period, everything was controlled by the state and its dictator. You may have still "owned" your farm under Nazism, but you had no control over it. Everything and everybody was forced to serve the state. The seventh key point of economics: *Ownership = Control. If you don't control something, you don't own it.*

Under both Nazism and Fascism (under Mussolini in Italy, 1922–1943), ownership by the state went one step further. The governments of Germany and Italy not only controlled (owned) everything within their own borders, they figured they owned *other* countries. The other countries didn't like that.

Your Turn to Play

1. If you were a citizen in a communist country, which owns 100% of everything, what percent would you personally own?

2. If you lived in England before the Industrial Revolution, on the average, four out of every five children you had died before the age of eight. What percentage lived to eight or older?

3. I could invent a function, which I'll call the socialist function. The domain will be {my car, my house, my doughnut factory}. The codomain will be {me, the state}. Here's how it would look:

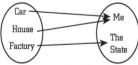

Draw similar pictures for a capitalist function and a communist function.

4. I worked this week at the rate of $12 an hour, and I got a bonus of $20. I made a total of $500. How many hours did I work?

........COMPLETE SOLUTIONS ....

1. 0% (Sometimes math is really easy.)

2. One out of five survived. $1 = ?\%$ of 5. You don't know both sides of the *of*, so you divide the number closest to the *of* into the other number.

$\frac{1}{5}$ which is $5\overline{)1.0}$ (giving 0.2) which is 20%.

3. The capitalist function:

The communist function:

4. The first step is to let x equal the thing we are trying to find.

Let x = the number of hours I worked this week.

The second step is to write one or more *Then XXX = YYYY* statements.

Then 12x = the wages I received for working x hours at $12/hour.

Then 12x + 20 = the total wages plus bonus I received.

At this point the equation becomes easy to write:

$$12x + 20 = 500$$
$$12x = 480 \qquad \text{Subtract 20 from both sides}$$
$$x = 40 \qquad \text{Divide both sides by 12}$$

I worked for 40 hours.

There is another aspect of Nazism that needs to be mentioned: Its hatred of many groups of people. About 11 million men, women, and children—innocent civilians—were rounded up, tortured, and killed. The Jews and Romani people (Gypsies) were hated by the Nazis on the basis of ethnicity. In the concentration camps, each prisoner wore a badge. The Jews wore a yellow star. The Gypsies, the homeless, the alcoholics, and the beggars wore a black triangular patch. The Jehovah's Witnesses, Adventists, Baptists, and other Christians wore purple triangular badges to indicate that they were *Bibelforscher* (Bible Students). Helmuth von Moltke wrote in 1942, ". . . what is happening is sin." At his trial the judge lectured Moltke, "Only in one respect does National Socialism resemble Christianity: It demands the whole man."

Chapter Thirteen
Interest Rates

Fred was on the street. He needed to get some money to start his business. He spotted another sign.

I can't believe my good luck! Fred thought to himself. *I don't have anything I want to pawn, but I do have a paycheck coming on July 1 from the university.*

Fred had no trouble finding 127 Main Street. In ten paces Fred was inside the store. (For adults, six steps would have been enough.)

Fred blinked. It was his friend, Mr. Coalback. "I didn't know you owned this store, too," exclaimed Fred.

Coalback did a little more smirking and said, "I own all the stores on this side of the street."* (He wasn't quite telling the truth. He was just renting.)

"I have a regular job at the University," Fred began. "I have been teaching there for five years."

"How much do you make?"

"I receive $500 on the first of each month."

"I can lend you $400, and you can pay me back on July 1st. I charge a fee of $100 for my service," Coalback told Fred.

Fred did the math: $100 is what percent of $400?

---

* If you must know—here is a list of some of those stores. We'll put the truth in [brackets].
Coalback's Day-Old [month-old] Bakery
The Take-And-Bake Crematorium
Tundra Tech Day Care [see *Life of Fred: Calculus* for the whole horror story]
Coalback Election Center [elect him to make the laws that take money from you]

Please note that there is nothing wrong with operating a bakery, a crematorium, a day care, or an election center. Almost everything—a match, a pencil, a gun, a birthday cake, an airplane—can be used for either good or evil.

$$100 \text{ is } ?\% \text{ of } 400$$

$$\frac{100}{400}$$

$$\frac{1}{4}$$

$$25\%$$

He would be charged 25% interest.

At first blush,* 25% didn't seem like such a large interest rate. Sometimes credit card default rates are over 30%.

The 30%, however, is an **annual percentage rate**. If you borrow $100, and pay back $130 a year later, the loan has had an annual percentage rate of 30%.

But Fred would be borrowing $400 for only a month. 25% is the *monthly* rate, not the annual rate.

The annual rate would be 25% times 12, which equals an annual percentage rate of 300%. That seemed a little steep. Fred thanked Mr. Coalback and left his payday loan store.

Your Turn to Play

1. Suppose Coalback starts the year with $400. He lends it out each month and collects $100 interest each month. Easy questions:

A) How much interest would he have collected in a year by lending out $400 each month?

B) His original $400 would have turned into how much at the end of the year?

★ *At first blush* is an **idiom**. It means "upon first considering something." *At first blush* has nothing to do with embarrassment or having a red face.

An idiom (ID-dee-m) is an expression that means something different than the individual words in the phrase. Do we really mean *a hot cup of coffee*?

2. Now suppose that Coalback starts the year with $400. He lends it out for the month of January and charges 25% interest. At the end of a month he would have *25% more than* he started with.

There are two ways to do a *25% more than* problem. (We showed both ways back in Chapter 24 of *Life of Fred: Decimals and Percents*.)

The Hard Way:

First, compute how much interest he was paid. 25% of $400 is $100.
Second, add that $100 to the $400 and get $500.

The Easier Way:

A 25% gain means the original $400 (100%) plus an extra 25%.
100% + 25% = 125%

$400 × 1.25 = $500

If each month Coalback lent out all the money he had, it would look like this:

$400	On January 1.
400 × 1.25 = 500	On February 1.
500 × 1.25 = 625	On March 1.

Or we could have written this as 400 × 1.25 × 1.25.
Or as $400 \times (1.25)^2$.

How much would Coalback have on January 1 of the following year if he lent out all the money he had each month for 12 months?

3. Suppose some of your ancestors received $24 when they sold a piece of New York real estate (Manhattan Island) 380 years ago. And suppose they invested that $24 in the stock market and earned 8% each year. And suppose they **compounded** their earnings by leaving all the money in the stock market. How much money would you and your relatives have today? You can leave your answer in the form ▬ × (▬)▬.

.......COMPLETE SOLUTIONS.......

1. A) He makes $100 in interest each month. At the end of 12 months he would make $1200 in interest.

    B) $400 + $1200 = $1600.   He would have quadrupled his money in one year.

2. He would have $400 × 1.25 × 1.25 × 1.25 × 1.25 × 1.25 × 1.25 × 1.25 × 1.25 × 1.25 × 1.25 × 1.25 × 1.25.

This could be written as $400 × $(1.25)^{12}$.

If you multiply it out . . .   400 × 14.551915228366851806640625

                              (I have a good calculator!)

which is $5820.77 (after rounding).

Some notes:

♪#1: If Coalback just lent out the $400 each month, he would have made $1200 in interest. (Question 1)

    If Coalback had lent out $400 plus any interest he received, he would have made $5820.77 – $400 = $5420.77 in interest. (Question 2)

    When interest builds on interest (as in question 2), it is called **compound interest**.

♪#2: If you put money in a bank and leave it there, each year* the interest will be added to your account. Your money will grow at a compound rate.

3. $24 invested at 8% for one year would yield 24 × 1.08 = $25.92.

For two years, $24 would yield 24 × 1.08 × 1.08 = 24 × $(1.08)^2$ = $27.99.

For 380 years, $24 would have turned into 24 × $(1.08)^{380}$.

$(1.08)^{380}$ is not too hard to figure out using logs, which you'll learn about in *Life of Fred: Advanced Algebra*. (You take the log of 1.08, multiply it by 380, and then take the antilog. $(1.08)^{380}$ = 5,023,739,194,020.) So today that $24 would be 24 × $(1.08)^{380}$ ≈ $120,569,740,656,492.

    $120 trillion is enough to easily buy all the land in the United States.

★ Some banks may pay interest every year. Some every month. Instead of paying you, say, 12% per year, they might pay you 1% per month.

    Some banks may pay you interest every day. Instead of paying a 12% per year, they might pay you 0.0329% per day. 0.0329% is 12% divided by 365.

Chapter Fourteen
The Tragedy of the Commons

Fred raced back to his office. He was eager to plan all the details of his hot dog business. As he sat at his desk, someone knocked on his door. It was the man whose office was down the hall.

"Other people and I here on the third floor have a wonderful idea," he began. "We all think it would be a great idea to have more fresh fruit in our diets. We are all going to chip in and buy a cherry tree. We will plant it out in the yard in front of the building, and when it produces fruit we can each go down and harvest the fruit."

"What a neat idea," said Fred.*

One problem that Fred had was that he only knew the fairy tale account of the Pilgrims' first years in America. Every Thanksgiving, Fred heard about how the Pilgrims came to Plymouth in the winter of 1620–1621. Fred heard the story of how the harvest in the fall of 1621 was bountiful, and how the Pilgrims along with the Indians celebrated the first Thanksgiving.

—It's chow time!

But that's only a half-truth. The harvest in the fall of 1621 was miserable. Famine and death followed that harvest. The harvest in the fall of 1622 was also miserable. More famine and more death.

What the Plymouth Colony was practicing was a form of socialism. Everything that was produced by farming, fishing, hunting, or sewing was put into a community storehouse. Each of the colonists was expected to

---

✶ When it came time to plant the tree, Fred had to do it because all the others said that they were busy.

When it came time to water the tree, Fred had to do it because all the others said that they were busy.

When it came time to harvest the cherries, there was one small cherry left on the tree for Fred. Everyone else on the third floor got there before Fred.

put in everything that he or she produced, and was allowed to take out only what was needed.

Nobody produced much since loafing gave you the same rewards as diligently working. This is the eighth key point of economics: *If you separate the rewards from the work, very little work will be done.*

After the poor harvests of the first two years, the colony switched from socialism to a free-market economy. Each family received its own separate parcel of land. What they produced was theirs to keep. No one had to tell them, "Work hard," because they knew that their success depended on their own efforts.

The governor of the colony, William Bradford, wrote, ". . . instead of famine now God gave them plenty. . . . Any general want or famine hath not been amongst them since to this day."

In the second year of operating under a free market system, they had so much food that they began exporting corn.

Many early colonies started out as socialist states. At Jamestown, for example, the harvests were so bad that during the winter of 1609–1610, the population fell from 500 to 60. Then they switched to a free market economy in which everyone owned what they produced. The colony secretary, Ralph Hamor, wrote that there was now, "plenty of food which every man by his own industry may easily and doth procure."

Hamor wrote that under the old communal system, "We reaped not so much corn from the labors of 30 men as three men have done for themselves now."

Fred didn't know the true account of the Pilgrims, but he did know about the community room down the hall from him. It was a room that the university had set aside several years ago for the use of the faculty on the third floor. Everyone on the third floor was expected to contribute peanuts for the peanut dish, candy for the candy dish, newspapers and magazines for the reading table, and help keep the place neat.

When the room was first set up, everyone thought that the community room was such a wonderful idea. Many of the faculty brought some peanuts for the peanut dish or some candy for the candy dish. But after a month the only one who was buying peanuts and candy was Fred. Every couple of days, Fred would go in and straighten up the newspapers and magazines and sweep the floor. Others would go in and eat peanuts and candy, read the newspapers, and leave the place a mess.

In economics books, this is called "The Tragedy of the Commons." It has happened over and over again in human history: something owned by everyone collectively is often abused by individuals.

✴ The ocean is owned collectively. Those who fish for whales get as many whales as they can. The results have been that some species of whales have been fished almost to extinction.

✴ The commons is a piece of land owned jointly by the members of the community. In the olden days the commons might have been a piece of pastureland on which everyone was allowed to graze their cattle. In a short time, the pastureland was destroyed. If a single person had owned that land, he might not have over-grazed it. But since everyone owned the

commons, everyone brought all their cattle there.

✴ If Fred decided to set up a big partnership for his hot dog business, he might have included Brenda, the math department secretary, to help with the clerical work of the business. He might have included the man down the hall to help with the advertising. He might have included Joe to help lift the cases of hot dogs. Fred's job in this partnership would be to do all the other jobs in business. And in this big partnership, Fred would promise each of them an equal share of the profits.

And if Fred decided to set up this partnership, he would be replaying another episode of The Tragedy of the Commons.

Instead of a partnership, Fred always could just own the business and *hire* others to do the clerical, advertising, and lifting.

Your Turn to Play

1. If Fred set up a partnership, there would be four partners: Fred, Brenda, the man down the hall, and Joe. What percentage of the profits would each of them receive?

2. Let's look at it from Brenda's point of view. She is supposed to contribute one-fourth of the work for the partnership and receive one-fourth of the profits. She thinks to herself, "If I work only half as hard, the profits of the hot dog business will suffer."

If Brenda did her 25% of the work, then 100% of the work would be done:

$$25\% + 25\% + 25\% + 25\% = 100\%$$
Fred   Brenda   man   Joe

100% of the work would be done, and 100% of the profits will be made. Brenda would receive 25% of that.

Now suppose Brenda worked only half as hard as she was supposed to. Fill in the question marks:

$$25\% + \ ?\% + 25\% + 25\% = \ ?\%$$
Fred   Brenda   man   Joe

3. If only 87½% of the work was done, the partnership would earn only 87½% of the potential profits. What would Brenda's share of the 87½% of the profits be? (In other words, what would 25% of 87½% be? Hint: this is most easily done using fractions instead of percents.)

4. If Brenda did all of her work, she would receive $\frac{1}{4}$ of the profits of the business. If she worked only half as hard as she should, she would still receive $\frac{7}{32}$ of the profits of the business. What fraction of the profits of the business would she lose? (Translation: $\frac{1}{4} - \frac{7}{32} = \ ?$)

5. By what percentage would Brenda's profits go down? (Translation: $\frac{1}{32}$ is $?\%$ of $\frac{1}{4}$)

·······COMPLETE SOLUTIONS·······

1. Each of them would receive one-fourth of the profits. 25%

2. $$25\% + 12\tfrac{1}{2}\% + 25\% + 25\% = 87\tfrac{1}{2}\%$$
   Fred   Brenda   man   Joe

   And if 87½% of the work was being done, the profits would be 87½% of what they might be.

3. 25% of 87½% is the same thing as $\dfrac{1}{4} \times \dfrac{7}{8} = \dfrac{7}{32}$

4. $\dfrac{1}{4} - \dfrac{7}{32} = \dfrac{1(8)}{4(8)} - \dfrac{7}{32} = \dfrac{8-7}{32} = \dfrac{1}{32}$

By working half as hard, she would lose $\dfrac{1}{32}$ of the potential profits.

5. $\dfrac{1}{32}$ is ?% of $\dfrac{1}{4}$ We don't know both sides of the *of,* so we divide the

number closest to the *of* into the other number.

$$\frac{1}{32} \div \frac{1}{4} = \frac{1}{32} \times \frac{4}{1} = \frac{4}{32} = \frac{1}{8} = 12\tfrac{1}{2}\%.$$

So if Brenda cuts her work in half, she only loses one-eighth of her income.

Fred, the man down the hall, and Joe would also each lose one-eighth of their incomes if Brenda worked at 50% of her capacity.

In any partnership, the math is easy. You gain 100% of the hours you slack off, and only lose a fraction of your income. In any endeavor in which the profits are shared communally, it's always in your personal best interest to work as little as possible. That's why the Pilgrims starved.

 # The Bridge
from Chapter 1 to Chapter 14

first try

Goal: Get 9 or more right and you cross the bridge.

1. Here are three different functions. Which of these, if any, is 1-1?

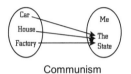
Communism

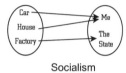
Socialism

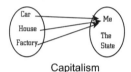
Capitalism

2. Joe once told Darlene that he would like to have a billion dollars.

"How are you going to do that?" Darlene asked.

"Easy," Joe answered. "I'm going to sell my bubble gum collection."

"But you chew up every piece of bubble gum you get the minute you get it," Darlene said.

"Yes, but I save the used bubble gum. The used pieces harden into all kinds of art shapes," Joe explained. "There is always someone who wants to buy modern art."

Joe's Gum Art

This is a billion dollars: $1,000,000,000. If you write it in the form of 10^x, what is the value of x?

3. C.C. Coalback didn't mind getting parking tickets because he never thought of paying them. When he was hauled in front of the judge, Coalback had 20 outstanding tickets. The judge added a $55 administrative fee on top of all the tickets, and Coalback owed $1,235. Each of the 20 tickets were for the same amount. How much was each ticket?

4. Joe's checking account was overdrawn by $100. His bank statement read: Checking account balance: −100. If Joe deposited $1000 into that account, what would his new balance be?

5. Every year, Joe's Gum Art collection is 9% heavier than the previous year. (So far, no one has bought his collection.) If his gum collection weighed 30 kilograms on January 1, 2005, how much did it weigh on January 1, 2007?

 # The Bridge
from Chapter 1 to Chapter 14

6. "What would you do with a billion dollars?" Darlene asked.

"First, I guess, I would have to pay the federal income tax of 43%, and the state income tax of 10%, and the city income tax of 3%.*"

How many dollars would Joe have to pay in income taxes?

7. "Then I would buy a whole lot of bubble gum and start chewing," Joe said.

Joe typically chews 7 pieces of gum every 18 minutes. How long would it take him to chew 200 pieces? Round your answer off to the nearest minute.

8. If a carton of gum (containing 400 sticks) costs $21, how much would x cartons cost?

9. If a function has a domain = {☎} and a codomain = {A, B, C, D}, must this function be 1-1?

10. The sales tax is 9%. How much sales tax would Joe have to pay to buy a $21 carton of gum?

---

* Yes. Some cities have their own separate income taxes to pay.

The rates used in this question vary from year-to-year and vary depending on what state and city you live in.

In 2005, California added what they called a "mental health tax" of 1% on incomes over $1 million. That certainly did not increase the mental health of those high income earners!

 # The Bridge
from Chapter 1 to Chapter 14

second try

1. Darlene told Joe, "You like to think about food and fishing all the time. Let's think about our future." She was thinking about their future *together*, but Joe went in a different direction.

Joe said, "Yeah. Someday I probably gotta go to work. I really don't want to, but my bubble gum collection hasn't sold yet. Okay. Help me think of a job."

Darlene wanted to shout out, "Husband!" but held back. Instead, she used a method she read in a supermarket tabloid:

She picked a letter at random and said, "P. What you should do starts with the letter P."

After she said that, she figured that her subconscious had supplied that letter, since P was the first letter in *partner*, *parent*, and *prenuptial*.

> *The Daily Blubber*
> **If you can't figure out what to do, just pick a letter.**
>
> New diet plan—Lose 24 pounds this weekend.

"That's it!" said Joe. "I'll be a park ranger. I always thought that would be a cool job."

Joe phoned in an order for 12 identical park ranger hats. The sales tax was $49, and the total bill was $613. How much was each hat?

2. While he waited for the hats to be delivered, he started packing.

His shirt went in his suitcase.	shirt → suitcase
His handkerchief went in a paper bag.	handkerchief → paper bag
His one sock went in his pocket.	sock → pocket
His puppy went in a crate.	puppy → crate

This is a function. The domain of this function is {shirt, handkerchief, sock, puppy}. What is the codomain of this function?

3. Is the function that was mentioned in the previous question a 1-1 function?

4. While he was waiting for his hats, he started making a sign. He knew park rangers spent almost all their time putting up signs. He didn't know what to write. He thought of "Litter Later—When You Get Home," but he wanted something that sounded more erudite. He telephoned Fred, and

 # The Bridge
from Chapter 1 to Chapter 14

Fred suggested that every morning he could put up a sign that read, "Et facta est lux."

Joe told Fred that all the words were misspelled. Fred giggled and told Joe that the words were in Latin and meant, "And there was light."

There are 13 letters in the phrase *Et facta est lux*, and Joe painted the first 3 letters in 11 minutes. How long did it take him to paint all 13 letters? Round your answer to the nearest minute.

5. The crate with the puppy in it weighed 47 pounds. Joe opened it up and dropped in some doughnuts. The crate gained 9% in weight. What was its new weight? Round your answer to the nearest pound.

6. Joe stopped his preparation. He didn't want to overwork himself. He sat in front of his television for a couple of hours and watched some drivel*. He heard the puppy scratching on the wall of the crate and knew what that meant. He let the puppy out. It weighed 4 kilograms. It headed out onto Joe's porch and did what puppies do when you "walk them." When it came back, it had lost 6% of its weight. How much (exactly) did the puppy now weigh?

7. Joe was flipping channels and stopped at a quiz program. The announcer told the contestant, "For $600 in prizes, name four consecutive even numbers where the largest of them is 88." What is the correct answer?

8. The next quiz show question was, "For $800 in prizes, what is the value of x that makes 2^x equal to 1024?" What is the correct answer?

9. This was too much for Joe. He flipped the channel to "Joy of Doughnut Cooking." The puppy licked the screen. The lady on the screen said, "Take $\frac{1}{3}$ cup of baking powder and add $\frac{3}{4}$ cup of flour." What is the volume of that baking powder and flour mixture? Do not leave your answer as an improper fraction. (An **improper fraction** is a fraction where the numerator is greater than or equal to the denominator.)

10. Solve $7x - 6 = 2x + 54$

★ *Drivel* is such a wonderful word. It has two meanings. Drivel is saliva (spit) that dribbles out of the mouth, and it is useless, idiotic communication.

 # The Bridge
from Chapter 1 to Chapter 14

third try

1. Joe suddenly realized that if he were a park ranger, he would have to go outdoors where the bears are. He mentally crossed off ~~park ranger~~.

He thought about Darlene's suggestion: "What you should do starts with the letter P."

A piece of paint drifted down from his apartment ceiling, and he knew in a flash that he should be a painter. He took a piece of paper and made up a business card.

> Joe
> I'm a
> painter.
> I'll paint
> your stuff
> cheaply.
> $80 per
> hour

Working at the rate of $80 per hour, how long would it take Joe to make a billion dollars? ($1,000,000,000.) (Hint: use a conversion factor.)

2. Joe had a stack of binder paper. Since he didn't have a copier, he wrote out his business card 19 more times. He figured that 20 business cards would be a good number to start out with. Those 20 sheets were 40% of his total sheets. How many sheets of binder paper did Joe own?

3. Joe looked in his closet and found an old bucket of paint. It had $\frac{3}{5}$ of a gallon of paint in it. Joe figured he needed a little painting practice before his first job so he painted his couch. That took $\frac{1}{2}$ gallon of paint. How much paint was left in Joe's bucket?

4. His couch weighed 80 pounds before it was painted. It gained 2% after Joe's paint job. How much did it weigh after being painted?

5. List five consecutive numbers where the middle number is 74.

6. Joe phoned the local hardware store and ordered 6 gallons of paint. When they asked him what color he wanted, he thought of what Darlene had told him and said, "**Pink**." With a sales tax of $8, the total came to $110. How much was each gallon of pink paint?

7. Let the first set (the domain) be the set of everything in Joe's apartment. Let the second set (the codomain) be the set of all possible paint colors that are sold in stores around the world. There are thousands of colors.

    Assign to each element of the domain the color pink.

    Is this a function?

    Is it 1-1?

8. Joe imagined that he would make $500 on each paint job. How much would he make on x jobs?

9. Express 16⅔% as a fraction.

10. Solve $3x + 7 = 4x - 32$

 # The Bridge
from Chapter 1 to Chapter 14

fourth try

1. Joe waited and waited, and no one phoned him to ask him to paint. There were several possible reasons: (1) He hadn't put his phone number on his business card, (2) he hadn't given anyone his business card, and (3) everyone who knew Joe. . . .*

 Joe thought of being a plumber, but when he thought of his apartment's leaking faucet that he had not been able to fix, he dropped the idea of being a plumber. Once he had counted the drips. It dripped 8 times in 5 seconds. How many drips would that be in a week? (Use conversion factors.)

2. Joe headed to his dictionary and looked at the words starting with P to see if that would give him any ideas for an occupation. He found *paleontologist*. He thought that would be cool, except that he didn't know what a paleontologist is.** All the dictionary told him was that a paleontologist is someone who studies paleontology. All Joe knew was that *paleontologist* was a much better word than *plumber* since it didn't have any silent letters in it. One-seventh of the letters in *plumber* are silent. What is $\frac{1}{7}$ as a percent? Round your answer to the nearest percent.

3. Right after *paleontologist* was *paperboy*. "Now that's a job I could do,"  he said to himself. He had seen the kid down the street deliver papers, and it didn't look like such a hard job. If the first set (the domain) was the set of 600 papers that he would be given, and the codomain was the 873 homes in the neighborhood, then all he needed to know was which 600 homes would each get a paper. This is a function. Is it one-to-one?

---

* One guy who knew Joe expressed it this way: "Joe couldn't paint the inside of a can full of paint." Others, more politely, just called him inept.

** A paleontologist is an individual who studies fossils.

The Bridge
from Chapter 1 to Chapter 14

4. If Joe makes x¢ for each paper he delivers, then how much would he make delivering 600 papers?

5. He said to himself, "If I do a really good job of delivering papers, then more and more people will subscribe." He would start his job delivering 600 papers. Assume that each month there would be 6% more subscribers than the previous month. How many subscribers would there be after 4 months? After you have done your computation, round your answer to the nearest whole number. (Whole numbers = {0, 1, 2, 3, . . . }.) You can't have "part of a subscriber."

6. Joe got ready to go out and get a job as a paperboy. It took him $\frac{1}{6}$ of an hour to get dressed, $\frac{1}{3}$ of a hour to comb his hair, and $\frac{1}{2}$ of an hour to get the pink paint off of his bicycle. How long did it take him to get ready?

7. Which of these, if any, are true? $2^3 > 3^2$ $(0.1)^2 = \frac{1}{100}$ $0 < 7$

8. Joe was hoping that the newspaper company would pay him in dimes. He liked dimes. They are so small and round.

   He fantasized that he would get a whole bunch of dimes and a bonus of 50¢ (in quarters) so his total income would be $12.40 (= 1240¢). How many dimes would he have gotten?

9. Solve $40x - 7 = 263 + 10x$

10. $-17 + 27$

The Bridge

from Chapter 1 to Chapter 14

fifth try

1. Then he hit *photographer* in his dictionary. "I would never have thought of that," he said to himself, "since *photographer* doesn't sound like a word beginning with P."

The more he thought about being a photographer, the better it sounded. He could charge $7 for a picture that took him only a sixtieth ($\frac{1}{60}$) of a second to take. How much could he make in one hour if he could earn $7 each sixtieth of a second? (Start with 1 hour and use conversion factors.)

2. Then he realized that somehow his camera had been painted pink and didn't work anymore. He turned one page past *photographer* in his

dictionary and found his dream job. He would become a pilot.

In a comic book, Joe once read that only 6 out of every 300 people can qualify to become an airline pilot. What percentage is that?

3. Joe imagined that his pay would be $10 per hour. That's what he had read in a comic book. After each year of flying, he would expect a raise of 6% over the previous year. What would be his pay after 20 years? You can leave your answer in the form ▬ × (▬)▪.

4. If Joe was a pilot, he knew he could fly his plane to any city in the world. (It's amazing the things you learn in comic books.) Invent a function where the domain is {Joe's plane} and the codomain is all the cities in the world. (Translation: Find a rule which associates to each element of the domain, exactly one element of the codomain.)

5. $6^3 = ?$

6. $(\frac{1}{2})^3 = ?$

7. Solve $2x - 7 = 3x - 15$

The Bridge
from Chapter 1 to Chapter 14

8. One of the first things that Joe had to do in order to get his pilot's license was get his eyes checked. He made an appointment with the "eye ball guy" (Joe's words) and went to see him.

Optometrist: *I see* * *you are here to get your eyes checked. Have you had any problems with your eyes?*

Joe: Nope. That was sure an easy exam. Thanks, doc. (Joe starts to leave.)

Optometrist: *Wait. That wasn't the exam. Please have a seat. Do you see the chart?*

Joe: Sure. It's on the wall. Thanks doc. (Joe gets up and starts to leave.)

Optometrist: *Please remain seated. Now we will start the exam. Can you read any line on the chart?*

Joe: Don't be silly. None of those are words.

Optometrist: *Can you read the letters?*

Joe: Yes, I can. Thanks, doc. That exam was easy. (Joe gets up.)

Optometrist: *Would you please read them?*

Joe: Okay. I've read them.

Optometrist: *No. I mean read them out loud.*

Joe: Oh. You didn't say that.

Joe read 80% of the 70 letters on the chart. How many did he read?

9. It took Joe a half hour to read the letters. The room was dark and he kept falling asleep. It took him a third of an hour to fill out the new patient form. It took him a quarter of an hour to get out his wallet and pay the optometrist's fee. How long did it take him to do all these three things? Do not leave your answer as an improper fraction. (An **improper fraction** is a fraction where the numerator is greater than or equal to the denominator.)

10. The fee had several parts to it: $38.20 initial visit charge; $10.58 for extended exam; $7.77 pilot fee. How much was the total?

✱ Optometrists use that verb a lot. A musician would have said, "I hear that you are here to get your eyes checked." A mathematician would have said, "I understand that you are here to get your eyes checked."

103

Chapter Fifteen
Fred Finds His Business

F red took out a sheet of paper and wrote down all the hot dog businesses he had thought of so far:

1. *Gourmet Gauss Dogs--sales to rich people*
2. *Hot dog delivery to homes*
3. *A hot dog stand on the street*
4. *Fred's Dog House restaurant*
5. *Wholesale to grocery stores*
6. *Going to the Dogs--hot dogs for dogs*

He added to the list:

7. *Smashed hot dogs as bookmarks*
8. *Dumbbells for people who don't want to lift a lot of weight*

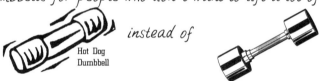

instead of

9. *Dog Logs--sell them as toys. Kids could build little houses using Dog Logs*
10. *Cut them in the shape of french fries. Then people could have potato "hamburgers" with meaty french fries*

When he thought about switching the roles of hamburgers and french fries, Fred suddenly realized what he was really good at. It was something that the world could certainly use.* He was good at ideas.

---

* Some people are really old—like 20 or 30—before they figure out their place in the world. I was 54 when I started writing the *Life of Fred* stories.

Short (true) story: When my younger daughter, Margaret, came home from kindergarten, she complained that the teachers kept asking her what she wanted to be when she "growed up."

I told her, "Tell them you want to be a ballerina."

Margaret responded, "But I don't want to be a ballerina."

I said, "That's okay. They'll like that answer, and it will give you time to think about what you really want to be."

He designed his business card.

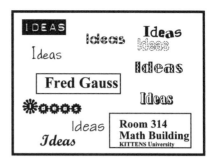

There are probably many, many businesses that could use Fred's skills.

On the other hand, many skills are needed to operate any business. Fred's ability to create ideas is just one part of the picture. On the other hand, he is not very good at lifting heavy boxes or at chopping down trees. This is called the **division of labor**.

The division of labor—you do your thing, and I'll do my thing—is necessary to create all the nice physical things that we enjoy.

Take, for example, a bottle of Sluice. Sluice is a clear lemon-lime soda not to be confused with Slice® / Sprite® / Storm® / Seven-Up® / Sierra Mist® / Squirt® which all start with S and which some people tend to confuse with each other. If Fred spent his whole lifetime, could he ever create—all by himself—a single bottle of Sluice?

Without the division of labor in our world, Fred would have to do everything himself.

✾ Getting the water might not be that hard. All he would need to do is find some stream. But he would need something to carry the water in. Where does he get that? We'll think about making a bucket some other time.

✾ Sugar is the main ingredient in Sluice. Fred will have to travel far from Kansas to find a place to grow sugar cane, which needs a tropical or subtropical climate. The best places in the world to grow sugar cane include India, parts of South America (Brazil, Peru, Bolivia, and Columbia), Australia, the Philippines, and Hawaii. Without a boat, Fred's best bet would be to get to South America. Without a car, bicycle, or airplane that trip is going to be llllloooooonnnnnnngggggggg. And without shoes, he would have a tough time getting there on foot. We'll think about making shoes some other time.

✾ Once the sugar cane grows, he will need to harvest it. The usual procedure is to first set the field on fire. That gets rid of any venomous

snakes that often inhabit those fields. The fire doesn't hurt the water-rich canes. Where does Fred get fire? We'll think about matches some other time.

❧ Fred will need a cane knife or a machete to cut the sugar canes down. He can't just use his teeth. He will need to make steel for his knife. He will need iron for the steel. He will need to find some iron-rich deposit, dig them up, and process the ore. We'll think about mining iron ore some other time.

❧ The label on the Sluice bottle is paper. He will need to cut down some trees. He will need an ax, which requires steel, which requires iron, which requires etc. We'll think about making paper some other time.

❧ To print the label, Fred will need to set up some kind of print shop, which will require ink. We'll think about making ink some other time.

❧ Fred will need plastic for the bottle and the cap. That requires oil. Digging an oil well requires all kinds of machinery. We'll think about drilling for oil some other time.

The division of labor means that each of us can pick one particular thing and learn to do that thing well. One of us can make buckets to carry water. One of us can grow sugar cane. One of us can make matches. One of us can dig iron ore. One can drill for oil.

Together, we can make bottles of Sluice—and other essential things—that make our lives comfortable.* With a good division of labor, all you need to do is be good at one (or a very few things). It can be taking care of babies or repairing air conditioning units.

What kills the division of labor? This is the ninth key point of economics: *The division of labor dies as you lose people you can trade with.*

✶ The thought of Sluice being essential is obviously untrue. The use of the word *essential* is an example of irony. Irony means saying something and obviously meaning the opposite of the literal meaning of the words.

Great literature will often use irony. It can be a powerful way of expressing something—unless the reader "misses it" and takes the words literally. When Amos (in the Old Testament) suggests that the people tithe every three days to Baal (NKJV), he is really screaming DON'T DO THAT! (Amos 4:4)

Your Turn to Play

1. Did you ever think about what it would be like if everyone else disappeared and you were the only person left on earth?

Or to be more extreme, eliminate all the books, all the machinery, all the things of civilization. You are naked in a forest. You have lost all the people you can trade with, and the division of labor has died.

Math question: What percent of all the things that have to be done will you need to do?

2. How do you catch a squirrel or kill a deer or find plants to eat? If you have ever walked in a forest—even with clothes on—did you notice that there weren't a lot of candy bars, milk shakes, or doughnuts? Here is a list of six things: 1) catch squirrels, 2) kill a deer, 3) separate the meat of the squirrel or deer from the rest of the animal (without a knife), 4) make a fire, 5) find 1500 calories of plant food every day for a year (that includes winter when there is snow on the ground), 6) pick your nose. What percentage of these things could you do?

3. Have you seen pictures of tribes of, say 100, people living in some remote jungle? Old issues of National Geographic are a good place to find those pictures. With 100 people the division of labor is still very small. Some of them will be hunters. Others may be gatherers of plant food. But in that small group there were no cell phones, no toilet paper, no filling of cavities at the dentist, and no mechanical pencils. Come to think of it, did any of those tribes invent and use the wheel? Getting calories is the big occupation.

Are these people stupid? No. Remember you would probably be dead if you were left in the jungle alone. They are smarter than you are at jungle survival.

Is it their fault that they don't have DVDs, nuclear power plants, or Swiss army knives? No. They just don't have enough people to trade with. Hence, no real division of labor. With no real division of labor, civilization doesn't develop.

Math question: What percentage of the kids in that tribe ever tell their parents that they want to grow up to establish a university (such as KITTENS University)?

4. Is it possible to invent a function that has a domain with 3 elements in it and a codomain with 2 elements in it that is 1-1?

5. The **cardinality of a set** is the number of elements in the set. What is the cardinality of {♡, ◊, ♧, ♤}?

6. Hard question: If a function is 1-1, what can you say about the cardinality of the domain and the cardinality of the codomain?

. . . . COMPLETE SOLUTIONS . . . .

1. Everything = 100%

2. For most of my readers, the response will be $\dfrac{1}{6}$ which is 16⅔%.

3. 0%

4. Suppose the domain is {A, B, C} and the codomain is {5, 8}.

Suppose that A is assigned to 5.   A → 5

Suppose that B is assigned to 8.   B → 8

C has to be assigned to either 5 or 8. In either case, the function will not be 1-1.

   If you have three mice and two pockets, and you put the mice in your pockets, some pocket will have more than one mouse.

   It is not possible for a function with a domain of 3 elements and a codomain of 2 elements to be 1-1.

5. The cardinality of {♡, ◊, ♧, ♤} is 4. There are four elements in the set.

6. If a function is 1-1, there have to be at least as many elements in the codomain as there are in the domain. Otherwise, we are in the situation described in question 4.

   If 17 cooks each make a recipe out of the *Joy of Squirrel Cooking* book, there have to be at least 17 recipes in order for each cook to have a different recipe.

   The cardinality of the codomain must be greater than or equal to the cardinality of the domain for a function to be one-to-one.

   If 90 students are in a classroom with 94 chairs, it is possible to assign each student to a chair so that no two students are assigned to the same chair. (You couldn't do that if there were only 89 chairs.)

Chapter Sixteen
Competition

F red knew that just making business cards was not enough to get customers. He put up posters all over campus advertising his new business.

> ### Ideas for Sale
> If you are stuck,
> I can supply ideas.
> Making things happen!
>
> Fred Gauss,
> Your Idea Man
> Room 314 Math Building

Lots of other people saw his posters, and they decided to go into the same business that Fred was in. Fred suddenly had competition.

Fred was dismayed. On the one hand, he was pleased that so many people thought that his plan to sell his ideas was such a good thing. But on the other hand, he wouldn't have 100% of the idea business. This was the first time in his life that he was in competition with a duck.

There are two different feelings about competition. People in business hate it; the rest of the world loves it.

Why people in business hate competition: If you're the only one who is selling a particular thing, you get all of the sales, and you never have to cut your prices.

Supposing you're selling tennis rackets, and you have no competition. Those who want to buy a tennis racket have to buy it from you. Recall the second key point of economics: *Customers are concerned about both the price and the quality of the product.* But if there's no competition, customers can't be very concerned about the price, and your rackets can be low quality.

With no competition you can make huge profits.

But if you are the only one selling tennis rackets and are making huge profits, other people are tempted to set up businesses selling tennis rackets. If you are selling tennis rackets at high prices, others will offer the same tennis rackets at cheaper prices and take away your customers. If you are offering shoddy tennis rackets, others will offer better tennis rackets at the same price.

Moral: If you have a **monopoly** (you are the only one selling something), you had better not set your prices too high or your quality too low, or others will enter your field of business and take away your customers.

> There is a natural tendency
> for monopolies to disappear.

Why consumers love competition: If I want to buy a tennis racket, I would be delighted to see that there are many companies selling them. They would all be competing to offer me the best racket at the cheapest price.

When Fred put up his posters, he followed a jogging route through the campus that he had used over the years. When he finished, he followed that same route back to his office.

While he was putting up the posters he averaged 3 mph. On the way back, he jogged at the rate of 9 mph.

It took him two more hours to put up posters than it did for him to jog back to the office.

How long did it take him to jog back to his office?

This is called a word problem, and it is considered by many students to be the hardest part of algebra. Back in Chapter 4, there were the three steps in finding the equation:

First: Read the problem and draw a picture if that helps.

Second: Write on a piece of paper: *Let x* = the thing you are trying to find out.

Third: Look at the *Let x* = statement that you have just written down. Look at the problem. You will then be able to write *Then XXX = YYYY* where *XXX* is some expression involving x, and *YYYY* is something in English.

The first step is pretty easy. You read the problem, and you draw a picture.

Office • ····   route   Fred   took   ⌒⌒⌒   —End

The second step isn't that hard. The question asks, "How long did it take him to jog back to the office?" so you write: *Let t = the time it took Fred to jog back to his office.* (You can use any letter you like for the unknown. If what we are looking for is a time, the letter t is sometimes chosen.)

It is writing the *Then XXX = YYYY* statements that is often the sticking point.

Experienced algebra students who have done a million of these kinds of problems will write out:

Then t + 2 = the time it took Fred to put up the posters.[*]

Then 9t = the distance Fred traveled to get back to his office.[**]

Then 3(t + 2) = the distance Fred traveled to put up the posters.

Since Fred traveled the same route back to his office as he did in putting up the posters, we have 9t = 3(t + 2).

---

[*] That is because we were told that "It took him two more hours to put up posters than it did for him to jog back to the office."

[**] It took Fred t hours to jog back to his office. (*Let t = the time it took Fred to jog back to his office.*) We are given that "he jogged at the rate of 9 mph." Going t hours at 9 mph will cover a distance of 9t miles.

But many beginning algebra students have trouble with that third step of writing the "*Then*" statements. In arithmetic, things were easy. They showed you how to do it, and then you did 40 identical problems. They gave you an example: $\frac{1}{5} \div \frac{3}{8} = \frac{1}{5} \times \frac{8}{3} = \frac{8}{15}$ and then your homework looked like this:

1. $\frac{1}{6} \div \frac{2}{3}$ 2. $\frac{3}{4} \div \frac{1}{4}$ 3. $\frac{2}{3} \div \frac{3}{4}$ 4. $\frac{5}{13} \div \frac{5}{6}$ 5. $\frac{11}{100} \div \frac{1}{4}$ etc.,

which you did—page after page—until you had filled the workbook. The work was easy but it was mind-numbing. You had the understandable thought: *How could anybody really enjoy doing this for a living? If this is what mathematicians like to do, I don't want any part of it.*

The truth: Mathematicians do not spend their days joyfully adding up columns of numbers. Most of them do not get a big thrill out of balancing their checkbooks. Most of them do not break out into happy singing when confronted with 40 division-of-fractions problems. Those 40 problems that are all alike have a special name among mathematicians. They are called **drill-and-kill** problems.

The first step in almost every field of learning involves a lot of drilling. Do you remember when you were first started to read? The teacher wrote an A on the board and said, "This is an A." Then she wrote a B on the board and said, "This is a B." Then you read, See Jack run. Jack's cat is Puff. See Puff run. Jack and Puff run. See them run. How much fun it is to see Jack run. At this point, some kids think to themselves, "If this is reading, I don't want any part of it. Reading is stupid." It is only later that reading becomes interesting: Jack got another cat. His name was Ralph. Ralph was a tiger. Ralph ate Puff.

What distinguishes mathematics from English or art or music is the amount of time it takes to get beyond the preliminaries. In the fifth grade, students are starting to read stuff that is truly interesting. In kindergarten, they are having fun drawing things. And somewhere in elementary school years, piano playing can become rewarding. In contrast, the fun part of mathematics takes a little longer. Geometry, if it's taught right, will emphasize the concept of proof, and it becomes a kind of puzzle to find a proof. There is often more than one way to do a proof.

Take for example the Pythagorean theorem. It's probably the most famous theorem in geometry. There are many proofs of this theorem. In 1876, a member of the United States House of Representatives found an original proof of this theorem. Later he became president (President Garfield). He is probably the only president to have found a proof of the Pythagorean theorem and have a famous cat with the same name. Elisha Scott Loomis wrote a book that listed 367 different proofs of that theorem.

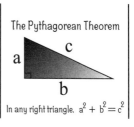

The Pythagorean Theorem

In any right triangle, $a^2 + b^2 = c^2$

Let's see if we can find a second way to find the equation for the Fred-puts-up-posters word problem. Here's the problem again so you don't have to look back.

This is a d = rt (distance equals rate times time) problem.

Count how many different quantities are involved. I count six of them:

two jogging speeds,
two lengths of time, and
two distances.

I could fill in six pretty boxes.

> When Fred put up his posters he followed a jogging route through the campus that he had used over the years. When he finished putting up the posters he followed that same route back to his office.
>
> When he was putting up the posters, he averaged 3 mph. On the way back, he jogged at the rate of 9 mph.
>
> It took him two more hours to put up posters than it did for him to jog back to the office.
>
> How long did it take him to jog back to his office?

	d	·r	t
Fred putting up posters			
Fred jogging back			

Filling in boxes is, perhaps, easier than writing *"Then"* statements.

What do they want to find out? Put an x (or a t) in that box:

	d	r	t
Fred putting up posters			
Fred jogging back			t

We know the two speeds (putting up the posters at 3 mph and jogging back at 9 mph):

	d	r	t
Fred putting up posters		3	
Fred jogging back		9	t

We know that it took him two more hours to put up the posters than it did for him to jog back to the office:

	d	r	t
Fred putting up posters		3	$t+2$
Fred jogging back		9	t

Since d = rt, we can fill in the last two boxes:

	d	r	t
Fred putting up posters	$3(t+2)$	3	$t+2$
Fred jogging back	$9t$	9	t

Since Fred traveled the same route both ways, we know that the two boxes on the left are equal.

$$3(t + 2) = 9t$$

We will show how to solve the equation in the next chapter. (Finding the equation is much harder than solving it.)

Your Turn to Play

1. Suppose you want to buy a new pair of shoes. There are already four shoe stores in the mall. Would you be happy or sad if a giant new shoe store opened up in town?

2. The man down the hall did not have very many original ideas. He started at one end of Main Street and walked to the other end, putting up posters everywhere he could. When he got to the far end of Main Street, he hopped on a bus and went back to its starting point. He put posters up on every lamppost, every fire hydrant, and every storefront. He averaged only 2 mph as he headed up Main Street. The bus took him back at the rate of 15 mph. It took him 13 more hours to put up his posters than it did for him to take the bus ride back. Find the equation to determine how long his bus ride was. (In the next chapter, we'll work on solving that kind of equation.)

3. Somewhere in the world there is always some weird weather happening. Fred heard on the radio about that desert that had a freak snowstorm. For several hours, it snowed at the rate of 10 inches per hour. Then the sun came out and melted all the snow. The melting took 7 more hours than the time it took to snow. The melting happened at 3 inches per hour. Find the equation to determine how long it snowed. (Again, in the next chapter we'll work on solving that kind of equation.)

4. Besides putting up posters, Fred had the opportunity to be interviewed on the local KITTENS University radio station. (The call letters of the station are MEOW.) In the time that he was being interviewed, he was gaining 54 customers per hour. He got the same number of customers by going door-to-door in the neighborhood and telling people about his new Ideas-for-Sale business, but he spent 4 more hours going door-to-door than he did in being interviewed. Door-to-door he was able to gain 6 customers per hour. Find the equation to determine how long his radio interview was.

Meow!

. . . . **COMPLETE SOLUTIONS** . . . .

1. The more places you have to shop for shoes—the more competition there is—the greater chance you will have of finding good shoes at a low price. As a consumer, you welcome more choices.

2. Count how many quantities are involved. I count six of them: two speeds, two lengths of time, and two distances. We'll use the six pretty boxes approach on this problem.

We want to find out how long his bus ride was, so we put a *t* in the appropriate box.

	distance	rate	time
Putting up posters			
Riding back			*t*

Since it took 13 more hours to put up the posters, the time to put up the posters is t + 13.

We are given the two rates, so we can put those in the boxes.

	distance	rate	time
Putting up posters		2	*t + 13*
Riding back		15	*t*

Since distance equals rate times time.

	distance	rate	time
Putting up posters	2(*t+*13)	2	*t + 13*
Riding back	15*t*	15	*t*

Since we know that the distance heading up Main Street is the same as the distance coming back, we have the equation: 2(t + 13) = 15t

3. If we do this problem using the traditional *Let x = . . .* approach, we have:

Let t = the length of time it snowed. (We always start a word problem by setting the variable equal the thing we are trying to find.)

Then t + 7 = length of time it took for the snow to melt. (The problem told us, "The melting took 7 more hours than the time it took to snow.")

Then 10t = the depth of the snow. (If it snowed for t hours at the rate of 10 inches per hour, there would be 10t inches of snow.)

Then $3(t + 7)$ = the depth of the snow that melted. (If that melted at the rate of 3 inches per hour for $t + 7$ hours, then $3(t + 7)$ inches of snow is melted.)

Since all the snow that came down was melted by the sun, we have: $10t = 3(t + 7)$.

Using the six pretty boxes approach:

	depth	rate	t
As the snow fell	$10t$	10	t
As the snow melted	$3(t + 7)$	3	$t + 7$

4. Let t = length of Fred's radio interview.

Then $t + 4$ = how long Fred spent going door-to-door. (He spent 4 more hours going door-to-door than he did being interviewed.)

Then $54t$ = the number of customers he gained from his radio interview.

Then $6(t + 4)$ = the number of customers to gain by going door-to-door.

Since we are told that he got the same number of customers by going door-to-door as he did in his radio interview, we have: $54t = 6(t + 4)$.

Here are the empty boxes, in case you would like to fill them in:

	Customers gained	rate of gaining customers	time
On the radio			
Going door-to-door			

Chapter Seventeen
Killing Competition

Originally, each of the five ideas-for-sale businesses received about 20% of the sales. Some people ordered from Fred because they thought he was cute. Some people ordered from the man down the hall because he looked experienced. Some people ordered from Zippo because they wanted some quick thoughts. Some people liked the idea of happy thoughts. And some people who really loved animals ordered from the Tall Duck.

The campus newspaper heard about all of these different ideas-for-sale businesses and did some investigative reporting.

THE KITTEN Caboodle

The Official Campus Newspaper of KITTENS University   Thursday 10:10 a.m. Edition 10¢

We Investigate

The Idea Business— An Inside Look

KANSAS: How is a consumer going to decide which Idea Man (or Woman or Duck) to hire? Your *KITTEN Caboodle* sent its best reporter to investigate each of these businesses.

We put the same question to each of them:

Our son is getting married and we are holding the wedding reception at our house. Give me ideas about what we should cook.

We first asked Zippo ("I can give you ideas faster than thought!"), and he came up with one thought: *Fast food! That's the way to go. Buy a whole bunch of $1 hamburgers, and everyone will be happy.*

We asked the man down the hall, and he informed us that he would have to think about it for several weeks.

We asked Ima Happy, and she was overjoyed: *I can't tell you how happy I am about weddings and receptions! They make me jump up and down. I love the roses and the wedding dresses and the music and the chatter of all the happy people.*

We asked the Tall Duck: *You can serve chicken or roast beef or fish or ham or turkey or lamb, but just don't serve duck!*

Finally we asked the little kid with a square head. His ideas came like fast-popping popcorn: *First, is this a lunch or dinner that you'll be serving? That makes a difference as to what you should cook. Second, who are the people who will be coming to the reception? Are they the meat-and-potatoes type or are they vegetarians? Third, will this be a formal reception or simply a gathering of close friends and relatives? If it's a formal reception, you probably can't serve pizza. Fourth, what you cook depends a lot on how much time you have and how big your kitchen is. Fifth,. . . .*

KITTEN Caboodle doesn't have the room in this article to list all 642 thoughts that Fred offered.

When people read the newspaper article, many of them flocked to Fred for their ideas. Fred has a high-quality product, and *customers are concerned about both the price and the quality of the product.* (That was the second key point of economics.)

When Zippo, the man down the hall, Ima Happy, and the Tall Duck saw their businesses going downhill, they decided to take action. Zippo, being the fastest mover in the group, acted first. He sent an email to all of the ideas-for-sale businesses:

Emergency Email

From: Zippo
To: Man down the hall, Fred Gauss, Ima Happy, Tall Duck
Subject: We gotta talk!

Dear Ideas-for-Sale friends,

Let's all meet for lunch today. I've got some quick ideas that will bring us a speedy recovery from our hard times.

Hurry on over to Stanthony's Pizza at noon.

In haste,
Zippo

When Fred received the email, he was delighted. He had thought of a new way of presenting the Ideas-for-Sale business to the public, and he wanted to share it with his friends. Instead of calling it, "Ideas for Sale," he thought that they could advertise their businesses as "Solutions to Your Problems." Since everyone has problems of one kind or another, the businesses would appeal to a wider audience.

The five met at noon at Stanthony's. Zippo began, "I have invited you here today because I have an idea. . . ." Everyone broke into applause. (What could you expect from a group whose business it is to produce ideas?)

"I'm going to suggest that we all work together to improve our business," Zippo continued. "I have an idea that. . . ." Everyone applauded again.

"I have an idea that we should all charge the same price for each of our ideas. If we each charge $100 for each idea, then we won't have any nasty price competition." Zippo glanced over at Ima who had been selling her ideas for a nickel apiece.

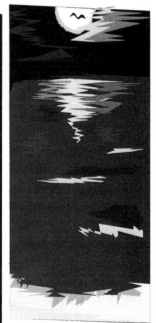

Collusion happens under cover of darkness.

Intermission

This method of restricting competition is called **collusion**. (ka-LOO-shun) Collusion is one of the oldest methods of getting more money from consumers.

Stockbrokers might collude to set minimum commission rates for selling stock.

Airlines might collude to set minimum prices for their tickets.

Producers of oil might collude to set the wholesale price of barrels of oil.

In Latin, *colludere* means to play together. However, in English, to *collude* takes on a more sinister meaning. When people collude, they meet in secret to plan things that will harm others. Did you notice that Zippo did not invite reporters from the *KITTEN Caboodle* newspaper to attend his noontime meeting?

Ima Happy was taking notes during the meeting. She wrote at the rate of eight words per minute. The man down the hall became impatient with Ima's slow writing. He grabbed the paper and continued the note taking at 20 words per minute. The meeting lasted 40 minutes. Ima and the man down the hall had written a total of 632 words.

How long had Ima written before the notes were snatched out of her hand?

How many quantities are involved in this problem? There's six of them: two writing speeds, two lengths of time, and two quantities of words written.

Using the six pretty boxes approach . . .   Ima writing

Words written	rate	time

writing

We want to find out how long Ima had written, so we put t in the appropriate box.

Ima writing

Words written	rate	time
		t

writing

Together, Ima and the man down the hall wrote for a total of 40 minutes. Ima wrote for t minutes. So, how long did the man down the hall write?

General Suggestion: If you are not sure how to write down something containing letters (an algebraic expression), do it with numbers first.

For example, if Ima wrote for 10 minutes, then the man down the hall must have written for 30 minutes.

If Ima wrote for 5 minutes, then the man down the hall must have written for 35 minutes.

If Ima wrote for 38 minutes, the man down the hall must have written for 2 minutes.

Now look to see what you have done in arithmetic. When you were given Ima's time, you subtracted it from 40 to get the amount of time that the man down the hall wrote.

If Ima wrote for t minutes, then the man down the hall wrote for 40 – t minutes.

Ima writing

writing

	Words written	rate	time
Ima writing			t
writing			$40 - t$

We are given the writing speeds, so we can fill those in.

	Words written	rate	time
Ima writing		8	t
writing		20	$40 - t$

Since the number of words written equals the rate of writing times the time,[*] we can fill in the last two boxes.

	Words written	rate	time
Ima writing	$8t$	8	t
writing	$20(40-t)$	20	$40 - t$

Word problems come in all different forms. It's not like in the old arithmetic days where you would get 20 problems that were all alike. In the previous chapter, when we filled in the last two boxes, we just set them equal to each other and we had the equation. That is because those last two boxes were distances that the word problem told us were equal.

One of the biggest difficulties in doing word problems is to read and understand the English. Doing word problems is not a mechanical procedure like brushing your teeth.

In *this* word problem, we are told, "Ima and the man down the hall had written a total of 632 words." They didn't write an *equal* number of words. Instead, what she wrote and what he wrote added up to 632.

So the equation is: $8t + 20(40 - t) = 632$.

---

[*] Using the **General Suggestion**, we look at some examples using numbers. If you write at 7 words per minute for 6 minutes, you will have written 42 words. If you write at 2 words per minute for 10 minutes, you will have written 20 words.

So, if Ima writes at 8 words per minute for t minutes, she will have written 8t words.

122

We are now going to solve $8t + 20(40 - t) = 632.$

Solving equations is much more mechanical than turning English into equations.

In Pre-Algebra 1, you first combined like terms.
Second, you added (or subtracted) the same thing to both sides of the equation in order to get the unknowns on one side of the equation and the numbers on the other side.
Third, you divided both sides by the same number, so that the unknown would be all alone.

for example

Start with	$13x + 19 + 2x = 21x + 1$
Combine like terms	$15x + 19 = 21x + 1$
Subtract 15x from both sides	$19 = 6x + 1$
Subtract 1 from both sides	$18 = 6x$
Divide both sides by 6	$3 = x$

Here in Pre-Algebra 2, we add one more step to the procedure.
In the equation $8t + 20(40 - t) = 632$, we must first get rid of the parentheses. Here are a zillion examples:

$5(x + 4) = 5x + 20 \quad 30(2t + 5) = 60t + 150 \quad 9(x + y) = 9x + 9y$
$2(6w + 1) = 12w + 2 \quad x(x + 7) = x^2 + 7x \quad \pi(z + 32) = \pi z + 32\pi$
$1.4(x + 4) = 1.4x + 5.6 \quad 4(x - 9) = 4x - 36 \quad -2(4x + 7) = -8x - 14$

$a(b + c) = ab + ac$ is called the **distributive law**.

So we start with the original equation $\quad 8t + 20(40 - t) = 632$
✓ Use the distributive law $\quad 8t + 800 - 20t = 632$
✓ Combine like terms $\quad -12t + 800 = 632$
✓ Add 12t to both sides of the equation $\quad 800 = 632 + 12t$
✓ Subtract 632 from both sides of the equation $\quad 168 = 12t$
✓ Divide both sides of the equation by 12 $\quad 14 = t$

So Ima wrote for 14 minutes before the man down the hall snatched the paper out of her hands.

Solving 8t + 20(40 – t) = 632 took five steps, but it didn't take much brain power because the whole process is mechanical. You could probably teach your kid brother how to solve these equations. You could just tell him:

1. Use 3(x + 7) = 3x + 21 if there are parentheses.
2. Combine like terms.
3. Put the x-terms on one side.
4. Put the numbers on the other side.
5. Divide both sides by the number in front of the X.

But your kid brother is not ready to turn English into equations. He will have to wait until he is as old as you are.

Your Turn to Play

1. If Zippo and Fred own a total of 18 pencils, and Zippo owns x pencils, how many pencils does Fred own?

2. If the man down the hall and the Tall Duck have a total of 30 clients, and the man down the hall has x clients, how many clients does the Tall Duck have?

3. 3(4x + 5) = ?

4. 7(8y – 6) = ?

5. When Zippo saw that the man down the hall and Ima were taking notes, he went crazy, and shouted, "Don't you understand that we are colluding to set prices? This must be kept secret." Fred started to feel a little uncomfortable as he realized that this wasn't just five friends going out for pizza.

Zippo took a big black felt tip pen and started crossing out each word that Ima and the man down the hall had written.

We met at noon and Zippo suggested that we collude and set all our prices alike. He said that we should set our prices at $100 per idea.

became, after Zippo started crossing out each word:

~~We met at~~ noon and Zippo suggested that we collude and set all our prices alike. He said that we should set our prices at $100 per idea.

He was crossing out words with his black felt tip pen at the rate of 62 words per minute. When his black felt tip pen ran out of ink, Zippo started to scratch out each word with his fingernail. This took a lot longer. He could only scratch out 2 words each minute.

It took him 16 minutes to obliterate the 632 words that Ima and the man down the hall had written. How long had Zippo worked with his black felt tip pen?

(It is important that you do not just look at the problem and then just look at the answer. If you take that shortcut, you may not learn how to do these problems on your own. Taking that shortcut may make it heaven now, but hell when you get to the Bridge.)

6. Ima loves to talk. During one 10-minute period she blinked 142 times. When Ima was telling the truth she blinks at the rate of 12 blinks per minute. When she's lying, she blinks at the rate of 16 blinks per minute. During that 10-minute period how long was she telling the truth?

.... COMPLETE SOLUTIONS ....

1. If there are a total of 18 pencils and Zippo owns x of them, then Fred would own 18 – x pencils.

2. If there are 30 clients and the man down the hall has x clients, then the Tall Duck would have 30 – x clients.

3. $3(4x + 5) = 12x + 15$

4. $7(8y – 6) = 56y – 42$

5. Let t = the amount of time that Zippo worked with his black pen.

Then 16 – t = the amount of time that Zippo used his fingernails.

Then 62t = the number of words he crossed out using his black pen.

Then 2(16 – t) = the number of words he scratched out with his fingernails.

Since he obliterated a total of 632 words:

$$62t + 2(16 – t) = 632$$

$62t + 32 – 2t = 632$	Use the distributive law
$60t + 32 = 632$	Combine like terms
$60t = 600$	Subtract 32 from both sides
$t = 10$	Divide both sides by 60

So Zippo used his black felt tip pen for 10 minutes before it ran out.

6. There are six quantities involved in this problem: two rates of blinking, two lengths of time (when she was telling the truth and when she was lying), and the number of blinks when she was telling the truth and the number of blinks when she was lying.

Using the six pretty boxes approach . . .

	Blinks	rate	time
Telling the truth			t
Lying			

Then . . .

	Blinks	rate	time
Telling the truth		12	t
Lying		16	$10-t$

And since the number of blinks is equal to the rate times the time* . . .

	Blinks	rate	time
Telling the truth	$12t$	12	t
Lying	$16(10-t)$	16	$10-t$

And since we know the total number of blinks is 142:

$$12t + 16(10 - t) = 142$$

$12t + 160 - 16t = 142$	Use the distributive law
$-4t + 160 = 142$	Combine like terms
$160 = 142 + 4t$	Add 4t to both sides
$18 = 4t$	Subtract 142 from both sides
$\dfrac{18}{4} = t$	Divide both sides by four

$\dfrac{18}{4} = \dfrac{9}{2} = 4\dfrac{1}{2}$ So Ima was telling the truth for $4\dfrac{1}{2}$ minutes.

✱ For example, if you blink 6 times per minute for 3 minutes, you will have blinked 18 times.

Chapter Eighteen
A Second Way to Kill Competition

Fred had started to feel uncomfortable. He excused himself and left the room.* He knew that you should never do anything that you would be ashamed to see reported in the newspaper.

The four conspirators wondered what to do next. Since Fred wasn't a part of their collusion to set prices, they had to think of a new way of stopping Fred from taking all the ideas-for-sale business. They knew that Fred was better at creating new ideas than they were.

They sat in silence for several minutes. The pizzas were getting cold. Then the Tall Duck said, "What if nobody brought their business to Fred? Then each of us would have a lot more business."

Ima suggested, "I know. I will spread rumors that Fred's ideas are second rate. I will tell people that they couldn't expect good ideas from someone who is only five years old. I'll say that a lot of people who went to Fred for ideas came away very dissatisfied."

The man down the hall couldn't figure that out. He said, "Fred's ideas are really great. No one has ever been dissatisfied with his work. How can you say those bad things about Fred?"

Zippo turned to the man down the hall and explained to him

that Ima would be LYING.

> The official word for this is **fraud**—lying, misrepresentation, or intentional concealment of the facts in order to gain some unfair advantage.

---

* Did you know that you could walk to heaven? It may never have been mentioned in Sunday school, but your feet can often be the best way to get out of a situation that may turn into hell. If your conscience says to you, "There is something wrong here," use your feet!

"But who is going to believe you?" the man down the hall asked. "Everyone knows that Fred has really good ideas."

Ima smiled. "I have such a pretty, happy face. I could tell people that the moon is made of green cheese, and they would believe me."

The four conspirators were enthralled with Ima's plan.

That afternoon Ima went to the *KITTEN Caboodle* newspaper and told them how bad Fred's work was. She was interviewed on MEOW, the local KITTENS University radio station. She telephoned all her friends. She wrote letters. She spread lies about Fred every way she could.

Did it work? Of course it did. Lying works ... in the short term. Stealing works ... in the short term. Getting drunk works ... in the short term. Punching somebody you don't like works ... in the short term. Every kind of evil works ... in the short term. That's why people do it.

In the fortnight* after Ima spread her lies, Fred's business had dropped to almost zero. Her fraud worked ... in the short term.

But a few customers that Fred had were so pleased with the ideas that Fred had furnished that they spread the news by word of mouth that Fred was really good. The people in the small community around KITTENS University soon realized that despite Ima's pretty, smiling face, she wasn't someone who could be trusted.

During those first 14 days, Ima was getting customers at the rate of r orders per day. Zippo was getting four more orders per day than Ima. At the end of 14 days, the pair of them had received a total of 252 orders. How many orders per day was Ima receiving?

There are six quantities involved, so we can put things in six pretty boxes.

---

* A fortnight has nothing to do with forts. It means 14 days and nights. *Fortnight* is a contraction of fourteen nights.

The first thing we do is let x (or t or r) equal the thing we are trying to find out. In the problem we were asked, "How many orders per day was Ima receiving?"

	Orders	rate	time
Ima		r	
Zippo			

We are told that Zippo was getting four more orders per day than Ima.

	Orders	rate	time
Ima		r	
Zippo		$r+4$	

Both Ima and Zippo were working for 14 days.

	Orders	rate	time
Ima		r	14
Zippo		$r+4$	14

And since the number of orders is equal to the rate per day times the number of days* . . .

	Orders	rate	time
Ima	$14r$	r	14
Zippo	$14(r+4)$	$r+4$	14

We know the total number of orders is 252:

$$14r + 14(r + 4) = 252$$

1. Finish solving $14r + 14(r + 4) = 252$.

2. At what rate was Zippo receiving orders during those first 14 days?

3. Some of the orders that Fred received were by mail. At first, things were slow because of Ima's lying. But after a couple of weeks, the mail

---

★ For example, if you get 5 orders per day for 7 days, you will receive a total of 35 orders.

orders increased. He then had to spend 3 more hours each day working on the mail orders.

If you look at one day during the first fortnight and one day after the first fortnight, he would have answered a total of 40 letters on those two days.

Fred could answer letters at the rate of five per hour.

How much time was he spending per day during the slow time?

. . . . COMPLETE SOLUTIONS . . . .

1.
$$14r + 14(r + 4) = 252$$

$14r + 14r + 56 = 252$ Use the distributive law

$28r + 56 = 252$ Combine like terms

$28r = 196$ Subtract 56 from both sides

$r = 7$ Divide both sides by 28

So Ima was receiving orders at the rate of seven per day.

2. We had let r equal the rate at which Ima had been receiving orders. In one of the six pretty boxes, we had written that Zippo was receiving orders at the rate of r + 4. Since r = 7 (by the previous problem), we know that Zippo was receiving orders at the rate of 11 per day.

3. Let t = the number of hours per day that Fred was spending during the first fortnight.

Then t + 3 = the number of hours per day that Fred was spending answering mail after the first fortnight.

Then 5t = the number of letters he answered during each day of the first fortnight.

Then 5(t + 3) = the number of letters he answered during each day after the first fortnight.

We are told that, "If you look at one day during the first fortnight and one day after the first fortnight, he would have opened and answered 40 letters on those two days," so 5t + 5(t + 3) = 40.

$5t + 5t + 15 = 40$ → $10t + 15 = 40$ → $10t = 25$ → $t = 2.5$

So Fred spent $2\frac{1}{2}$ hours per day during the first fortnight.

Chapter Nineteen
A Third Way to Kill Competition

For a fortnight, Ima's lying had worked. But Ima's lies only worked ... in the short term. The four conspirators met at lunch again. Price collusion hadn't worked. Fraud hadn't worked. Somehow they needed to eliminate the competition that Fred offered.

"We've got to do something quick," Zippo said.

"I'm really unhappy about the situation," Ima complained.

The Tall Duck didn't know what to say.

They all looked at the man down the hall. He looked angry. He stood up, and suddenly they realized that he was no lightweight.* It sounded like he had gravel in his throat when he said, "I'll take care of this problem. He's not going to bother us anymore."

Ima swallowed hard when she heard his words. They frightened her. The meeting was adjourned. As they left, the Tall Duck was still silent, but was thinking, *I am glad it's Fred and not me.*

That afternoon, Fred was in his office opening his mail. The orders had been coming in requesting his help for difficult situations. He was reading a letter from a farmer:

> Dear Fred,
>
> I'm new at farming, and I have a problem. I have about 100 chickens, and I get plenty of eggs. In fact, every one of those hens lays eggs. I want to get some baby chicks, so I don't gather the eggs but let the hens sit on the eggs. But weeks go by and nothing happens. Are they sitting on their eggs incorrectly? I await any ideas you may have.
>
> Yours,
> Miss Helen Huntenpecker

---

* ... *that he was no lightweight* is another example of litotes. Litotes is saying the negative of the opposite. An example of litotes is saying that a meal consisting of a rack of beef ribs, a large milkshake, a combination pizza, a salad with blue cheese dressing, and a boysenberry pie for dessert is *not a small meal.*

The man down the hall was 6'4" tall and weighed almost 300 pounds.

Fred started to write to Helen suggesting that she read Prof. Eldwood's *All Hens and No Rooster Gives You Lots of Eggs and No Chicks,* 1847, when he heard a loud knock on the door.

Fred hopped off of his chair and ran to the door. It was the man from down the hall.

"Hi!" Fred said. "I hope your teaching has been going well. I know that the first year of teaching is always the hardest. If there is any way I can help, please let me know."

The man walked into Fred's office and looked at all the mail on Fred's desk. He picked up the letter that Fred was writing to Miss Huntenpecker, read it, and slowly tore it up. He took the other mail and threw it into the trash. He looked at Fred and said, "Listen kid. You are out of the ideas-for-sale business starting now. Do I make myself clear?"

Fred was speechless. He nodded. The man left the room, leaving the door open.

Fred was shaking. He had wet his pants.

Your Turn to Play

1. Fred weighs 37 pounds. The man down the hall weighs 295 pounds. Fred's weight is what percent of the man's weight? Round your answer to the nearest percent.

2. If you have been reading carefully, you can guess exactly how to answer this question: Does force work?

3. Fred changed clothes. He figured it was time to do a load of laundry. He took his plastic basket of dirty clothes down several flights of stairs to the basement of the math building where the washing machines are.

Carrying the basket, he headed down the stairs at the rate of 2 steps per second. He put his clothes in the washing machine and ran up the stairs at the rate of 5 steps per second. It took him 9 fewer seconds to go up the stairs than it did to go down the stairs.

How long did it take him to go down the stairs?

4. $\dfrac{5}{6} - \dfrac{2}{3} = ?$

. . . . COMPLETE SOLUTIONS . . . .

1. 37 is what percent of 295. $37 = ?\%$ of 295. $295\overline{)37.0000}^{\,0.1254}$ $= 12.54\%$
which is closer to 13% than it is to 12%.

2. Lying works ...in the short term.

    Stealing works ...in the short term.

    Getting drunk works ...in the short term.

    Punching somebody you don't like works ...in the short term.

    Fraud works ...in the short term.

    And, yes, force works ...in the short term.

3. There are six quantities involved: the two rates, the two lengths of
time, and the number of steps in each direction.

The first thing we do is let x (or t or r)
equal the thing we are trying to find out.
In the problem we were asked, "How long
did it take him to go down the stairs?"

Stairs	rate	time
Down the stairs		t
Up the stairs		

We are told it takes him 9 seconds less to
go up the stairs than to go down the stairs.
We are also given his speed in each direction.

Stairs	rate	time
Down the stairs	2	t
Up the stairs	5	$t\text{-}9$

Since the number of steps is equal to the
rate times the time* . . .

Stairs	rate	time
Down the stairs	$2t$	2	t
Up the stairs	$5(t\text{-}9)$	5	$t\text{-}9$

Since the number of steps going down is the same as
the number of steps going up: $2t = 5(t-9)$.

$2t = 5(t-9) \rightarrow 2t = 5t - 45 \rightarrow 2t + 45 = 5t \rightarrow 45 = 3t \rightarrow 15 = t$

It took Fred 15 seconds to go down the stairs.

4. $\dfrac{5}{6} - \dfrac{2}{3} = \dfrac{5}{6} - \dfrac{2(2)}{3(2)} = \dfrac{5-4}{6} = \dfrac{1}{6}$

★ For example, if you take 9 steps per minute and go for 4 minutes, then you will have
traveled 36 steps.

Chapter Twenty
A Fourth Way to Kill Competition

Now that Fred was out of the ideas-for-sale business, the four conspirators could divide up all the sales among themselves. Their first concern was that other people might want to enter the business. If it became known that the four of them were making lots of money, others would be tempted to put up posters and also sell their ideas.

Zippo contacted his legislator and told him, "We need to establish a system so that the public is protected. Not everyone should be allowed to sell their ideas to the public. People who sell their ideas should be licensed."

And so Public Law #805 was passed:

Public Law #805:

(A) No person shall sell their ideas without a state license.

(B) Requirements for the license:

    (1) Payment of $3500.

    (2) Take eight state-approved courses in Ideas Production.

    (3) Pass a three-hour state examination.

(C) (Grandfather clause) All persons currently engaged in the sale of ideas are exempt from having to obtain a license.

The four conspirators loved that law. It would really cut down on the number of competitors. The government officials loved the law since it would bring in "free" money—money that didn't cost them anything.*

---

* This particular Kansas law is fictitious. But in most places, if you start a business, you will need a business license.

    Even if you just write a poem on a sheet of binder paper and mail copies to people who send you a dollar, even if you are just sitting at home alone and never leave your house, even if you have no employees, even if no customers come to your door—you have to apply to the government for permission to do that. And you have to pay the government for that permission.

Next week Ima went to her lawmaker and told him, "We need to protect the public. Are you aware that there are non-humans who are selling their ideas to the public?"

And so Public Law #805 had a new paragraph added to it:

Public Law #805:

. . .

(D) Only natural human beings are permitted to sell their ideas.

Now, instead of four conspirators, there were only three. The Tall Duck was excluded by law.

With only three people in the business, they each had roughly 33⅓% of the profits instead of 25%.

Zippo headed back to the government and argued, "We don't want sickly, unhealthy, or physically unfit persons selling ideas, do we?"

And so Public Law #805 had another paragraph added to it:

Public Law #805:

. . .

(E) In order to promote the general health of our population and to protect them from sickly, unhealthy, or physically unfit persons selling ideas, each person selling ideas must pass these basic physical tests:

  (i) Lift a 25-lb. weight above their head using only one arm;

  (ii) Run a mile in under 8 minutes.

Ima couldn't do the weight lifting. The man down the hall had no problem with the weight lifting. He bragged that he could do that with a 50-lb. weight. But his age and his 295 lbs. made it impossible for him to cover a mile in under 8 minutes.

Zippo now had a monopoly. Nowadays, the easiest way to create a monopoly is to use the force of government law. And when you have a monopoly, you invariably have high prices and poor quality.

Ever see a long line in a post office? You hardly ever see lines that long in stores. Why? Congress has passed a law making the United States Postal Service a monopoly. By law, no one else is allowed to set up a business delivering first-class mail.

It's usually very difficult to create a monopoly unless you have the government's help.

Using the government is probably the best way to eliminate your competitors. History is loaded with instances of this. For example, in the 1930s, the democratically elected government of Germany passed a law that Jews could not teach at the universities.

In the United States, democratically elected governments at the federal, state, and local levels have passed laws that have discriminated against the Chinese, the Irish, blacks, Catholics, women. . . . (The list might fill a page.)

Your Turn to Play

1. Without looking back, can you name the four ways that people in business have used in order to eliminate competition?

2. When Zippo put up his posters it cost him $100. So his business was $100 in debt. In his first two weeks of business he received $532 in orders. What was his net income after expenses? $-100 + 532 = ?$

3. Fred wanted to check how his laundry was doing. Because he wasn't carrying a heavy basket of clothes, he could head down the stairs at a rate of 3 steps per second. When he got to the bottom of the stairs, he heard the washing machine was still running, so he ran back up the stairs at the rate of 5 steps per second.

The trip up the stairs took 4 seconds less than the trip down the stairs. How long did it take for him to go down the stairs?

4. Forty steps per minute is how many steps per hour?

```
.......COMPLETE SOLUTIONS.......
```

1. First, they can collude to set prices. Second, they can use fraud—lying, misrepresentation, or intentional concealment of the facts. Third, they can use force, or the threat of force. Fourth, they can run to the government and use the force of government to suppress their competitors.

2. $-100 + 532 = 432$. His net income was $432.

3. Let t = the time it took Fred to go down the stairs.

Then t – 4 = the time it took Fred to go up the stairs.

Then 3t = the number of steps going down.

Then 5(t – 4) = the number of steps going up.

Since the number of steps going down is the same as the number of steps going up,

$$3t = 5(t-4)$$

$3t = 5t - 20$	Distributive law
$3t + 20 = 5t$	Add 20 to both sides
$20 = 2t$	Subtract 3t from both sides
$10 = t$	Divide both sides by 2

It took Fred 10 seconds to go down the stairs.

4. Using a conversion factor,

$$\frac{40 \text{ steps}}{1 \text{ minute}} \times \frac{60 \text{ minutes}}{1 \text{ hour}} = \frac{2400 \text{ steps}}{\text{hour}}$$

 # The Bridge
from Chapter 1 to Chapter 20

first try

---

1. Joe liked to watch football on television. In order to show that he really supported his team, he bought a whole bunch of football helmets. They cost $60 each. He also bought a lot of autographed footballs, which cost $200 each.

He purchased 10 more footballs than helmets. When the bill came at the end of the month, Joe owed $9800.

How many helmets had he purchased?

2. Darlene called Joe and asked if she could come over and watch football with him. She really was more interested in sitting next to him than watching the game. She brought over her set of wedding books, which she liked to read while she sat next to Joe. It was supposed to give Joe a hint about getting married. Her set was {Prof. Eldwood's *Guide to Church Weddings,* Prof. Eldwood's *Setting the Date,* Prof. Eldwood's *Make Your Marriage Last Longer than the Wedding Cake*}. What is the cardinality of this set?

3. "What would you think about weddings where a thousand people are invited?" Darlene asked Joe. (She knew that she wasn't supposed to talk to him during the game, but only during the commercials.)

"Why would someone want that many people to attend?" Joe asked.

"Think of all the presents we would get," she hinted. She had subtly changed to the pronoun *we*, instead of talking about weddings in general.

Joe liked presents. His current television screen is 4-feet wide. If he got one that was 20% wider, how wide would the new one be?

4. The commercials were over, and Darlene fell silent as the game went on. She opened her *Setting the Date* book, and read, "The important thing is to pick one of the days of the year as the wedding date." Darlene liked that. She thought that Prof. Eldwood was pretty smart.

 # The Bridge
from Chapter 1 to Chapter 20

      If the domain is {Joe} and the codomain is all the days of the year, Darlene invented the function that would assign Joe to July 5th. Is this function 1-1?

5. Joe paid special attention when one of the football players was injured. There were 12 injuries in the first 16 minutes of play. At that rate, how many injuries would be expected in one game (which has 60 minutes of play)?

6. Solve $15w + 7 + 2w = 5(w + 8) + 27$

7. As Darlene read her *Setting the Date* book, she started to feel uncomfortable. For several minutes, she couldn't figure out what it was. And then she realized that she had been sitting on one of Joe's football helmets. She pulled it out from underneath her and looked at it. The goofy-looking thing weighed $2\frac{3}{8}$ pounds. How much would 7 of those helmets weigh? Do not leave your answer as an improper fraction.

8. Each year Joe watches 5% more hours of football than the previous year. When Darlene first met him, he was watching 400 hours per year. Five years later, how much was he watching? You can leave your answer in the form ▬ × (▬)▪.

9. Darlene's 3 Prof. Eldwood books all weighed the same. She carried them in a canvas bag that weighed 2 pounds. The books and the bag together weighed 6 pounds. How much did each book weigh? (No credit if you just supply the answer. Show your work, starting with *Let x* =. . . .)

10. $(1.8)^2 = ?$

 # The Bridge
from Chapter 1 to Chapter 20

second try

1. When halftime came, Darlene suggested to Joe, "Why don't we get up and do something?" She was thinking that anything would be better than sitting there hour after hour.

Joe shook his head. "We can't. The halftime is the educational part where they do marching and singing. I don't want to miss that."

For Darlene, the marching seemed too militaristic, and the singer sounded like two cats fighting. She headed outside to take a little walk. Joe didn't notice that she had left.

She headed up the street at 3 mph (miles per hour) looking in each of the store windows. When she got out of the commercial area and into the residential area—where there were no stores—she walked at 4 mph.

She walked for an hour longer in the residential area than in the commercial area. She went a total of $6\frac{1}{3}$ miles. How long did she walk in the commercial area?

2. As Darlene walked in the residential area, she looked at each house and decided whether it would be a good house for Joe and her when they got married. Let the domain be the set of all houses that she looked at and let the codomain be {yes, no}.

Let the function be Darlene's assignment of either *yes* or *no* to each house. Is there a way that Darlene could have made that assignment so that the function would be 1-1?

3. Darlene suddenly realized that the halftime was probably over. She headed back to Joe's apartment. When she got back, it was still halftime. People were still marching around and singing.* What she noticed was that his collection of 30 helmets had increased by 20%. How many helmets did Joe have now?

★ Explanation: Darlene had been gone so long that the first football game had finished and this was the halftime of a second game that Joe was watching.

 # The Bridge
from Chapter 1 to Chapter 20

4. She waited until this halftime was over (and the commercials began) and then asked, "Where did you get the new helmets?"

"There was a special," Joe answered. "I bought these special helmets with pizzas on them. Now you can tell what the players are thinking about." How many of these pizza helmets had Joe bought? (See the previous question for more data.)

5. Solve $90(z - 4) = 42z - 240$

6. Joe's favorite commercial came on. He always laughed when he saw

the little Sluice Doll wave its little arms and sing the Juicy Sluicy song. Joe asked Darlene to go out to the kitchen and pour him some Sluice. He didn't want to miss any part of the song. He sang along with the puppet; Darlene was happy to leave.

Sluice Doll

She found three opened bottles of Sluice in the kitchen. One had $\frac{1}{3}$ liter. Another had $\frac{2}{7}$ liter. Another had $\frac{1}{2}$ liter. She poured them all into one big glass. How much Sluice was that? (Do not leave your answer as an improper fraction.)

7. $(1/3)^3 = ?$

8. "Did you know," Joe said after the song was over, "that you can trade in 6 Sluice bottle caps and get 80 Sluice Points?"

Darlene was confused and asked, "What good are Sluice Points?"

Joe explained, "Everybody knows that with 120 Sluice Points you can get a free Sluice Doll."

How many bottle caps would it take to get 9 Sluice Dolls? (Use conversion factors. Start with 9 Sluice Dolls.)

9. $7\frac{1}{6} \div \frac{1}{3} = ?$

10. If Joe sang x verses of the Juicy Sluicy song, and then, as an encore, sang 24 more verses, how many verses did he sing?

 # The Bridge

from Chapter 1 to Chapter 20

third try

1. As Darlene sat there on the sofa, she looked over at Joe, the man she hoped would some day be her husband. In his lap was a little Sluice Doll. The label on the doll said, "Not for children under the age of two. Choking hazard since the eyes are removable. Doll weight = 0.4 kilograms."

To the nearest ounce, how much did Joe's doll weigh? (1 kilogram = 2.2 pounds. 1 ounce = 0.0625 pounds.)

2. Joe called his doll Sluicy. Since Joe had the habit of throwing Sluicy up in the air whenever his team scored a touchdown, her eyes had fallen out months ago. Now, since Sluicy was blind, Joe would describe every play to her. Joe would say either, "They ran with the ball," or "They kicked the ball," or "They passed the ball." Hour after hour, Darlene heard these three sentences. She couldn't figure out how the game of football—with its runs, kicks, and passes—could fascinate an adult for hours every weekend.

While the game was on, she turned to her bridal magazines, which had the following set of topics: {setting the date, dieting, picking a cake, choosing a dress}. What is the cardinality of this set?

3. When she turned to the picking-a-cake section in one of her magazines, Darlene read an article entitled, "A 10^6 Flavors." Written out in words, what does 10^6 equal?

4. She asked Joe, "Which flavor do you like best? Vanilla almond, chocolate devil's food, orange creamsicle, marble swirl, lemon poppy seed, carrot, cherry chip, tiramisu, lemon, fresh banana walnut, apple pecan, pumpkin, coconut mango, or cream cheese."

Joe said, "I didn't know Sluice came in all those flavors."

"No, silly," Darlene said. "Those are wedding cake flavors." She figured that if she couldn't get him to think about a date for the wedding, at least she could get him to commit to a wedding cake flavor.

Pumpkin Flavor

The Bridge

from Chapter 1 to Chapter 20

If {Joe} is the domain, and if {vanilla almond, chocolate devil's food, orange creamsicle, marble swirl, lemon poppy seed, carrot, cherry chip, tiramisu, lemon, fresh banana walnut, apple pecan, pumpkin, coconut mango, and cream cheese} is the codomain, Darlene was looking for a function that would assign to each element of the domain exactly one element of the codomain.

Joe said, "Sluice flavor." Is this a function with the given domain and codomain?

5. Darlene ran to the phone and called the Main Street Bakery. "Can you make a wedding cake with Sluice flavor?" she asked breathlessly.

"That will be awfully sweet," the baker replied, "but we can do it. Our regular 3-layer cakes are $24, but with this special flavor, it'll be 15% extra."

How much will the Sluice-flavored cake cost?

6. As Darlene came back into Joe's living room, Sluicy was launched vertically as a touchdown was scored. Sluicy weighed 9 ounces before being thrown up in the air. When Joe tossed her up, she lost some more of her stuffing. She lost one-tenth of her weight. How much did Sluicy weigh when she landed back in Joe's lap?

7. During the first game that Joe watched, there were 3 touchdowns for each hour he watched television. During the second game, which lasted an hour longer than the first game, there were 4 touchdowns for each hour watched. All together, the two games had 25 touchdowns. How long was the first game? (No credit given if you don't show your algebra. In fact, I'll even give you the final answer: 3 hours.)

8. Name 5 consecutive odd numbers where the last number is 17.

9. If x is equal to some odd number, what is the value of the next consecutive odd number?

10. Joe took his $21\frac{1}{2}$ ounces of Sluice that Darlene had given him and gave one-fifth of it to Sluicy. He opened her cloth mouth and poured it in. How much did he pour?

The Bridge

from Chapter 1 to Chapter 20

fourth try

1. Darlene really liked one of the houses that she had seen on her walk. During one of the commercials she showed Joe a picture of it that she had taken with her digital camera. "What do you think of this house, Joe?"

Joe and his Sluice doll looked at it. "What do you think, Sluicy?" he asked. Joe knew it was a rhetorical question, since Sluicy wasn't very talkative. This gave Joe time to think. Then he said to Darlene, "Are you thinking of buying it? I didn't think you made enough money to buy a mansion like that."

Joe couldn't have given a better answer. Darlene said, "No, I couldn't afford it on one salary. It would take *two* salaries." The minute she said that, she knew what Joe was going to say.

Joe said, "That is terrible—you holding down two jobs just to buy a house." Darlene knew she should have said that it would take two *people's* salaries.

One little word can make all the difference. For example, what is the value of $55 \times 3.7 \times \frac{1}{3} \times 10^6 \times 0.33987962 \times 0 \times 3.1415926$?

2. "What if *we* owned that house?" Darlene asked. "Then we could sit out on the front porch *together*."

"That's a silly idea," Joe said. "If we put the TV out there, it'd get wet when it rained."

The game resumed and took Joe's attention away from their conversation. Joe thought that was such a silly conversation—her wanting to work two jobs and the idea of putting a television out on the porch.

Joe's television, which was worth $600, would lose 70% of its value if it were left in the rain. How much would it then be worth?

 # The Bridge

from Chapter 1 to Chapter 20

3. When Sluicy drank 4.3 ounces* of Sluice (see problem #10 two pages ago), she gained 1.29 pounds. To the nearest pound, how much would 80 ounces of Sluice weigh?

(The conversion factor is $\frac{1.29 \text{ pounds}}{4.3 \text{ ounces}}$)

4. Darlene wandered into Joe's kitchen while he watched his football game. A second later she heard two sounds from the living room. The first was Joe's usual, "Hooray!" that he always yelled when his team made a touchdown. The second was a cry of distress that brought Darlene running back to see what was wrong.

Joe's doll was stuck to the ceiling. All the sugary Sluice that she had drunk had made her very sticky.

For the first 20 minutes that Sluicy was stuck to the ceiling, she was dripping at the rate of r drips/minute. In the next 20 minutes, her dripping rate slowed to r – 2 drips/minute. In those 40 minutes, Joe received 240 drops on his head (as he continued to watch his game). Find the value of r.

5. $2^6 = ?$

6. Solve $4(x + 5) = 7(x + 2)$

7. Express 83⅓% as a fraction.

8. Three consecutive even numbers add to 630. What is the smallest of the three? (Hint: Let x = the smallest of the three. Then x + 2 = the second consecutive even number.)

9. $2\frac{1}{3} - \frac{2}{3}$

10. $-13 + 7$

---

* There are two kinds of ounces. Sluicy drank 4.3 *fluid* ounces. There are 8 fluid ounces in a cup. It is a measure of volume.

In contrast, there are 16 ounces in a pound—a measure of weight. The metric system doesn't have this craziness.

It gets worse. When you weigh precious metals, black powder, or gemstones, you use troy ounces. Troy ounces are heavier than "regular" (avoirdupois) ounces. 14.5833 troy ounces = 16 avoirdupois ounces. So an ounce of gold weighs more than an ounce of lead.

 # The Bridge
from Chapter 1 to Chapter 20

fifth try

1. In Darlene's Child Psychology course at KITTENS University, the teacher talked about parallel play. The teacher said that there were four stages that young kids go through in learning to play. First, children play by themselves. Then they engage in parallel play where they play alongside other kids, but not with them. This begins at ages 2 or 3. Then comes associative play where the kids play together and share things. Finally, is cooperative play in which they can take complementary roles—"You be the mommy, and I'll be the daddy."

The teacher wrote on the board: {solitary, parallel, associative, cooperative}. What is the cardinality of this set?

2. When Darlene sat next to Joe watching football on television, she believed they were doing parallel play. Darlene hoped that would change after they got

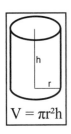

$V = \pi r^2 h$

married.* Sluicy dropped from the ceiling into Joe's lap, and he gave the doll a big hug (a mistake). Joe's lap became wet with Sluice. Darlene was miffed.** She headed back into Joe's kitchen. She found a can of spaghetti and opened it.

She called to Joe, "I'm heating spaghetti. Do you want any?"

Open before heating

"How much do you have?" he asked.

The can was 4-inches tall with a radius of 2 inches. Use 3 for π. What was the volume of the can?

---

* The mistaken belief that your partner will change after marriage is one of the root causes of marital unhappiness. Just picture Joe at the age of 80 watching football with his doll on his lap.

** To be miffed is to be put in a bad mood. When vexatious (troubling, annoying) events occur, it is much better to say, "I am miffed," than to utter its vulgar modern equivalent.

3. On the stove, the spaghetti heated up at the rate of 8° per minute. If she had turned up the heat so that it heated at the rate of 12° per minute, she could have heated it in 2 minutes less. How long did it take Darlene to heat it up (at the original 8° per minute rate)?

4. The spaghetti can was labeled 250 grams. Just as Darlene was taking it off the stove, Joe called out, "I'd like 2% of it."

"You mean something like 20%, don't you?" Darlene said.

"No. I'd like 2% of it. I'm pretty full of Sluice."

How much is 2% of 250 grams?

5. As everyone knows, the weight of a nickel is approximately 5 grams. Darlene brought Joe's dinner out to him.

Joe's entire dinner.

That strand of spaghetti was 8 inches long. Joe cut it into 15 equal pieces and gave one of them to Sluicy. How long was Sluicy's piece?

6. Joe put Sluicy's piece in her mouth. She must not have been very hungry either. She wasn't chewing.

Joe put the other 14 pieces in his right hand and held Sluicy with his left hand. (He had put the fork in his shirt pocket.) When the Sluice commercial came on, Joe sang the Juicy Sluicy song. This was the shorter song. It lasted 18 seconds. The other Sluice commercial has a song that lasted 20% longer. What is the length of the longer song?

7. $4\frac{1}{4} \div 5\frac{1}{5}$

8. $(\frac{1}{5})^3$

9. Solve $20x + 4(x + 3) = 18$

10. Darlene carried in her plate full of warm spaghetti and sat down next to Joe. He put his 14 pieces of spaghetti on her plate and announced that he wasn't very hungry.

What percentage of the spaghetti had Joe eaten?

Chapter Twenty-one
Government Regulation

Ima Happy wasn't very happy with that Kansas law that put her out of the ideas-for-sale business. She decided to move to Maryland where her sister Mia lived. She decided that she would become a hairdresser. When she was in Kansas, she had been cutting and coloring her friends' hair for free. They loved her work.

Mia had a hair salon and invited Ima to come work with her.

Mia warned her sister that she would have to get a hairdresser's license from the State of Maryland. She would have to pay a fee to the government to get the license.

Ima said, "Okay."

Then Mia said she would have to pass an examination given by the State Board of Cosmetologists. It has two parts to it: Practical and Theory. That would cost her another $75.

Ima said, "I know how to cut and color. That should be a cinch."

Then Mia gave her sister the really bad news. Maryland requires 1,500 hours of training at a cosmetology school in order to get a license to be allowed to cut and color hair.*

"Fifteen hundred hours!" Ima screamed. "That's insane."

Mia added, "It's not just learning to cut and color. You will also learn how to clean fingernails and put on polish. You learn how to shampoo and condition hair and apply creams to soften customers' skins. But, of course, the training isn't free."

"Fifteen hundred hours!" Ima repeated. "That will sure cut down on the number of hairdressers in Maryland."

✶ This is not fiction. These are the real, actual requirements.

There was still a lot of summer vacation ahead for Fred. He sat at his desk in his office and wondered what he would do now that he was out of the ideas-for-sale business.

He wanted to think first—and then act. He knew that gave a different result than acting first—and then thinking about what you did. Fred giggled. It was like putting on your shoes and socks. It does matter which one you do first. They are not **commutative**.

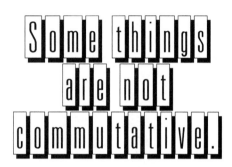

Addition: $5 + 3 = 3 + 5$

Multiplication: $4 \times 7 = 7 \times 4$

Putting a stamp on an envelope and sealing the envelope.

Brushing your teeth and combing your hair.

Putting on shoes and socks.

Subtraction: $8 - 2 \neq 2 - 8$

    ($\neq$ means "not equal")

Division: $3 \div 8 \neq 8 \div 3$

Putting the toothpaste on your brush and brushing your teeth.

Getting in the airplane and flying.

Licking the stamp and putting it on the envelope.

Counting your change and putting it in your pocket.

The phone rang. "Hello. Is this Fred Gauss—the one who is famous for having lots of good ideas?"

Fred didn't know how to answer that double question. He said, "This is Fred."

"Hello. My name is Mia Happy. I am Ima's sister. You knew her when she lived in Kansas. My sister and I were trying to think of a slogan we could use to advertise my hair salon here in Maryland. I would be delighted to pay you for some memorable phrase."

Fred gulped. He didn't want the man down the hall to come back and beat him up. "I'm no longer in the business of selling my ideas, but let me think about it for a moment." After 0.000027 seconds passed, which is plenty of time for Fred to think, he said, "Here's my suggestion for a slogan: *You'll be happy with Mia.*"

Fred heard a squeal of delight. Mia said, "Oh! That's perfect! Thank you so much."

Fred went back to thinking about how he might go into hot dog sales as Mr. Coalback had urged him to do. Fred had already thought of ten different businesses, from Gourmet Gauss Dogs, which could be sold to rich people, to cutting the hot dogs into the shape of french fries.

Fred thought of his simplest idea: a hot dog stand on the street. That would be so neat, he thought.

☆ I could sell my Gourmet Gauss Dogs to the rich people.

☆ I could sell Double Dogs—two dogs in one bun—for married couples celebrating an anniversary.

☆ On the hot days, I could sell Cold Dogs.

Then a gloomy thought hit him. In fact, two g̶l̶o̶o̶m̶y̶ thoughts.*

First gloomy: If I'm successful, some big guy who is operating a competing hot dog stand is going to threaten to knock my brains out if customers come to me instead of him.

Second gloomy: The other hot dog vendors are going to go to the government and get laws passed that will make it almost impossible for me. They will require that all new businesses like mine have to get a license, and to get the license I will need to go to hot dog school for 1500 hours.

∗ That's the way that double gloomy thoughts look: g̶l̶o̶o̶m̶y̶

Your Turn to Play

1. The commutative law of addition is written in algebra $a + b = b + a$.
It is true for any a and b.

   Is there a commutative law of subtraction?

2. If you went to hot dog school 4 hours each day, 5 days per week, how
long would it take you to receive 1500 hours of training? (Use conversion
factors. Start with 1500 hours.)

3. This is just a fun question. Imagine you are the owner of a Maryland
cosmetology school where people are forced to get 1500 hours of training
if they want to work in a beauty salon. How would you fill those 1500
hours? Write out what would occupy your students for those hours.

   I'll give you a start:

Cutting women's hair	40 hours
Trimming women's hair	15 hours
Shaping fingernails	5 hours

4. Mia's Happy Hair Haven offers haircuts and manicures (nail jobs).
When she's cutting hair, she makes $10/hour. When she's doing nails, she
makes $12/hour. One day she did nails for an hour more than she cut hair.
That day she made $111. How long did she spend cutting hair?

. . . . **COMPLETE SOLUTIONS** . . . .

1. Of course not. It isn't true. $5 - 2 \neq 2 - 5$

2. $\dfrac{1500 \text{ hours}}{1} \times \dfrac{1 \text{ day of school}}{4 \text{ hours}} \times \dfrac{1 \text{ week of school}}{5 \text{ days of school}} = 75 \text{ weeks}$

3.
Cutting women's hair	40 hours
Trimming women's hair	15 hours
Shaping fingernails	5 hours
Cleaning fingernails	3 hours
Polishing fingernails	30 hours
Shaping women's hair	7 hours
Cutting men's hair	30 hours
Trimming men's hair	10 hours
Shaping men's hair	4 hours
Shaping toenails	4 hours
Cleaning toenails	1 hour
Polishing toenails	10 hours
Sweeping the floor	1 hour

Tossing clipped hair in the garbage	1 hour
Shaping eyebrows	12 hours
Coloring eyebrows	8 hours
Plucking eyebrows	2 hours
Applying cosmetics	50 hours
Applying lotions	4 hours
Applying creams	4 hours
Answering the phone	2 hours
Booking appointments	6 hours
Organizing the daily schedule	7 hours
Massaging scalps	4 hours
Shampooing	14 hours
Applying conditioner	10 hours
Talking to customers	9 hours
Coloring hair	20 hours
Tinting hair	8 hours
Bleaching hair	8 hours

Stop! This is impossible. So far I've accounted for 329 hours of instruction. And the amount of time allotted to each of these topics has been generous. For example, would it really take you 10 hours to learn how to apply conditioner?

I have no idea how you would fill the remaining 1171 hours. Maybe advanced techniques of sweeping for another hour. Maybe nose hair plucking.

Maryland requires 1500 hours of schooling to become a hairdresser. How does this compare with a full college education? Going to a university for four years and getting a bachelor's degree requires about 120 semester units. A unit is about 15 hours of instruction (one unit = 1 hour per week for 15 weeks). So graduating from college involves about 1800 hours of classroom time (plus homework). During the first two years you will learn about many different academic subjects: English, math, history, music, science, anthropology, a foreign language, and/or philosophy.

After those first two years, you select a major field of study (like math!) and spend the last two years taking lots of courses primarily in that field. There are a zillion possible majors. For example, some of the majors beginning with the letter A are: accounting, actuarial science, advertising, aerospace engineering, agriculture, agronomy and crop science, American history, American literature, anatomy, ancient studies, animal science, anthropology, applied mathematics, applied physics, aquatic biology, Arabic, archeology, architecture, art, artificial intelligence and robotics, astronomy, astrophysics, athletic training, and atmospheric science.

4. We want to know how long she spent cutting hair, so we . . .

Let t = the number of hours she spent cutting hair.

Since we know that she spent an hour more doing nails than cutting hair, we know . . .

Then t + 1 = the number of hours she spent doing nails.

Since she gets $10/hour cutting hair and she spent t hours doing that, we know . . .

Then 10t = the amount of money she earned cutting hair.

Since she gets $12/hour doing nails and she spent t + 1 hours doing that, we know . . .

12(t + 1) = the amount of money she earned doing nails.

Since the total amount of money she received was $111, we know . . .

$$10t + 12(t + 1) \; = \; 111$$

Solving the equation is the easy part.	$10t + 12(t + 1) \; = \; 111$
Distributive law	$10t + 12t + 12 \; = \; 111$
Combine like terms	$22t + 12 \; = \; 111$
Subtract 12 from both sides	$22t \; = \; 99$
Divide both sides by 22	$t \; = \; \dfrac{99}{22}$
	$t \; = \; 4\frac{1}{2}$

Mia spent 4½ hours cutting hair.

If you like to do it with six pretty boxes:

	Money earned	rate	time
Cutting hair	10t	10	t
Doing nails	12(t+1)	12	t+1

Chapter Twenty-two
Freedom

Fred was feeling sad.* He couldn't see how he could possibly operate a hot dog stand. He was stopped by the threats of physical violence from his competitors and by the government's laws that his competitors used to keep Fred out of the hot dog business.

He wanted to be *exempt from those external controls*. That's the definition of **freedom**. Nobody (and nothing) pushing you around equals freedom.

Intermission

How about Perfect Freedom? How nice does that sound? No rules to follow. No laws you have to obey. No external constraints.

Perfect Freedom would mean that you wouldn't have to get up in the morning unless you wanted to.

Perfect Freedom would mean that you wouldn't have to go to the dentist unless you wanted to.

It would mean that you could choose to eat as much chocolate as you wanted to.

. . . live in the nicest house that you would want to have.

. . . take revenge on anyone you considered an enemy.

. . . never be constrained by the threat of death.

★ The psychology teacher at KITTENS University gives a lecture each semester entitled, "The Four Basic Emotions." On the board he writes, "Glad, Sad, Mad, and Afraid." Darlene looked at Joe's notes: Glad, Sad, Mad, and Afrad, and told him he had misspelled *afraid*.

"No, I didn't," Joe answered. "I just made them all rhyme."

❀ ❀ ❀

I, your author, get up at about 4 a.m. every day. I don't have to. I want to. I write at this time of day.

I choose to go to the dentist. I am happy that my dentists (they are a husband-and-wife team) do what they do.

Like most adults, I have enough money that I could eat all the chocolate, pizzas, beef ribs, and cheesecake that I want. But I choose to (sometimes) limit my pizza intake.

I could afford to live in a house twice as expensive as the one that my wife and I live in. But we are happy where we are.

I take lots of revenge on all my enemies. I kill them all. But I should mention that I don't have any enemies to begin with. I choose not to have enemies. The worst thing that an enemy can do to you is cause you to hate him.

Death? If I live as long as my grandfather, I have about 183,960 hours left. But even if it is only 183 hours, I treasure those hours, but I don't own them. Since I don't own them, they can't be taken away from me.

I used to own my life, but I put it "in the offering plate" on Sunday morning.

Perfect Freedom. Yes!

Fred was not free to set up a hot dog stand. The threat of physical violence from his competitors and the anti-competitive laws of government were stopping him. The solution was in liberty (which is slightly different than freedom). Fred's road to a hot dog stand is in liberty. That is the topic of our next chapter. Now it is . . .

Your Turn to Play

1. Convert 183,960 hours into years.

2. Let's suppose on some day Fred sold x Gourmet Gauss Dogs and made a profit of $3 per dog. On that day he also sold x − 2 Double Dogs and made a profit of $2 per dog. And on that day he sold x − 8 Cold Dogs and made a profit of $1 per dog. If he made $168 on that day, how many Gourmet Gauss Dogs did he sell?

. . . . COMPLETE SOLUTIONS . . . .

1. $\dfrac{183,960 \text{ hours}}{1} \times \dfrac{1 \text{ day}}{24 \text{ hours}} \times \dfrac{1 \text{ year}}{365 \text{ days}} = 21 \text{ years}$

2. Not every word problem has six pretty boxes. In this case we have three rows of boxes instead of two.

We want to find out how many Gourmet Gauss Dogs were sold.

	Total Profit	Profit per Dog	Number Sold
Gourmet			X
Double			
Cold Dogs			

We know that he sold 2 less Double Dogs than Gourmet and 8 less Cold Dogs than Gourmet.

	Total Profit	Profit per Dog	Number Sold
Gourmet			X
Double			X-2
Cold Dogs			X-8

We fill in the profit per dog. The profit per dog times the number sold, gives the total profit.*

	Total Profit	Profit per Dog	Number Sold
Gourmet	3X	3	X
Double	2(X-2)	2	X-2
Cold Dogs	X-8	1	X-8

Selling all three kinds of dogs, Fred made $168.

Therefore,

$3x + 2(x - 2) + x - 8 = 168$	
$3x + 2x - 4 + x - 8 = 168$	Distributive law
$6x - 12 = 168$	Combine like terms
$6x = 180$	Add 12 to both sides
$x = 30$	Divide both sides by 6

Fred sold 30 Gourmet Gauss Dogs on that day.

✻ If, for example, you made a profit of $8 per dog sold, and you sold 3 dogs, your total profit would be $24.

Chapter Twenty-three
Liberty

Fred pulled some coins out of his pocket. He had 90 cents. By the commutative law of addition, he knew that he would get the same answer regardless of the order in which he added the numbers.

$$5¢ + 10¢ + 25¢ + 50¢ = 25¢ + 5¢ + 10¢ + 50¢$$

On some of the coins, the head faced left, and on one, the head faced right.

Three had the date on the front.

Only one had "The United States of America" on the front.

Every coin declared, "IN GOD WE TRUST." This is the official motto of the United States.

And every coin has the word "LIBERTY." None of them have the word *freedom*. It is liberty that a government will provide or deny.

The first definition of **liberty** from my favorite dictionary* is: "1. freedom from arbitrary or despotic government. . . ."

A **despotic government** is a government with unlimited power.

Wait a minute! I, your reader, have a question. I thought all governments have unlimited power. Wouldn't that make all governments despotic?

★ *Random House Webster's College Dictionary*

What do you mean by "unlimited powers"?

Can't the government take away your money (taxes)? Can't the government draft you into the army and ship you overseas and make you do all kinds of things that you might not want to do?

Yes.

Well . . . where's the limitations? The federal government of the United States of America can do whatever it wants to me. Name one limitation it has!

Let me name some limitations on the federal government:

Limitation #1: The government cannot interfere with: a) religion

b) speech

c) the press

d) assembly

e) petitioning

Limitation #2: The government cannot interfere with the right of people to keep and carry weapons.

Limitation #4: The government cannot do unreasonable searches. Any searches must be made according to strict legal guidelines.

Limitation #5: The government cannot take your property for public use without paying you a fair price.

Limitation #10: Congress is strictly limited to only those powers specifically granted by the Constitution.

Those limitations sound familiar.

Those are from the Bill of Rights of our Constitution.

Rights is a word that gets messed up in everyday conversation. A right is something that you have that no government can give to you or take away from you.

You have the right to practice your religion.

You have the right to publish your thoughts.

You have the right to protect yourself and your family—not just with words—but with weapons if you choose to.

We are endowed by our Creator with certain unalienable Rights. That's in the second paragraph of the Declaration of Independence. Life and liberty are unalienable (= they are not to be taken away from you).

I, your reader, ask what's this all boil down to? Where's Fred in all this?

Our "nation conceived in liberty"* must act to protect Fred's rights. Fred has a right not to be beat up by his competitors. Fred has the right not to experience arbitrary or despotic government.

If government operates as it should, Fred will be protected against the bullies, and he will not face crazy laws that are designed merely to eliminate competition. No laws that require 1500 hours of hot dog school. No laws that require that you be able to lift a 25-pound weight above your head.

With good government—with liberty—Fred is instantly on the street with his little hot dog cart.

❁   ❁   ❁

Did you ever wonder why the United States of America has such a high standard of living? Answer this question and you have gone to the heart of economics.

★ Is it because our people are somehow superior?

That's a laugh. Read U.S. history. From the very beginning, it has been the "scraps" from other nations that have come here, those who had trouble in the "old country." Many were religious minorities, or criminals, or those coming to make a quick buck in the new country.

★ Is it because we have a ton of natural resources?

We have a bunch, but so do many other countries that have much lower standards of living.

Sweden has about the same amount of natural resources as Cuba, but it has fewer people and a much harsher climate. Yet Sweden's gross domestic product (a measure of economic production) is eleven times that of Cuba.

Hong Kong has about 6.5 million people crowded into 402 square miles. Tanzania has over four times as many people and over 850 times as

---

* From Lincoln's Gettysburg Address.

much land. Hong Kong's gross domestic product is over eight times larger than Tanzania's. Natural resources (including the size of the country) don't make a country's people rich.

★ Is democracy the key to a high standard of living?

Suppose C. C. Coalback, his salesclerk, and Fred were on a desert island. Coalback would announce, "Democracy is the only fair way to have a government."

The first law under that democracy would be that all people under the age of 12 have to give up all their possessions. The vote was: Coalback—yes; salesclerk—yes; and Fred—no.

Fred would end up naked.

In the United States Constitution and the Bill of Rights, there is no mention of "democracy." And there was no tax on income. Any direct tax on the people had to be apportioned according to the population of each state (Article 1, Section 2).

One problem with a democracy is that the voters eventually figure out how to outvote the minorities. It doesn't happen just on desert islands where Fred is outnumbered. Currently, 1% of the people (those with the highest earnings) in the United States pay more taxes than the bottom 95%.*

Economist Walter Williams has written, "Two-thirds of the federal budget consists of taking property from one American and giving it to another."

What makes the difference in the wealth of various nations? It is liberty. It is governments that promote competition among those who want to operate a hot dog stand.

That competition-promoting government can come in many forms. It can be a democracy, an aristocracy, or an all-powerful king.

---

* For the tax year 2007, 40% of all federal personal income taxes were paid by the top 1% of earners. The bottom 95% paid 39%.

1. Having no government is called **anarchy** (ANN-er-key). Why wouldn't anarchy promote wealth in a society?

2. Is it always true that $a^b = b^a$?

3. Fred pushed his hot dog cart down Main Street for 5 hours. Then he headed onto the KITTENS campus and sold for 3 hours. On campus he was selling at the rate of 8 more dogs per hour than he was on Main Street. (Students love hot dogs.) In those 8 hours, Fred sold 504 hot dogs. At what rate was he selling hot dogs on Main Street?

. . . . COMPLETE SOLUTIONS . . . .

1. Without a government, Fred would be in great physical danger. Look at what happens every time a big hurricane blows through and there is temporary anarchy. Looters run wild, smashing store windows.

2. No, for example:
$$2^3 = 2 \times 2 \times 2 = 8$$
$$3^2 = 3 \times 3 = 9$$

3. Let r = the rate of hot dog sales on Main Street.

Since on campus he was selling at the rate of 8 more dogs per hour than he was on Main Street . . .

Then r + 8 = rate of hot dog sales on campus.

Then 5r = number of hot dogs sold on Main Street.

Then 3(r + 8) = number of hot dogs sold on campus.

Since he sold a total of 504 hot dogs . . .

$$5r + 3(r + 8) = 504$$

Distributive law	$5r + 3r + 24 = 504$
Combine like terms	$8r + 24 = 504$
Subtract 24 from both sides	$8r = 480$
Divide both sides by 8	$r = 60$

Fred was selling hot dogs on Main Street at the rate of 60 per hour.

Chapter Twenty-four
Creating Wealth

During the school year, Fred had been making $500 per month teaching at KITTENS University. He loved that job. In his geometry class he loved showing that the angle bisectors of any triangle always meet at the same point.

Selling hot dogs wasn't as much fun as teaching math, but Fred enjoyed being out in the sunshine. On his first day, he sold 504 hot dogs. He made a profit of about $2 per dog. That works out to about $1000 a day.

Fred did the math: $1000/day > $500/month

How much would that be per year? If he worked 5 days per week and 50 weeks per year,

$$\frac{\$1000}{day} \times \frac{5\ days}{week} \times \frac{50\ weeks}{year} = \$250,000 \text{ per year}$$

Fred stopped breathing for a moment. A quarter of a million dollars a year.

And that computation was based on his first day. He knew that his sales would go up as people told their friends how wonderful "Fred's dogs" were.

People happily traded their money for Fred's dogs. They benefitted. Fred happily traded his dogs for money. He benefitted.

Did government create Fred's wealth? No. It allowed Fred to create wealth. The government did its proper job by encouraging competition.

How do individuals create wealth? They do it by moving low-value things to higher value. When Fred teaches, he moves chalk from sticks into diagrams on the board. He moves students from less educated to more educated.

There is only <u>one way to create wealth,</u>

but there are <u>three ways to get wealthy</u>.

One Way to Create Wealth

Move stuff from lower value to higher value.

☞ Take some land, plow it, plant it, and harvest the crop.

☞ Take some paint and create art.

Mona Freda Lisa

☞ Take snow from Alaska and sell it in New Mexico.

☞ Change a baby's diaper.

Three Ways to Get Wealthy

Way #1: Create wealth. Move stuff from lower value to higher value. This is called "working."

Way #2: Get a gun and rob other people's hot dog stands.

Way #3: Have the government destroy your competition or take money from others and give it to you.

Price supports, tariffs, minimum wages, licensing, subsidies, job stimulus programs, and government-sponsored stadiums, schools, power companies, parks, swimming pools. . . . The list is almost endless.

Government can be very good when it promotes competition. It can be very evil when it kills competition.

Suppose I'm good at pruning roses. People will pay me $17/hour to prune their roses. If I want to get wealthy, I ask the government to pass a **minimum wage law**: Those who prune roses must get paid at least $17/hour.

What happens to those who are just learning how to prune roses and are willing to work for $15/hour? They can't work. The minimum wage law has put them out of work. And I benefit.

Remember the fourth key point of economics: *You have to look at the whole picture.*

Any minimum wage law discriminates against those who are less skilled. They are willing to work but are forced to be unemployed.

A minimum wage law directly results in forced unemployment. This is *looking at the whole picture.*

Those who vote for minimum wage laws say that they prevent people from having to work for only $5/hour. What they fail to say is that they prevent people who would be happy to work for $5/hour from working.

How about a $100/hour minimum wage? Wouldn't we all then be rich? A better question: Would you be working, or would you have to go on welfare?

❀   ❀   ❀

On the second day that Fred sold hot dogs, he made $1020. That was a 2% increase over the first day's $1000.

$$\frac{\$1020}{\$1000} = 1.02 \quad \text{a 2\% increase}$$

Customers who had tasted Fred's dogs wrote blogs: "No one can do a dog like Fred. You gotta try one."

On the third day, his sales increased by another 2%.

$1020 × 1.02 = $1040.40

On the fourth day, another 2%

$1040.40 × 1.02 = $1061.21

After n days, his sales were $1000 × $(1.02)^n$.

How long would it be before Fred's sales doubled?
Restated: How long would it be before he was making $2000/day.
Restated: What n will make $(1.02)^n$ equal 2?
The exact solution of the **exponential equation** $(1.02)^n = 2$ is something we do in *Life of Fred: Advanced Algebra* using logs. (It's called an exponential equation because the unknown n is an exponent.)

But why wait? There is a fast, easy way to find out approximately how long it takes things to double. It's called the **Rule of 72**.

To find out how long something will take to double if it is growing at 2%/day:

$$\frac{72}{2} = \text{approximately 36 days.}$$

To find out how long it will take your bank account to double if it is growing at 8%/year:

$$\frac{72}{8} = \text{approximately 9 years.}$$

A fast and easy approximation.

Your Turn to Play

1. If I'm gaining weight at the rate of 3% per year, how long will it be before I weigh twice as much as now?

2. If I'm gaining weight at the rate of 3% per year, how long will it be before I weigh four times as much as I do now?

3. How long before Fred's hot dog business is making money at the rate of a million dollars a year? (Facts: He started at the rate of $1000/day, which we computed three pages ago to equal a quarter of a million dollars per year. His profits are increasing by 2% per day.)

4. Sometimes Fred would have a lot of customers lined up to buy his hot dogs. Other times things would get quiet. He used those quiet times to prepare more dogs for sale.

  In one 20-minute quiet time, he first prepared his Gourmet Gauss Dogs. He could do that at the rate of 22/minute. Then for the rest of the 20 minutes he prepared his Hot Hot Dogs.

> The Hot Hot Dogs were Fred's newest creation. He took a regular hot dog and dusted it with some red pepper flakes. Then he split it open and poured in cayenne, chili powder, jalapeño peppers, curry, red savina habanero, and bhut jolokia.

He could prepare his Hot Hot Dogs at the rate of 18/minute.

  In that 20-minute period, he made as many Hot Hot Dogs as Gourmet Gauss Dogs. How long did he spend making the Gourmet Gauss Dogs?

.......COMPLETE SOLUTIONS.......

1. 72/3 = approximately 24 years.

2. In 24 years, I'll double my weight. In another 24, it will double again. So it will take me 48 years to quadruple my weight.

3. If he started at a quarter of a million dollars per year, then he will have to double his profits twice. The first double will bring him up to $500,000 per year, and the second double will bring him up to $1,000,000 per year. At an increase of 2% per day, it will take 72/2 = about 36 days to double once and another 36 days to double again. In 36 + 36 = 72 days he will be making hot dog profits at the rate of a million dollars per year.

4. Using six pretty boxes . . .

We are asked how long he spent making Gourmet Gauss Dogs.

	Dogs made	rate	time
Gourmet			t
Hot Hot Dogs			

If he spent a total of 20 minutes, and he spent t minutes on the Gourmet Gauss Dogs, then he must have spent 20 − t on the Hot Hot Dogs.

	Dogs made	rate	time
Gourmet			t
Hot Hot Dogs			$20-t$

Next, fill in the rates. Then, since he made 22 Gourmet Gauss Dogs/minute and worked for t minutes, he must have made 22t dogs.

	Dogs made	rate	time
Gourmet	$22t$	22	t
Hot Hot Dogs	$18(20-t)$	18	$20-t$

Since he made the same number of each kind of dog, $22t = 18(20 - t)$.

Distributive law $22t = 360 - 18t$
Add 18t to both sides $40t = 360$
Divide both sides by 40 $t = 9$

Fred spent 9 minutes making Gourmet Gauss Dogs.

F red bought his hot dogs from Whole Dog, a company in Texas. Its official name is Wholesale Hot Dog Supply Company of Lampasas, Texas, but everyone just calls it Whole Dog. Whole Dog would sell Fred hot dogs at $100/case.

Fred found out that he could buy the same hot dogs from Freedonia, a floating island nation in the middle of the Atlantic.

This fabulous* country of Freedonia offered their hot dogs to Fred for $90/case.

Fred was delighted. Since his costs were less, he could make more money.

His customers were delighted. Their hot dogs cost less.

Can you guess who was miffed? It was the Wholesale Hot Dog Supply Company of Lampasas, Texas. They had lost their business to a competitor in Freedonia. Whole Dog had three choices:

A) Sell their dogs for $90/case to match their competitor's price.

B) Use violence. Whole Dog could destroy the shipments of hot dogs that were being sent to Fred from Freedonia.

C) Whole Dog could send lobbyists to Senator Snow of Texas and tell him, "American jobs are being lost! You gotta protect us! You can't let those foreigners interfere with our business!" They also promised Senator Snow lots of votes if he "protected a Texas industry." And Whole Dog made a $30,000 tuition payment for Senator Snow's daughter.

Senator Snow did not realize that the proper function of government is to promote competition. He did realize that getting votes was important for his re-election, and he had been wondering how he would pay for his daughter's tuition. He thought of two possible bills that he could present to the United States Congress. First, he could ask

---

* The word *fabulous* has several meanings. We are not using *fabulous* in the sense of extremely pleasing. If you own a dictionary. . . .

Congress to declare war on Freedonia. Then Freedonia couldn't ship their hot dogs to Fred or anyone else in the United States.

An easier way would be to impose a tariff on Freedonian hot dogs. A **tariff** is a tax on goods coming into or going out of a country. Senator Snow's bill proposed a tariff of $40/case on hot dogs from Freedonia. That would make Freedonian hot dogs cost $130/case (= $90 + $40).

Who benefitted from this tariff? The Whole Dog company and Senator Snow.

Who was hurt by this tariff? All the hot dog eating people in the United States and the company in Freedonia.

Every time you restrict competition, society as a whole is poorer.

Every tariff contributes to scarcity.

Every tariff works against the division of labor. (Key point #9 was *The division of labor dies as you lose people you can trade with*.) And the division of labor (specialization) is central to a higher standard of living.

Intermission

The Civil War Was a Tariff War
Not a War to Free the Slaves

Wait a minute! I, your reader, object. Everyone knows that the Civil War was fought to free the slaves. None of my teachers ever mentioned tariffs. You're kidding me, aren't you?

Which of these facts will your teachers deny?

Fact #1: Government should treat everyone equally under the law with no special privileges to any group.

Fact #2: The steel and manufacturing industries were located mainly in the North. The South was mainly agricultural.

Fact #3: The South was much more dependent on imports than the North.

Fact #4: For years before the Civil War, the South had been complaining about the high tariffs.

Fact #5: At the beginning of the war, the South had been paying as much as 80% of the tariffs.

Fact #6: A high tariff benefitted the industries of the North. It helped eliminate competition from other countries.

Fact #7: Just before Lincoln became president, the Morrill tariff became law. The Morrill tariff greatly increased the rates and expanded the number of items subject to the tariff.

Fact #8: The Morrill tariff almost tripled the tax burden.

Fact #9: The outrage of the South must have been on Lincoln's mind. In the speech he gave at his swearing in, he said, "*The power confided in me will be used to hold, occupy, and possess the property belonging to the government, and to collect the duties and imposts; but beyond what may be necessary for these objects, there will be no invasion—no using force against, or among the people anywhere.*" (Does this translate as: "You pay the tariffs, and I won't invade"?)

Fact #10: Fort Sumter was a tariff collection point. The first shots of the Civil war were fired here. This was five weeks after Lincoln's threat-of-invasion speech.

Fact #11: Lincoln later admitted that he manipulated things so that the South fired the first shot. (The same thing probably happened in 1941 at Pearl Harbor.) That made the North "the good guys."

Fact #12: Here is the order of events in 1861:

C. S. A.

February—Seven states had issued their declarations of independence from the Union. They formed a new nation (the Confederate States of America). They expected to be able to leave peacefully.

March—Morrill tariff enacted and Lincoln warns about invasion.

April—The South forces the surrender of Fort Sumter in South Carolina—a Union tariff collection point in the Confederacy. There were no deaths on either side during the battle.

Fact #13: At Lincoln's inaugural speech in March he also said, "*I have no purpose, directly or indirectly, to interfere with the institution of slavery in the States where it exists. I believe I have no lawful right to do so, and I have no inclination to do so.*"

Fact #14: In a public debate in 1858, Lincoln said:

"*I will say then that I am not, nor ever have been, in favor of bringing about in any way the social and political equality of the white and black races—that I am not, nor ever have been, in favor of making voters or jurors of Negroes, nor of qualifying them to hold office, nor to intermarry with white people; and I will say in addition to this that there is a physical difference between the white and black races which I believe forever forbids the two races living together on terms of social and political equality. And in as much as they cannot so live, while they do remain together there must be the position of superior and inferior, and I as much as any other man am in favor of having the superior position assigned to the white race.*"

Fact #15: The Emancipation Proclamation (issued over a year after the war began) only freed slaves in the Confederate States of America. It did not free slaves in the North.

Fact #16: When the Emancipation Proclamation went into effect, thousands of Union soldiers deserted in protest.

Fact #17: The largest insurgency (rebellion against the government) in the history of the United States (not counting the Civil War itself) happened in New York City in response to the Emancipation Proclamation and the draft law.

You are old enough to know the truth about:
✓ The Easter Bunny who lays chocolate eggs,
✓ Santa Claus, and
✓ Why the Second War for Independence was fought.

Those that want tariffs imposed often cry, "It's to save jobs here in this country." *But you have to look at the whole picture—especially the consequences that are not immediately obvious.*

Having a job is not the final goal of economics. It is enjoying abundant, inexpensive things. This happens when you have a division of labor (specialization) and are permitted to freely buy and sell. Tariffs limit competition. It's the difference between having only one store in town that you can shop at and having lots of stores (and the Internet).

Those that want tariffs imposed often cry, "That other country is dumping their products on us. Unfair competition." Selling stuff at less than the cost of producing it is called **dumping**.

Suppose some company in another country offers to sell their microwave ovens to us for 6¢ each. Do we want to stop them? Heavens no! I'll buy one for each room in my house. Come to think of it, I would like one for the garage. And one for my car. I will gladly trade 54¢ for nine microwaves. I'm rich in microwaves.

Those that want tariffs imposed will cry, "What about the microwave manufactures in this country? No one is going to buy from them if they can get 6¢ microwaves from the foreign competitors."

Consumers are concerned about both the price and the quality of the product. If the microwave ovens are of the same quality, the consumer should be free to choose. One group of competitors—in this case, the American microwave manufacturers—should not be allowed to use the force of government to eliminate their foreign competition.

Competitors don't have a right* to force customers to buy their products. They earn their sales by offering quality and price. Some companies that can't offer good quality and price will fade away. If you are really old (like people who are 30), you might remember Polaroid cameras that offered instant pictures. If you are fairly old (like 15), you may remember when everyone used film in their cameras. This process of

---

✶ A right is something that you have to begin with. No government gives you your rights.

unsuccessful companies giving way to newer companies is called **creative destruction**.* If you are not making things that consumers want at prices they like, then wouldn't it seem reasonable that you should change what you are doing?

Speaking of doing, we are long overdue for . . .

Your Turn to Play

1. Let the countries of the world be the domain. Let {☹,✿,☺} be the codomain. Assign a country to ☹ if it doesn't have any companies that make microwave ovens. Assign a country to ✿ if it has only one company that makes microwave ovens. Assign a country to ☺ if it has more than one company that makes microwave ovens.

Is this a function?

Is it 1-1?

2. Is it possible to invent a function whose domain is {3, 7} and whose codomain is {☎}?

3. Is it possible to invent a function whose domain is { ✗ } and whose codomain is the **natural numbers** {1, 2, 3, 4, . . . }?

4. Fred didn't want his hot dog business to be caught in a wave of creative destruction. He kept innovating. His newest invention was the *Polka Dot Hot Dog*. He did that by sticking the dogs in a waffle iron.

He first ran a batch of hot dogs through the microwave one at a time at the rate of 4 dogs/minute. Then he unplugged the microwave and plugged in the waffle iron. The waffle iron added polka dots to the dogs at the rate of 3 dogs/minute.

Makes Polka Dot Hot Dogs

Since the waffle iron could process fewer dogs/minute it took 3 minutes longer to do the whole batch.

How long was the microwave used to do a batch?

----

* Back in 1913, Werner Sombart wrote "from destruction, a new spirit of creation arises" describing how coal was displacing wood for heating. The term *creative destruction* was popularized by Joseph Schumpeter, an economist from the Austrian School in *Capitalism, Socialism and Democracy.*

.... COMPLETE SOLUTIONS ....

1. Since every element in the domain is assigned to exactly one element in the codomain, it is a function. Since more than one country has no companies that make microwave ovens, more than one element in the domain is assigned to ⊗. The function is not 1-1.

2. There is only one possible function with a domain of {3, 7} and codomain of {☎}. Assign 3 to ☎ and assign 7 to ☎.

3. Easy. Assign, for example, ✗ to 1743. Then every element of the domain has been assigned to exactly one element of the codomain.

4. This first step in solving a word problem is almost always the same: you let t (or x or r) equal what you are trying to find out.

Let t = how long it takes to process a batch through the microwave.

Then t + 3 = how long the waffle iron is used for the batch.

Then 4t = how many dogs are microwaved in a batch.

Then 3(t + 3) = how many dogs are polka dotted in the waffle iron.

Since the same number of dogs are microwaved as are waffle ironed,
$$4t = 3(t + 3)$$
$$4t = 3t + 9$$
$$t = 9$$
The batch of dogs takes 9 minutes in the microwave.

Dumping. One standard way companies in foreign countries are able to sell their microwaves for 6¢ is to have their governments subsidize their companies. Translation: Their taxpayers pay the government, which then pays the company.

This is wonderful for us. Wonderful! Wonderful! Wonderful! The other country's taxpayers are paying to make our purchases cheaper.

Of course, if our government subsidizes our products that we export, we are the dummies.

Chapter Twenty-six
Opportunity Costs

Everyone liked Fred's **Polka Dot Hot Dogs**. The idea was a winner. He would pop a dog into his microwave, then into his waffle iron, and immediately sell it.

Hold it! I, your reader, have a small question. In the previous Your Turn to Play, you wrote that Fred was sticking the dogs into his microwave "one at a time." That seems awfully silly.

It really isn't. Fred couldn't put a full-sized microwave on his cart. The microwave he used could only hold one dog at a time. It was this size:

Thank you for clearing up that important point.

Of course, with such a small microwave oven, Fred has to make choices. If he chooses to put in a dog to make a **Polka Dot Hot Dog**, then at that moment he is not able to put in a dog to make a Gourmet Gauss Dog.

Now featuring
Polka Dot Hot Dogs

This would be silly.

Every choice in life means that you are giving up something else. When Fred elects to push a hot dog cart on the streets around KITTENS University, he is giving up . . .

teaching summer school,
being assistant manager at Terry's Taffy & Taco,
washing dishes at Stanthony's pizza, and
mowing lawns.

The **opportunity cost** is the value of the nicest thing you are giving up.

For Fred, teaching summer school would give him, say, $300. Being assistant manager at T's T & T, $200. Washing dishes, $180. And mowing lawns, $150.

So, the opportunity cost to Fred for pushing a hot dog cart is $300, which is the value of the next-best thing—teaching summer school.

174

I, your reader, have a thought. This "opportunity cost" is the wrong name. It should be called the "lost opportunity cost." It is measuring the thing you gave up. What do you think of that?

I like that. *Lost opportunity cost* is much more descriptive.

Are you going to use my suggestion?

No.

Why in blazes aren't you? We both like "lost opportunity cost." What's holding you back?

There are two of us, but there are seven billion (7,000,000,000) other people on the planet who call it "opportunity cost."* There is a real advantage for:

- using the same language as others you converse with,
- driving on the same side of the road as everyone else,
- saying "Hello" instead of "Goodbye" when you meet someone,
- using the same table manners as those you are with, and
- singing as loudly or softly as the rest of the choir.

❀   ❀   ❀

The opportunity cost to Fred in choosing to push a hot dog cart is the $300 (teaching summer school) that he gives up. That means *his profit for pushing the hot dog cart is more than $300.* (Otherwise, he wouldn't have been doing it.)

Oh! Do I feel like an idiot. When Fred chooses to take the opportunity to do something, he pays the cost of the nicest thing he isn't doing. Do you get it? Opportunity cost = what it costs to seize a particular opportunity. The phrase "opportunity cost" makes a lot of sense.

I still like "lost opportunity cost."

There are 7,000,000,001 of us and only one of you. Mr. Author, you lose.

What can I say?

You can say, "Okay."

Okay.

★ . . . in whatever language they use.

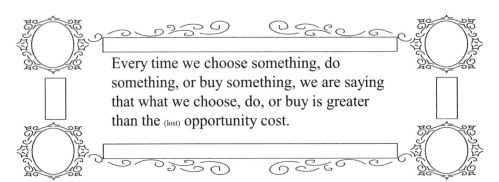

Every time we choose something, do something, or buy something, we are saying that what we choose, do, or buy is greater than the (lost) opportunity cost.

If I buy Prof. Eldwood's *Modern Guide to Yodeling,* I won't have enough money to buy Goodbye Cat stickers for my sticker album. My opportunity cost for buying the yodeling book is not getting the stickers.

Goodbye Cat

Opportunity cost is the important thing to look at in making any decision (economic or otherwise).

Simple example: Joe is trying to decide whether he should apply to become a cashier at Terry's Taffy & Taco. The job pays $8/hour. Joe's other alternatives are either going fishing, which gives him $2/hour, or watching television, which gives him 25¢/hour.*

Joe's opportunity cost in choosing to be a cashier is $2/hour. If Terry offered him anything more than $2/hour, Joe would benefit by taking the cashier's job.

A second simple example: Suppose Darlene is also considering becoming a cashier at Terry's Taffy & Taco. Her other alternative is being a manicurist, which pays $11/hour. Darlene's opportunity cost in choosing to be a cashier at Terry's is $11/hour. Terry would have to offer Darlene more than $11/hour in order for her to accept the cashier's job.

Who will get the cashier's job? Joe will. He can underbid Darlene since his opportunity cost is less than hers. He can sell his labor more cheaply than Darlene can.

---

* The 25¢/hour comes from his watching the ads and seeing where he can save money.

The tenth key point of economics is: *If you and the other guy are selling identical products, the one with the lower opportunity cost is the one who makes the sale.*

The one with the lower opportunity cost has a **comparative advantage**.

In a diagram:

	Cashier at T & T	Next best choice
Joe		$2/hr
Darlene		$11/hr

Joe's opportunity cost is $2/hr

Darlene's opportunity cost is $11/hr

Your Turn to Play

1. Suppose working as a cashier at Terry's Taffy & Taco is pleasant work that you could do easily. Suppose that they offer the job to you and will pay you $80/hour. Creative writing assignment: *Invent an economic reason (involving opportunity cost) that would cause you to turn down that job offer.*

2. Joe applied for the cashier's job. Terry wanted to find out how good Joe was and gave him a test. For the first part of the test, Joe was checking out tacos. They are 30¢ each. For the second part of the test, Joe was checking out pieces of taffy, which cost 6¢ each. He checked out 80 more pieces of taffy than tacos.

He checked out the same dollar amount of tacos and taffy. How many tacos did he check out?

3. What is the cardinality of {2, A, ✂}?

4. Solve $4x - 4 = 6(x - 3)$

5. $\dfrac{3}{4} + \dfrac{1}{5}$

6. $\dfrac{3}{4} \div \dfrac{1}{5}$

.......COMPLETE SOLUTIONS.......

1. Your answer will, of course, probably be different than mine since this is creative writing. I picture that I am a gifted musician who could make $90/hour playing my harmonica. I am also an artist who could make $45/hour selling my art. I am also a brain surgeon who makes $450/hour doing brain surgery.

    My opportunity cost to work as a cashier at Terry's is the value of the best thing I am giving up. In my case, it is the most valuable item in the set {musician ($90/hour), artist ($45/hour), brain surgeon ($450/hour)}. So my opportunity cost for getting the $80/hour cashier's job would be $450/hour.

2.
You let x equal the thing that you are trying to find out.

	how much $ checked	rate	number of items
Tacos			x
Pieces of Taffy			

Fill in the given information.

	how much $ checked	rate	number of items
Tacos		30	x
Pieces of Taffy		6	$x + 80$

    If you check 3 tacos at 30¢/taco, you will check out 90¢ worth of tacos.
    Joe had checked out x tacos at the rate of 30¢/taco. So he will have checked out 30x¢ of tacos.

	how much $ checked	rate	number of items
Tacos	$30x$	30	x
Pieces of Taffy	$6(x+80)$	6	$x + 80$

    Since we are told that he checked out the same dollar amount of tacos and taffy, we have $30x = 6(x + 80)$
    Solving that, we arrive at $x = 20$. Joe had checked out 20 tacos.

3. The cardinality of a set is the number of elements in a set. The cardinality of $\{2, A, \text{✂}\}$ is 3.

4. Solve $4x - 4 = 6(x - 3)$

$$4x - 4 = 6x - 18 \qquad \text{Distributive law}$$
$$4x + 14 = 6x \qquad \text{Add 18 to both sides}$$
$$14 = 2x \qquad \text{Subtract 4x from both sides}$$
$$7 = x \qquad \text{Divide both sides by 2}$$

5. $\dfrac{3}{4} + \dfrac{1}{5} = \dfrac{3(5)}{4(5)} + \dfrac{1(4)}{5(4)} = \dfrac{15 + 4}{20} = \dfrac{19}{20}$

6. $\dfrac{3}{4} \div \dfrac{1}{5} = \dfrac{3}{4} \times \dfrac{5}{1} = \dfrac{15}{4} = 3\dfrac{3}{4}$

Chapter Twenty-seven
Most Important Concept in Economics

Before Fred invented **Polka Dot Hot Dogs**, he had been making about $1000 a day. Now, with his new hot dogs, he was making gobs of money, heaps of money, tons of money.* It got to be so much that it wouldn't all fit in his pockets. So every time he passed the KITTENS Bank ATM, he would stop and empty his pockets into the machine.

Fred had a choice. He could work an extra hour until 6 p.m. Doing that, he could sell to the "dinner crowd," as it's called in the hot dog business. An extra hour could give him another $500. (I did mention, didn't I, that he was no longer making just $1000 a day.)

He chose not to work the extra hour. Instead, he decided to spend that crepuscular time taking a walk around the Great Lake near the KITTENS University campus. He liked to see the rabbits playing on the lawn and the sailboats silently moving in the distance.

I really hate to interrupt your wonderful narrative, but I, your reader, think that you, Mr. Author, are getting foggy in your old age.

Foggy?

Yes. Inconsistent. You are losing your grip. The medical word is senile.

What makes you think that?

In the previous chapter you wrote, "Opportunity cost is the important thing to look at in making any decision (economic or otherwise)." Now you have Fred giving up $500 to go walking around the lake. Since Fred is giving up at least $500, his opportunity cost is at least $500. In that fancy box on page 176, you said that when we choose something, it is always greater than the opportunity cost.

Yes, I said that.

---

* Some people call that *making serious money*, but if I were making $500 an hour, I would start giggling.

Are you telling me that Fred is going to get more than $500 by walking around the lake?

No. I'm not. When I defined opportunity cost, I was careful to write that opportunity cost is the "value" of the nicest thing you are giving up—not the "greatest dollar value."

I'm using this example to introduce what I consider the <u>M</u>ost <u>I</u>mportant <u>C</u>oncept in <u>E</u>conomics.

M.I.C.E.
Why do we study economics?

Why do we study really hard to get a good job?

Why do we work overtime?

Is it so we can make lots of money?

If money is so important, why do we spend it? Why do we trade it for clothes or for pizzas?

What comes next is intended only for my human readers. If you are a robot or a computer program reading this book, you won't understand this M.I.C.E. (Most Important Concept in Economics).

The thing that really counts is happiness.

M. I. C. E.

If this is your book, which you bought with your own money, feel free to use a highlighter on that sentence.

Surprise! Ⅲ➡ The object is not to make as much money as possible. It is to be as happy as possible.

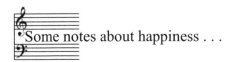

Some notes about happiness . . .

♪#1: For every choice you make, the critical thing is the opportunity cost. In 1992, I, your author, married Lynn. My opportunity cost was the greatest value in the list { , , , , or staying single}.

Hold it! I, your reader, can't believe this. Did you really assign dollar values to each item in that set? That is really gross.

No. The whole point of M.I.C.E. is that money is not the final measure of everything. You don't want a tombstone that looks like this.

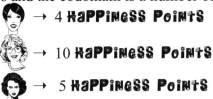

Here lies somebody who lived just to make money

The Most Important Concept in Economics is that happiness is what counts. If you like to make things mathematical, we could invent **HaPPiNeSS PoiNtS**.

You create a function. The domain is the set of all the alternatives and the codomain is a number of **HaPPiNeSS PoiNtS**.

→ 4 **HaPPiNeSS PoiNtS**

→ 10 **HaPPiNeSS PoiNtS**

→ 5 **HaPPiNeSS PoiNtS**

→ 11 **HaPPiNeSS PoiNtS**

staying single → 7 **HaPPiNeSS PoiNtS**.

So the opportunity cost associated with marrying Lynn was 11 **HaPPiNeSS PoiNtS**.

When we choose something, it is because it is greater than the opportunity cost. The value of marrying Lynn was 3,298,899 **HaPPiNeSS PoiNtS**.

♪#2: Looking at your **HaPPiNeSS PoiNtS** when you pick something does not mean you have to be **GREEDY**, **SELFISH**, **COVETOUS**, or **AVARICIOUS**.

Consider an Albanian woman who was named Agnesë Gonxhe Bojaxhiu when she was born. For over 45 years she worked in India helping the poor, the orphaned, and the dying.

She chose to do that. Nobody forced her.

Her opportunity cost for choosing that work in India was the value of the most **HaPPiNeSS PoiNtS** that she gave up.

A trip to Disneyland might have been worth 6 **HaPPiNeSS PoiNtS** to her.

Getting married and having a bunch of kids might have been worth 985 **HaPPiNeSS PoiNtS** to her.

Working as a teacher at a university might have given her 104 **HaPPiNeSS PoiNtS**.

In order to work with the sick and dying, her opportunity cost was at least 985 **HaPPiNeSS PoiNtS**. She did something that was worth more than that to her.

She looked at her **HaPPiNeSS PoiNtS**, but hardly anyone would call her **GREEDY** or **SELFISH**.

Agnesë
Gonxhe
Bojaxhiu

When she died in 1997, her funeral was broadcast on television around the world.*

♪#3: Each of us assigns different happiness points to the different choices. That's why not everyone is married to Lynn.**

---

* I watched it. It was over four hours long. Lots of people cried. The television announcers did not use her birth name, Agnesë Gonxhe Bojaxhiu. Instead, they called her Mother Teresa.

** . . . or Pat, or Kelly, or Chris, or Robin, or Terry, or Ashley, or Leslie, or Jackie, or Lee—all of these can apply to either gender. And while I'm at it: Gomer, Morgan, Dale, Dakota, Joyce, Sam, Sig, Shirley, Sandy, Shelly, Drew, Jan, Kim, Sidney, and Jean are also on that list. Did you know that before 1940, Lynn was more frequently a boy's name than a girl's? After about 1975, it became almost exclusively a girl's name.

That's why not everyone goes to India to work with the orphans or likes the same kind of pizza.

Not everyone gets the same haircut.

It makes a difference **who** is assigning **HaPPiness PoiNts**.

♪#4: It also makes a difference **when** those **HaPPiness PoiNts** are assigned.

✓ When you are really poor, an extra $600 will mean a lot of **HaPPiness PoiNts**. Later in life, when you are a millionaire, an extra $600 is hardly worth one **HaPPiness PoiNt**.

✓ When you are dying of thirst, a glass of water is worth 1,000 **HaPPiness PoiNts** and a glass full of diamonds is worth 3 **HaPPiness PoiNts**. You will gladly exchange the glass full of diamonds for a glass of water.

✓ When Fred starts his work day at 8 a.m., pushing his hot dog cart for an hour gives him 400 **HaPPiness PoiNts**, but at 5 p.m. he might only get 70 **HaPPiness PoiNts** pushing his cart for an hour.

The Bridges are coming up very soon. In order for you to have as many **HaPPiness PoiNts** as possible, let's use this *Your Turn to Play* to get ready.

Your Turn to Play

1. Fred is walking around the Great Lake near the KITTENS University campus. He gets sand in his shoes at the rate of 0.12 grams for every 4 minutes he walks. How much sand would he get in 9 minutes of walking? (Use a conversion factor.)

2. If you have *n* quarters, how many cents is that worth?

3. Solve $7(8 + x) = 16x + 2$

4. Here are the Eleven Conversions. Write each of these fractions as a percent: $\dfrac{1}{2}$ $\dfrac{1}{3}$ $\dfrac{2}{3}$ $\dfrac{1}{4}$ $\dfrac{3}{4}$ $\dfrac{1}{8}$ $\dfrac{3}{8}$ $\dfrac{5}{8}$ $\dfrac{7}{8}$ $\dfrac{1}{6}$ $\dfrac{5}{6}$

5. In an hour of walking, Fred spent 12 minutes watching the rabbits play on the lawn. What fraction of the hour was that?

.......COMPLETE SOLUTIONS.......

1. Since 0.12 grams matches up with 4 minutes, the conversion factor will either be $\dfrac{0.12\text{ g}}{4\text{ min}}$ or it will be $\dfrac{4\text{ min}}{0.12\text{ g}}$

We are given 9 minutes. So that the units will cancel we choose $\dfrac{0.12\text{ g}}{4\text{ min}}$

$$\frac{9\ \cancel{\text{minutes}}}{1} \times \frac{0.12\text{ grams}}{4\ \cancel{\text{minutes}}} = 0.27\text{ grams}$$

2. If you have 1 quarter, it is worth 25 cents.

If you have 2 quarters, they are worth 50 cents.

If you have 10 quarters, they are worth 250 cents.

Using that same pattern, we know that *n* quarters are worth 25*n* cents.

3. $7(8 + x) = 16x + 2$

$56 + 7x = 16x + 2$	Distributive law
$56 = 9x + 2$	Subtract 7x from both sides
$54 = 9x$	Subtract 2 from both sides
$6 = x$	Divide both sides by 9

4. Here are the Eleven Conversions that you memorized:

$$\frac{1}{2} = 50\% \qquad \frac{1}{4} = 25\% \qquad \frac{3}{8} = 37\tfrac{1}{2}\% \qquad \frac{1}{6} = 16\tfrac{2}{3}\%$$

$$\frac{1}{3} = 33\tfrac{1}{3}\% \qquad \frac{3}{4} = 75\% \qquad \frac{5}{8} = 62\tfrac{1}{2}\% \qquad \frac{5}{6} = 83\tfrac{1}{3}\%$$

$$\frac{2}{3} = 66\tfrac{2}{3}\% \qquad \frac{1}{8} = 12\tfrac{1}{2}\% \qquad \frac{7}{8} = 87\tfrac{1}{2}\%$$

5. Twelve minutes is what fraction of 60 minutes? 12 = ? of 60.

We divide the number closest to the *of* into the other number.

$$\frac{12}{60} \text{ which reduces to } \frac{1}{5}$$

 # The Bridge
from Chapter 1 to Chapter 27

first try

1. "What do you think about children?" Darlene asked Joe. She wanted Joe to marry her. She had tried talking about wedding cakes, bridal dresses, and wedding gifts, but those topics didn't seem to work.

"What do I think about children?" Joe repeated her question. That was a habit of his. It gave him time to think.

"Yes," Darlene responded. "Do you ever think about children?"

Joe thought for a moment. "I don't like it when they stand in front of the television when I'm watching it."

Darlene continued, "But you could look at the kid instead of looking at the TV. It could be one of your children."

"But I'm not married," Joe answered.

It had taken Darlene 42 minutes to get Joe to say the word *married*. Forty-two minutes is what fraction of an hour? (Reduce your answer to lowest terms.)

2. Darlene read an article in one of her romance magazines. It was entitled, "How to Spend 20% More Quality Time with the Guy You Love."

In Darlene's mind, "quality time" wasn't time spent watching television with Joe. The only quality time she currently had with him was the 30 minutes they spent walking to classes together. How much quality time could they have if that 30 minutes were increased by 20%?

3. The article suggested, "Unplug his TV when he isn't watching." During one of the commercials, Joe headed into the kitchen to get some more snacks. Darlene unplugged the TV.

Joe headed to the kitchen at the rate of 4 feet/second. On his way back with his arms full of bottles of Sluice, a bag of cookies, a slice of pie, and some taffy, he moved more slowly—3 feet/second.

The trip from the kitchen back to the TV took 2 seconds longer than the trip to the kitchen. How long did it take him to get to the kitchen?

4. When Joe got back to his couch, he sat down and arranged the bottles of Sluice, the bag of cookies, the slice of pie, and the taffy around him. Since Darlene was sitting next to him, Joe had Darlene hold the taffy.

Joe ate the whole bag of cookies (70 Calories per cookie) and the piece of apple pie (600 Calories). He had consumed 2000 Calories. How many cookies were in the bag?

5. Then Joe noticed that the TV screen was black. He pressed the power button on his remote control but nothing happened. He asked Darlene to go and get his bag of batteries. He couldn't do that because he had a bottle of Sluice balanced on each knee. Darlene set down the taffy and headed to the closet where Joe kept his bag of batteries.

Each battery weighed 65 grams. There were 100 batteries in the bag. How many pounds did all those batteries weigh? (One gram is 0.002 pounds.)

6. While Darlene was gone, Joe had consumed two-thirds of a cup of Sluice. When she came back and sat down next to him, he consumed another two-fifths of a cup. How much had he drunk? (Do not leave your answer as an improper fraction.)

7. Darlene was thinking to herself *Is this quality time?*

She offered to hold his bottles of Sluice while he changed the batteries in his remote control. "That won't be necessary," he said. He had watched so much television ➠ used the remote so often ➠ needed to change the batteries so often ➠ that he could do it with just one hand.

He popped out the old batteries and put them in between the cushions on the couch. He slipped in two new batteries and closed the cover. He pressed the power button . . . and the screen was still black. If each change of batteries required two new batteries, how many batteries would be required for *n* changes?

8. $2^5 = ?$

9. What is the volume of a glass of Sluice (it is a cylinder) that has a radius of 2 inches and a height of 8 inches? Use 3 for π.

10. Create a function whose domain is {A, B} and whose codomain is the set of all natural numbers {1, 2, 3, 4, 5, . . .}.

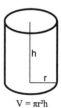

$V = \pi r^2 h$

The Bridge

from Chapter 1 to Chapter 27

second try

1. Write each of these fractions as a percent:

$$\frac{1}{2} \quad \frac{2}{3} \quad \frac{3}{8} \quad \frac{7}{8} \quad \frac{1}{6}$$

2. Joe had changed the batteries in his remote control 50 times, and still the TV screen was black. "Something must be wrong," he announced. He never noticed that the TV was unplugged.

   "We could go out walking together," Darlene suggested. "When we come back, maybe the TV will be better. They sometimes fix themselves."

   "Let's go to the hardware store," Joe said. Darlene agreed; she would have gone anywhere with him. Even a hardware store was nicer than watching Joe sit in front of the television and eat.

   Joe put the Sluice and the taffy in a bag to take along saying, "In case I get hungry." He had carried 8 pounds of food from the kitchen to the television. He had consumed 40% of that food (by weight). How much did the stuff he put in a bag weigh?

3. Joe put on his left shoe first and then put on his sweater. Were these two commutative?

4. Joe seemed to be getting slower in his old age. (He was around 20 years old.) Darlene noticed that as each month passed, it took him 4% longer to get ready to go anywhere than the previous month. If it now takes Joe 10 minutes to get ready, how long will it be before it takes him 20 minutes?

5. Darlene carried the bag of food. She knew that if she carried the food, they could travel at the rate of 5 feet per second. If he were carrying the food, they would go 4 feet per second, and the trip from his front door to his car would take 3 seconds longer.

   How long would it take for them to get from his front door to the car if Darlene carried the food?

6. Joe's car wouldn't start. It rarely did. In fact, only 2 times out of the last 25 times that they had gotten into his car had he been able to start it. What percent of the time did it start?

7. "Let's walk," Darlene suggested. "It's only 3 blocks to the hardware store." How far is that in feet?

(1 block = 110 meters. 1 foot is approximately 0.3 meters.)

8. After walking a block, Joe complained that his feet hurt. Darlene noticed that Joe had put his shoes on the wrong feet. She pulled out a "Putting Shoes on the Correct Feet" chart that Prof. Eldwood had created.

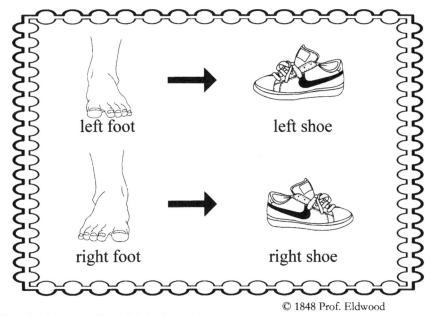

left foot → left shoe

right foot → right shoe

© 1848 Prof. Eldwood

What is the domain of this function?

9. Is this function 1-1?

10. $\frac{1}{2} + \frac{1}{3} + \frac{1}{5}$

 # The Bridge
from Chapter 1 to Chapter 27

third try

1. If you have *n* dimes, what are they worth?

2. Which of these pairs of operations (if any) are commutative?

$\begin{cases} \text{cooking a pizza} \\ \text{eating the pizza} \end{cases}$

$\begin{cases} \text{putting on your socks} \\ \text{putting on your shoes} \end{cases}$

$\begin{cases} \text{brushing your teeth} \\ \text{reading your mail} \end{cases}$

3. When Joe and Darlene arrived at the hardware store, they found that remote control batteries were on sale. Darlene put 20 batteries on a scale. They weighed 3.2 pounds. Joe bought 50 of them. How much would they cost? Use conversion factors and show your work. In fact, showing your work is the important part of this problem.

Batteries!!! $1.10 per pound!!!

4. The 50 batteries cost $8.80. The tax was 7%. How much did Joe have to pay including tax? Round your answer to the nearest cent.

5. Joe was getting thirsty after all this shopping. Darlene handed him a bottle of Sluice and a paper napkin. He drank most of the bottle, wiped his mouth with the napkin, and threw the napkin in the garbage. This snacking cost $6.14. (Let's call it 614¢ so we don't have to work with decimals.) How many ounces of Sluice did he drink? (An ounce of Sluice costs 40¢ and a paper napkin costs 14¢.)

6. Find the value of n so that 10^n equals 10,000.

7. The aisles at the south end of the hardware store were numbered 1, 3, 5, 7, 9. . . . (At the north end of the store they were consecutive even numbers.)

Question 7A: Will the sum of 3 consecutive even numbers always be even or odd?

 # The Bridge

from Chapter 1 to Chapter 27

Question 7B: Will the sum of 3 consecutive odd numbers always be even or odd?

Question 7C: Will the sum of 4 consecutive odd numbers always be even or odd?

8. Suppose the domain is {aisle 6, aisle 11, aisle 12} and suppose the codomain is {nuts, bolts, paint}. Suppose we assign to each element of the domain the things that are found in that aisle.

$$\text{aisle } 6 \ \rightarrow \ \text{paint}$$
$$\text{aisle } 11 \rightarrow \text{nuts}$$
$$\text{aisle } 12 \rightarrow \text{nuts and bolts}$$

Is this a function?

9. $2\frac{3}{4} \div 1\frac{2}{3}$

10. $2\frac{3}{4} + 1\frac{2}{3}$

 # The Bridge
from Chapter 1 to Chapter 27

fourth try

1. "Oh look Joe!" Darlene exclaimed. "Isn't this just darling! You could build this for our children, and then they wouldn't stand in front of the TV when you are trying to watch it."

Darlene was introducing too many different concepts to Joe at one time:

✓ Joe building something.
✓ Our children.
✓ Kids standing in front of the TV.

Build a Crib!
Complete Plans
Available!

One new concept every $4\frac{2}{3}$ minutes was about all that Joe could handle. How long would it take Joe to handle 3 concepts?

2. He immediately liked the idea of children not standing in front of the television when he was trying to watch it. Minutes later, the words "our children" registered in his brain.

A little over nine minutes later, he was able to show his deep insight* when he said, "Our children?"

Darlene smiled. "Yes. Wouldn't that be wonderful?"

"Yes. But . . . but . . . we aren't married," Joe sputtered.

Darlene seized the opportunity. "Oh you big, wonderful man. Are you proposing to me? How wonderful. Right here in aisle 14 of our favorite hardware store. I accept!"

Joe asked Darlene for some pieces of taffy and some Sluice. He wasn't sure what had just happened, and he desperately needed time to think. Chewing taffy always helped him figure things out. He ate 6 pieces of taffy (one at a time) and took a 16-second slurp of Sluice. The whole

---

* *His deep insight* is an example of irony. Irony means saying something and obviously meaning the opposite of the literal meaning of the words.

thing took 160 seconds. How long did each piece of taffy take? Show your work, starting with "Let t =. . . ."

3. After 160 seconds, Joe figured out that Darlene had accepted something, but he wasn't sure what it was. All he knew was that Darlene was hugging him, which made it difficult for him to eat his taffy.

When Darlene let go of Joe, she got out her cell phone and called her mother. "Mom! He finally did it! He did it! He did it!"

Joe wasn't sure what Darlene was talking about, but she seemed very happy. He wandered over to look at the crib plans that listed the set of items needed: {one pile of lumber, one box of nails, a hammer, a saw}. What is the cardinality of this set?

4. Darlene grabbed Joe's hand. "Come on you big, wonderful man. We've got plans to make." Joe wrinkled his forehead. He thought she wanted him to buy the crib plans, not make the plans.

Darlene was almost running as she pulled him down the street. They were going at the rate of 6 feet/second. When they had been heading toward the hardware store, they had been walking at the rate of 3 feet/second and it had taken them 80 seconds longer. How long did it take Darlene to drag Joe back to his apartment?

5. Solve $5(x - 12) = 3(x + 2)$

6. When Joe got back to his apartment he sat down on his couch. He opened the bag containing the 50 new batteries that he had purchased and tried a new pair in his remote. As he pointed the remote control toward his TV he noticed that the TV was unplugged.

He wanted to brag to Darlene that he had fixed the television, but she was on the phone with the florists finding out the prices for bridal bouquets. She wrote down:

Every 5 flowers in a bouquet cost $16.

How much would an 88-flower bouquet cost?

7. Write each of these fractions as a percent: $\dfrac{2}{3}$ $\dfrac{3}{4}$ $\dfrac{7}{8}$ $\dfrac{5}{6}$

8. $9^5 \times 9^7 = 9^?$ (The answer is not 9^{35}.)

9. $\dfrac{1}{6} + \dfrac{1}{8}$

10. $\dfrac{1}{6} \div \dfrac{1}{8}$

fifth try

1. Write each of these fractions as a percent:

$$\frac{1}{2} \quad \frac{1}{3} \quad \frac{2}{3} \quad \frac{1}{4} \quad \frac{5}{6}$$

2. "Are you free next Saturday?" Darlene asked Joe.

She was trying to create a function whose domain is {the wedding date} and whose codomain is the set of all days in the year, {January 1, January 2, . . . , December 30, December 31}.

Joe answered, "No way. Next Saturday is when the Winnows take on the Flags in the playoff."

"How about the following Saturday?"

"No way," Joe said. "Don't you know that's the Saturday that the Flamingos play the Yellows."

Darlene tried every day of the year and nothing worked. Finally, she said, "Okay. It's going to be June 25th." (Darlene had always wanted a June wedding.)

Is this function—wedding date assigned to June 25th—a one-to-one function?

3. Joe asked, "What's going to be June 25th?"

Darlene said, "You know. Our plans."

"You mean the plans for the crib?"

Darlene winced.* "No. For the wedding."

There was silence for a moment. Joe was watching a TV commercial of a little guy selling timeshares. Joe thought his hair was funny. Then Joe asked, "What wedding?"

Every minute of this conversation increased Darlene's blood pressure by 6% over the previous minute. Approximately how long would it take to double her blood pressure?

4. After many minutes, Darlene walked around and stood between Joe and his television. She asked, "Joe, are you in love with me?"

---

* To wince is to tense up as if you were kicked.

194

 # The Bridge
from Chapter 1 to Chapter 27

"Sure," he answered. He waved his hand, indicating that she should move over so that he could see the screen.

Darlene put her hands on her hips. "And how do you know that you are in love with me?"

Joe thought that was a silly question. "That's easy. You told me."

Darlene's heart had been beating at 160 beats per minute. She shut her eyes and tried to calm herself. Her heart rate dropped by 20%. What was her heart rate now?

5. In her heart she knew that, at least for now, "our plans" were only "her plans." She went in the other room and phoned her mother.

She said, "Mom, he . . . he. . . ."

Darlene's mother tried to comfort her, "I know, dear. Sometimes men get cold feet."*

"I'm afraid Joe's feet were never warm in the first place," Darlene half-joked. She had a tear in her eye.

One teardrop weighs 0.3 grams. How much would 2000 tears weigh in ounces? (One gram = 0.035 ounces.)

6. $\dfrac{3}{4} \div \dfrac{7}{8}$

7. $44^5 \times 44^8 = 44^?$

8. $\dfrac{1}{6} + \dfrac{4}{9}$

9. $(\dfrac{1}{7})^2$

10. told Joe that 8 people could share 5 years' worth of a house equally. How much would each person get?

---

* *To get cold feet* means to lose your nerve about something you were going to do. The expression originally came from soldiers whose feet were frozen, and they could no longer fight.

Chapter Twenty-eight
Demand Curve

Fred felt as if he were stuffed with **HaPPiNeSS PoiNtS**. He had worked hard all day. He had supplied people with something (hot dogs) that they enjoyed. He had made more money in a single day than he would have made in six months of teaching. Now he was enjoying well-earned leisure time walking around the Great Lake near the KITTENS University campus.

It's been fun to make so much money Fred thought to himself but with the $500 per month that I receive from KITTENS, I have more than enough for everything that I need or want. I give $50 each month to Sunday school. I sleep under my desk in my office, so I don't have to pay rent. I don't have to keep buying new clothes like other five-year-olds, because I don't seem to outgrow my clothes.

My main clothing expense is the bow ties that I like to wear when I teach. I think that bow ties look cool.

Fred sat on a bench and looked out over the lake. He thought about somehow making a bow tie hot dog.* No one in Kansas had ever seen one. He thought of putting a little clip on the hot dog so it would stay attached to the bun. He thought of squishing the hotdog in the middle to make it look like a bow tie. Neither of these ideas were very good but that did not discourage Fred. He knew that the general rule was that only one idea out of a hundred (1%) would be a really great idea.

Bow tie. Bow tie. Bow tie. Bow tie. Tie. Tie. Tie. That's it! Fred thought to himself. I have to tie the hot dog to the bun somehow. My customers have always complained that when they add too much mustard, and ketchup, and relish, their hot dogs tend to slip out of the bun. If I could tie the dog to the bun, it would be a winner.

And so was born Fred's famous Dog on a Leash.

---

* One of the best ways to create new ideas is to combine things that have never been combined. Certainly hot dogs and bow ties are a combination that few people have ever considered.

What to make the leash out of? Fred had seen dried fruit strips in the grocery store. He could cut those into narrow thin ropes to make the leashes. Then that could be the dessert after they ate the hot dog.

What price should he set for his new Dog on a Leash?

If he sets the price at one dollar, he could sell 100 of them each day. $1 → 100 sold. (This is starting to look like a function.)

Sometimes $1 → 100 is written as (1, 100). This is called an **ordered pair**.

Another way to write $1 → 100 is to put (1, 100) on a graph.

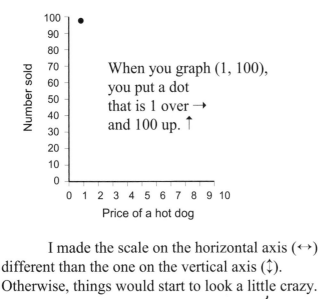

When you graph (1, 100), you put a dot that is 1 over → and 100 up. ↑

I made the scale on the horizontal axis (↔) different than the one on the vertical axis (↕). Otherwise, things would start to look a little crazy.

If he set his price at $2, only 25 people would buy his 𝔇𝔬𝔤 𝔬𝔫 𝔞 𝔏𝔢𝔞𝔰𝔥. $2 → 25 sold. This assignment of 2 to 25 is written as the ordered pair (2, 25).

If he priced it at $5, only those people who didn't pay any attention to how much something costs would buy it. $5 → 4 sold. The ordered pair would be (5, 4). Graphing all these ordered pairs . . .

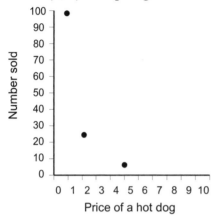

The number of hot dogs sold *depends* on the price that Fred sets. The number of hot dogs sold *is a function of* the price.

Once we have drawn enough points (dots), we can draw a curve through those points. Here is where you get to use your artistic skills.

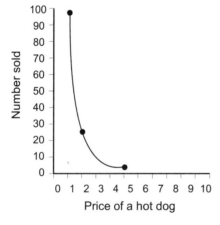

The value on the horizontal axis is always named first. We use that value to find the number on the vertical axis.

The horizontal axis is called the **x-axis**, and the vertical axis is called the **y-axis**. You tell me the value of x, and I will tell you the value of y. In other words, y is a function of x.

For Fred's $\mathbb{D}\mathbb{o}\mathbb{g}$ $\mathbb{o}\mathbb{n}$ $\mathbb{a}$ $\mathbb{L}\mathbb{e}\mathbb{a}\mathbb{s}\mathbb{h}$, the equation in algebra that related his price (x) with the number sold (y), is given* by

$$y = \frac{100}{x^2}$$

If I set x equal to 1, then y is equal to 100.   (1, 100)
If I set x equal to 2, then y is equal to 25.   (2, 25)
If I set x equal to 5, then y is equal to 4.   (5, 4)**

Surprise! You can now **graph any equation**. It is really easy. You are given the equation. Find some points (ordered pairs). Plot the points (dots). When you have enough points, sketch the curve.

Suppose we had a demand curve that was given by the equation

$$y = 8 - 2x$$

You first find some points (ordered pairs). Name any number you like for the value of x. Then find out what y is equal to.

For example, if I select 3 as the value of x, then y will equal 2.*** I get the ordered pair (3, 2).

If I select 0 as the value for x, then y will equal 8.   (0, 8)
If x = 2, then y = 4.   (2, 4)
If x = 1, then y = 6.   (1, 6)

---

* Much later in your mathematics career we will show you how to get the equation. Right now, we will start with the equation and show you how to turn it into a graph.

** Here is the math: If x is equal to five, then $y = \frac{100}{x^2}$ becomes $y = \frac{100}{25} = 4$

*** Here is the math: If x is equal to three, then $y = 8 - 2x$ becomes $y = 8 - 6 = 2$

Then we plot those four ordered pairs.

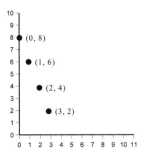

You keep plotting points until the shape of the curve becomes obvious, and then you become an artist and sketch in the curve.

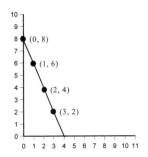

After plotting four points, I draw in the curve, which in this case is a straight line.

Notice that when the price is equal to 4 on the horizontal axis (the x-axis), the number of hot dogs sold is equal to 0. Nobody is buying hot dogs at that price.

Your Turn to Play

1. Graph $y = 3x + 4$ for values of x between 0 and 4.

2. Graph $y = \sqrt{x}$ for values of x from 0 to 100.

$\sqrt{x}$ is pronounced "the square root of x." Recall, $\sqrt{9} = 3$ and $\sqrt{100} = 10$. You can find square roots using your calculator. For example, punch in 17 and hit the $\sqrt{\ }$ key. Out will come something like 4.1231056 or if your calculator is really fancy it might say

---

4.12310562561766054982140985597741. In either case, you would round things off a bit and graph the point (17, 4.1). I don't know of anyone with eyes good enough to plot (17, 4.12).

Hint: The graph of $y = \sqrt{x}$ is not a straight line.

.... COMPLETE SOLUTIONS ....

1. First, we need to find some ordered pairs.

If we let x = 0, then y = 3(0) + 4 = 4 and we have the ordered pair (0, 4).

If x = 1, then y = 3(1) + 4 = 7.   (1, 7)

If x = 2, then y = 10.   (2, 10)

If x = 3, then y = 13.   (3, 13)

If x = 4, then y = 16.   (4, 16)

Then plot those five points.

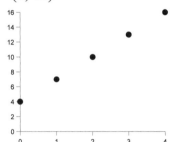

Notice that since the x values go from 0 to 4, I make the scale on the x-axis go from 0 to 4. Since the y values go up to 16, I make the vertical axis go to 16.

You have a lot of freedom in choosing the scales for the two axes.★

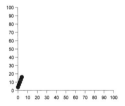

You could even make your scales on each axis go from 0 to 100 if you wanted to but things would get a bit scrunched up.

★ Small English lesson: The plural of axis is axes (pronounced AK-sees). The plural of axe is axes (pronounced AK-sis).

2. You have to get enough points so that you can figure out the shape of the curve.

If $x = 0$, then $y = \sqrt{0} = 0$.   (0, 0)

If $x = 1$, then $y = \sqrt{1} = 1$.   (1, 1)

If $x = 4$, then $y = 2$.   (4, 2)

Similarly, I get (9, 3), (16, 4), (25, 5), (36, 6), (49, 7), (81, 9), (100, 10).

If I needed more points, I could try some harder-to-compute numbers such as $x = 55$. Then $\sqrt{55} = 7.4161984870956629487113974408007$ (You can tell that I love my calculator!)   I get the ordered pair (55, 7.4).

Plotting these points and sketching the curve . . .

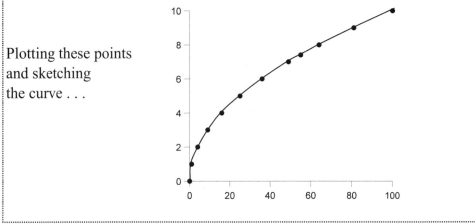

Sad historical note about demand curves . . .

Everybody in mathematics, in physics, in chemistry, in biology, in ornithology (the study of birds), and in ophthalmology (the study of eyes) knows that when you graph a function, you put the independent variable on the horizontal x-axis. Virtually everyone does it this way.

Number sold is a function of the price. Price is the independent variable. You tell me price, and I'll tell you how many are sold. The demand is a function of price.

Almost Everyone

Everyone does it this way, except economists who, because of tradition, draw their demand curves with their axes reversed.

Economists

Chapter Twenty-nine
Whom Should You Trade With?

Fred looked out over the Great Lake. It was beautiful. He took a piece of paper out of his pocket, unfolded it, and drew a picture of the lake scene.

He had created something that wasn't there before: a piece of art.

Some people grow apples.

Some people mine diamonds.

Some people raise sheep.

Some people create computer programs.

The way we have abundant, cheap things is the division of labor—people specializing in the things that they do best. Fred wasn't very good at making bow ties but he realized that some of the bow ties he wore when he was teaching were starting to look a bit ragged.

It was getting dark so Fred walked back to his office in the math building. Using his computer, he located several bow tie manufacturers that were willing to trade their bow ties for his art.

The one in Arizona would give Fred five bow ties for his picture. The one in Freedonia offered him eight bow ties for his picture. Both companies offered free shipping, and their bow ties were all of the same quality.

One difference was that Arizona was in the United States, and Freedonia was a foreign country. Should Fred trade for five bow ties from Arizona or eight bow ties from Freedonia?

Fred had seen the signs that said, "Buy American!" He had even seen a sign that said, "Buy Kansas Products!" (Fred lived in Kansas.) If he had ever visited Freedonia, he might have seen a sign that said, "Buy Freedonia Products!"

Each of these signs urges that you restrict the number of people you trade with. The ninth Key Point of Economics is: *The division of labor dies as you lose people you can trade with.* As the division of labor dies, you become less prosperous. If you have to do everything for yourself—grow your own food, make your own clothes, do your own surgery—you would probably end up starving, wearing rags, and dead.

Who would put up a sign that said, "Buy Kansas Products!"? It certainly wouldn't be people who lived in Arizona. It would be people who had Kansas products to sell. It was a way of eliminating competition.

The Tall Duck would put up a sign that read, "Buy only products made by local ducks!"

If a company in Arizona made five bow ties and Fred made one piece of art, and they traded . . .

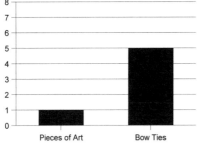

If a company in Freedonia made eight bow ties and Fred made one piece of art, and they traded . . .

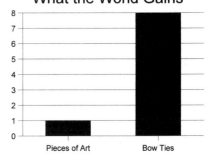

(These graphs are called **bar graphs**.)

Getting the best deal not only benefits you, but it adds to the world's abundance.

On his computer, Fred placed his order for eight bow ties.

The first key point of economics is: *Your labor is something you sell. It has a price.* So when you sell your labor (become employed) or, like bow ties, when you buy labor (employ someone), getting the best deal benefits both you and the rest of the world.

Buyers of bow ties discriminate. They note differences in both price and quality. A second key point of economics is: *Consumers are concerned about both the price and the quality of the product.* There is nothing surprising about that.

Buyers of labor discriminate. They note differences in both the price and quality of labor they purchase. Employers are consumers.

There is a second meaning of the word *discriminate*. It means to make a choice not on the basis of price and quality, but on the basis of the group or class that a person comes from.

Some employers (buyers of labor) will not hire people if they belong to particular groups such as:

> those under the age of 16
> homosexuals
> blacks
> Orientals
> women
> those with tattoos
> the overweight
> Catholics
> atheists
> Irish
> those in wheelchairs
> those over the age of 40
> redheads
> people whose last name begins with C.

The list is almost infinite.

Some discrimination makes sense. You wouldn't want to hire Fred, who is five years old and weighs 37 pounds, to lift 80-pound boxes in your warehouse. You wouldn't want to hire the Tall Duck to be your chauffeur if you are extremely allergic to duck feathers.

What about employers who practice stupid **discrimination**? Do we need to have government pass laws that prevent employers from practicing irrational choices in hiring? The answer is no. A free economic system will automatically punish employers that have prejudices that are not based in reality. A simple example will make this clear.

Suppose you and I are in the business of painting houses. Each of us needs to hire painters to get the work done. Let us say that I have an irrational prejudice against hiring people with purple hair. You, in contrast, don't care what color their hair is—all that matters to you is whether they are good painters.

When you hire painters, you have a wide circle of choices. You can choose good painters with normal colored hair (✳) or good painters with purple hair (✴).

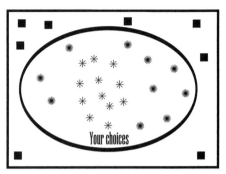

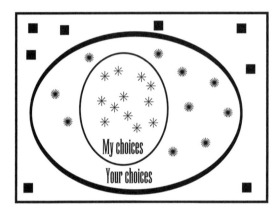

If I won't consider good painters with purple hair (✴), my choices are more limited.

(The people represented by ■ are those that neither one of us would hire—such as the blind, the hospitalized, or the criminally insane.)

My choices are a subset of your choices. Who has the best chance of hiring good painters at low cost? You do. You could choose anyone I could choose (✳), and in addition, you could choose (✴).

The result is that if I irrationally discriminate against ✴, my crew of painters will be more expensive than yours.

If someone wants their house painted, you will get the job, because you can underbid me. Without painting jobs, I will go out of business.

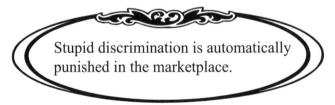

Stupid discrimination is automatically punished in the marketplace.

On the other hand, it should also be noted that . . .

Intelligent discrimination* is
automatically rewarded
in the marketplace.

If you carefully choose the painters that you will hire—and not just hire anybody who says that they want to work for you—you will deliver a better quality product, and your business will prosper.

Your Turn to Play

1. If my painting company ("Pizza Painters") makes $12,000 a year, and your painting company ("Perfect Painters") makes $60,000 a year, draw a bar graph to illustrate this.

2. The boxes on the previous page are examples of **Venn diagrams**.

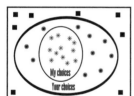

My choices are a **subset**** of your choices. Everything that is inside of my circle is also inside of your circle.

   Draw a Venn diagram that shows that the natural numbers are a subset of the whole numbers. N = {1, 2, 3, 4, . . .}
   W = {0, 1, 2, 3, 4, . . .}

3. $\sqrt{144} = ?$

4. Graph y = 2x + 3 for values of x between 0 and 5.

5. Express as a percent: $\frac{2}{3}$ $\frac{5}{6}$ and $\frac{7}{8}$

---

* Here we are using the word *discriminate* in its first meaning: to note differences in the objects being examined—not in the groups they came from.

** Here is the official definition of "is a subset of": Set A is a subset of set B if every element of A is also an element of B.

·······COMPLETE SOLUTIONS·······

1.

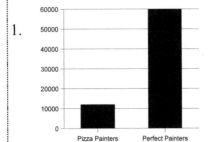

2.

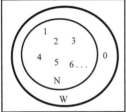

3. $\sqrt{144} = 12$

4. To graph y = 2x + 3, we first find some ordered pairs that satisfy the equation.

If x = 0, then y = 2(0) + 3 = 3.	(0, 3)
If x = 1, then y = 5.	(1, 5)
If x = 3, then y = 9.	(3, 9)
If x = 5, then y = 13.	(5, 13)

We plot those points and sketch in the curve (which, in this case, is a straight line).

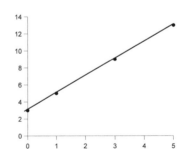

5. $\dfrac{2}{3}$ = 66 2/3% $\dfrac{5}{6}$ = 83 1/3% $\dfrac{7}{8}$ = 87 1/2%

Chapter Thirty
David Ricardo's Law of Comparative Advantage

F red rubbed his eyes. It was getting near his bedtime. He turned off his computer and thought about the people in Arizona who made bow ties. Their bow ties were the same quality as those made in Freedonia, but they cost more.

Fred could imagine many different reasons why they cost more:

❖ The materials used in the production cost more. (For example, cotton might be more expensive in Arizona.)

❖ Taxes might be higher in Arizona. (For example, United States income taxes, Arizona income taxes, tariffs, sales tax, property tax, business license taxes, taxes on phone, electricity, lights. . . .) Freedonia is very much like the United States in its early years—each adult pays the same amount and a light tariff on imports.

❖ Litigation (suing and going to court) is much less common in Freedonia. There, the loser in a court fight has to pay the attorneys' fees and court costs for both sides. (This is not true in the United States.) The effect of Freedonia's loser-pays-all-the-costs rule is twofold: (1) There are fewer frivolous lawsuits, and (2) if you are in the middle of a court fight that you know you're going to lose, you're much more inclined to settle the case out of court rather than continue increasing legal costs. In the United States, litigation can be a significant business expense. Ask any doctor.

❖ Government regulations drive up the expense of making bow ties in Arizona. There are thousands of laws affecting Arizona businesses, and virtually every one of them adds to the cost of doing business.

With the higher cost of materials, taxes, litigation, and regulation, the Arizona bow tie manufacturer may go out of business and sell its tools and cloth inventory to the manufacturer in Freedonia.

I, your reader, am concerned about lost American jobs! What are you going to do about that Mr. Author?

We could cut or eliminate the tariff on imported cotton. The bow tie manufacturers could buy cotton more cheaply.

We could cut or eliminate many of the taxes that American bow tie manufacturers have to pay.

We could pass laws that discourage silly lawsuits.

We could cut or eliminate the amount of regulation a business faces.

What about those people that are out of work today?

Unless government passes a minimum wage law, there is work for everyone. *Each person—regardless of his education, his talents, his age, his physical ability—has work to do that no one else can do as economically as he can.*[*]

That's crazy! It couldn't be true!

Everyone knows that most of economics is either boring or trivial. You already knew that when you increase the price of something that the demand will go down before we drew the graph.

It was trivial to learn the Rule of 72. If you have a wart that is growing at the rate of 12% a week, it will double in size in six weeks,

since $\frac{72}{12}$ equals 6.

But the fact that *every person, every firm, every country has work to do that no one else can do as economically* is mind blowing. This is David Ricardo's Law of Comparative Advantage.

---

[*] And, of course, every *he* and *his* can be replaced by *she* and *her*.

David Ricardo's Law of Comparative Advantage

There is some economic activity
in which you
have a comparative advantage*
over everyone else.

Suppose you have a comparative advantage over everyone else in raising zebras. By definition, your comparative advantage means that you have a lower opportunity cost than anyone else. That means that no one else can underbid you in selling zebras.

Fred knew it was time to F & B (floss and brush his teeth). He grabbed his towel, his dental floss, his toothbrush, and a tube of toothpaste. As he headed down the hall to the restroom, he looked at his tube of toothpaste.

FReedoM TooTH PaSTe
Cleans Sluice scum like no other paste!

Product of Freedonia

Why in the world Fred thought to himself do we import toothpaste from Freedonia when we can make it cheaper here in the United States? The answer is David Ricardo's Law of Comparative Advantage.

---

* **Comparative advantage** = your ability to produce a particular good or service at a lower opportunity cost than anyone else.

About 200 years ago (in 1817), Ricardo wrote a book, *On the Principles of Political Economy and Taxation*, in which he introduced his Law of Comparative Advantage. It explains why it is to our economic advantage to buy our toothpaste from Freedonia even though we could make it more cheaply here.

I, your reader, have a whole bunch of questions before you go one step further.

First question: If we buy our toothpaste from Freedonia, don't we lose American jobs?

Answer: On the contrary, Ricardo's Law of Comparative Advantage tells us that we will lose lower-paying jobs and gain higher-paying jobs.

Second question: Why haven't I ever heard of this Law of Comparative Advantage?

Answer: Few adult Americans can explain this Law even though it is central to many economic decisions we have to make. Every member of Congress should know about this Law of Comparative Advantage before passing bills restricting the right of Americans to buy toothpaste from Freedonia.

Third question: How bad is the mathematics in Ricardo's Law of Comparative Advantage? Is there a lot of algebra, trigonometry, or calculus? You've got to remember I haven't had any of that stuff yet.

Answer: This is the perfect time in your math career. All that it will involve is . . . fractions!

My fourth and last question: You keep calling it Ricardo's Law. Is it really a law, or is it just his opinion, his personal bias, his pronouncement?

Answer: In the next chapter, I will *prove* that it is true using mathematics.

Let's start with a very simple example—two locations and two products.

In Kansas, they can either raise zebras or make toothpaste.
In Freedonia, they can either raise zebras or make toothpaste.

If Kansas uses all of its labor and resources, it could raise 4000 zebras. Or it could make 8 tons of toothpaste.
If Freedonia uses all of its labor and resources, it could raise 2000 zebras. Or it could make 5 tons of toothpaste.

Kansas has an **absolute advantage** over Freedonia. It is better in raising zebras, and it is better in making toothpaste.

The data are* summarized in this **p̶r̶o̶d̶u̶c̶t̶i̶o̶n̶ ̶c̶h̶a̶r̶t̶**:

	🦓	🧴	
Kansas	4	8	Zebras in thousands
Freedonia	2	5	toothpaste in tons

This chart indicates that if Kansas put all of its labor and resources into raising zebras, it could raise 4000 zebras. If it put all of its labor and resources into making toothpaste, it could make 8 (tons) of toothpaste.

Many people looking at this chart and noticing that Kansas has an absolute advantage over Freedonia—both in zebras and toothpaste— would suggest that Kansas do some of each. That suggestion would hurt Kansas.

We need to look at the opportunity costs . . .
If Kansas raises 4 zebras, its opportunity cost is 8 toothpastes. (The opportunity cost for selecting something was defined to be the greatest of the things that you are giving up.) So the opportunity cost for each zebra is 2 toothpastes. $2 = \frac{8}{4}$

If Freedonia raises 2 zebras, its opportunity cost is 5 toothpastes. So the opportunity cost for each zebra is $\frac{5}{2}$ toothpastes.

---

* English lesson: *Datum* means individual items of information. In academic or scientific writing, *data* is a plural word, and you write *the data are*.

In everyday life (on television, in e-mails, or at football games), you will encounter *the data are* when the speaker is thinking of the individual items and *the data is* when the speaker is thinking of all the items as a single collection.

Doing that for each of the four items in the production chart on the previous page, we obtain an **opportunity cost chart** ...

	🦓	🫧
Kansas	$\frac{8}{4}$	$\frac{4}{8}$
Freedonia	$\frac{5}{2}$	$\frac{2}{5}$

This opportunity cost chart indicates, for example, for Freedonia to raise a zebra, its opportunity cost is $\frac{5}{2}$ of a toothpaste. For Freedonia to produce a toothpaste, its opportunity cost is $\frac{2}{5}$ of a zebra.

Look at that opportunity cost chart. The opportunity cost for Freedonia to produce a tube of toothpaste ($\frac{2}{5}$) is less than the opportunity cost for Kansas to produce that tube of toothpaste ($\frac{4}{8}$).

In decimals, 0.4 < 0.5.

Freedonia has a comparative advantage over Kansas in toothpaste production.

In zebra raising, Kansas has the lower opportunity cost. 2 < 2.5

So Freedonia should sell toothpaste, and Kansas should sell zebras.

Your Turn to Play

If Joe uses all of his labor and resources, he can catch 4 fish or he can make 1 cake. If Darlene uses all of her labor and resources, she can catch 9 fish or make 2 cakes.

1. Does Darlene have an absolute advantage over Joe?
2. Make a production chart for these data.
3. Make an opportunity cost chart for these data.
4. Who should be fishing and who should be making cakes?

·······COMPLETE SOLUTIONS·······

1. Darlene does have an absolute advantage over Joe. She can catch more fish, and she can make more cakes.

2. The **production chart** . . .

	🐟	🎂
Joe	4	1
Darlene	9	2

3. The **opportunity cost chart** . . .

	🐟	🎂
Joe	$\frac{1}{4}$	$\frac{4}{1}$
Darlene	$\frac{2}{9}$	$\frac{9}{2}$

4. Now how do you tell which is smaller: $\frac{1}{4}$ or $\frac{2}{9}$?

   The easiest way is to pretend you were going to add the two fractions together. In other words, you make their denominators alike.

   $\frac{1}{4}$ becomes $\frac{9}{36}$ (having multiplied top and bottom by 9)

   $\frac{2}{9}$ becomes $\frac{8}{36}$ (having multiplied top and bottom by 4)

So $\frac{2}{9}$ is less than $\frac{1}{4}$. Darlene's opportunity cost for choosing fishing is less than Joe's. She should fish.

   Joe's opportunity cost (4) for making cakes is less than Darlene's (4.5), so Joe should be making cakes.

Chapter Thirty-one
Why Ricardo Is Right

Fred headed into the restroom. Since this was the math building, each restroom was equipped with a blackboard.* He was thinking so much about zebras and tubes of toothpaste that he squeezed a dab of Freedom toothpaste on his dental floss.

In mid-floss, Fred drew the production chart for zebras and toothpaste on that blackboard. Since he couldn't floss with just one hand, he let the string dangle.

	🦓	🦷
Kansas	4	8
Freedonia	2	5

According to the opportunity cost chart (two pages ago), Kansas should be selling zebras and buying toothpaste.

A Comparison

Following Ricardo's Law . . .	Ignoring Ricardo's Law . . .
Step one: Kansas just raises zebras and sells 2 of them to Freedonia.	Step one: Kansas spends half of its resources raising zebras and half of it making toothpaste. It does no trading with Freedonia.
Step two: Freedonia puts all its resources into making toothpaste and sends the 5 toothpastes to Kansas in trade for the 2 zebras it received.	
Result: Kansas has 2 zebras and 5 toothpastes.	Result: Kansas has 2 zebras and 4 toothpastes.

---

*In the physical education building, their restrooms were equipped with soap dispensers that were hard to push. That gave them a little more exercise.

   In the restrooms in the music building, there were harmonicas at every sink.

Even though Kansas is better at making toothpaste than Freedonia, every tube of toothpaste that Kansas workers make results in less prosperity for Kansas. Raising zebras is a higher-paying job.*

With Ricardo's Law of Comparative Advantage, both countries become more prosperous. Their workers are more productive, and hence, will tend to have higher-paying jobs.

Fred put on his headphones while he brushed his teeth. He was listening to the recordings of Shakespeare's plays. He figured that by the age of 10, he will have heard all 37 plays** during his toothbrushing time.

Fred was working on *All's Well That Ends Well*, a dark comedy in contrast to the livelier, romantic comedies that Shakespeare wrote (such as *Twelfth Night* and *As You Like It*).

Fred stopped brushing when he heard the line, "There's place and means for every man alive." Iambic pentameter verse Fred thought to himself.

／　　　／　　　／　　／　　　／
There's place and means for every man alive.

Pentameter = a line of verse with five feet.

A foot = a group of syllables with the same stress pattern as other groups on the line.

Iambic = feet with the pattern <unstressed><stressed>. "There's pláce" is an iamb. So is "and méans."

---

* The same analysis could be done from Freedonia's point of view. If Freedonia just concentrates on making toothpaste, where it has a comparative advantage, and trades some of its toothpaste for zebras raised in Kansas, it will be more prosperous than if it tried to both raise zebras and make toothpaste.

In other words, in Freedonia, the higher paying jobs are found in making toothpaste.

** Thirty-seven is the traditional number of plays ascribed to Shakespeare, but we are really not sure. Should we count *Henry VIII*? It appears that Shakespeare and John Fletcher were co-authors. Some scholars contend that Shakespeare wrote less than 20 percent of *Henry VI, Part 1;* the rest was written by a team of playwrights working together.

"There's place and means for every man alive," Fred repeated. Oh my! Shakespeare must have been thinking about Ricardo's Law of Comparative Advantage!

Intermission

If Shakespeare had been thinking about Ricardo's Law of Comparative Advantage, he probably would not have given it that name, since he lived centuries before Ricardo. But Shakespeare had the right idea.

Ricardo's Law states, in essence, if you and someone else each have two jobs available, one of those jobs is guaranteed to be yours. In one of those jobs you will have a comparative advantage over the other person. "There's place and means for every man alive."

Many other economic books ignore Ricardo's Law. This is crazy. This is one of the most interesting and nontrivial parts of economics.

Those books that talk about Ricardo's Law just give examples. I've never seen another economics book that shows that Ricardo's Law must be true.

The Proof of Ricardo's Law

Start with two people, Dale and Pat. Each has a choice of either being a cook in a chicken soup restaurant or being an apple farmer. The production chart looks like this:

	🍲	🍎
Dale	a	b
Pat	c	d

Dale can make a servings of soup.
Pat can make c servings of soup.
Dale can grow b apples.
Pat can grow d apples.

The corresponding opportunity cost chart would look like this:

Dale	$\frac{b}{a}$	$\frac{a}{b}$
Pat	$\frac{d}{c}$	$\frac{c}{d}$

Case one: $\frac{b}{a} < \frac{d}{c}$

This means that Dale's opportunity cost for making chicken soup is less than Pat's.
Since $\frac{b}{a} < \frac{d}{c}$ implies $\frac{a}{b} > \frac{c}{d}$ * this means that Pat's opportunity cost for growing apples would be less than Dale's. Each has a job.

Case two: $\frac{b}{a} > \frac{d}{c}$

In this case, Pat has a lower opportunity cost for making soup.
Since $\frac{b}{a} > \frac{d}{c}$ implies $\frac{a}{b} < \frac{c}{d}$ this means that Dale's opportunity cost for growing apples is less than Pat's. Each has a job.   (End of proof.)

---

* How do you start with $\frac{b}{a} < \frac{d}{c}$ and end up with $\frac{a}{b} > \frac{c}{d}$?

Here are the steps from algebra:

You start with $\frac{b}{a} < \frac{d}{c}$

You multiply both sides by $\frac{ac}{bd}$ and get $\frac{bac}{abd} < \frac{dac}{cbd}$

You cancel like factors from the top and bottom of each fraction: $\frac{c}{d} < \frac{a}{b}$

If $\frac{c}{d}$ is less than $\frac{a}{b}$ then it must be true that $\frac{a}{b}$ is greater than $\frac{c}{d}$

Some notes about this proof:

♪#1: There is a third possible case. That is $\dfrac{b}{a} = \dfrac{d}{c}$.

In this case the opportunity costs for Dale and Pat are equal. One of them chooses one job, and the other can have the other job. Each has a job.

♪#2: The statement $\dfrac{b}{a} < \dfrac{d}{c}$ implies $\dfrac{a}{b} > \dfrac{c}{d}$ (which we proved in the footnote of the previous page) is expressed in English, "If one fraction is less than another, inverting the fractions reverses the sense of the inequality."

♪#3: Ricardo's Law of Comparative Advantage is useless unless you use it in your everyday life. Suppose your calling in life is to buy houses, fix them up, and sell them. You're much better at buying and selling houses than your brother-in-law. You're also much better at painting houses than your brother-in-law. You have an absolute advantage over your brother-in-law. But if you do both the buying and selling and the painting, David Ricardo will be very unhappy with you.

You will make less money than if you do the thing for which you have the comparative advantage, and let your brother-in-law do the thing for which he has the comparative advantage.

How do you tell where you have the comparative advantage? Make the opportunity cost chart. Who knows? Maybe your brother-in-law should do the buying and selling. You can't tell until you do the math.

Your Turn to Play

1. If you put in all your time and effort, you can either sell 5 houses or paint 8 of them. If your brother-in-law puts in all his time and effort, he can either sell 3 houses or paint 6 of them.

    Make a production chart and an opportunity cost chart for these data.

    Who should be selling houses and who should be painting?

2. Not until you put all four numbers in a production chart (and its corresponding opportunity cost chart) can you tell who has the comparative advantage.

    You can either give 200 haircuts, or you can design 7 houses. Your sister-in-law can either give 100 haircuts, or she can design x houses.

Question 2A: For what values of x will you have an absolute advantage over your sister-in-law?

Question 2B: How many houses should your sister-in-law be able to design, so that she would have a comparative advantage over you in designing houses? [Hint: You will find the answer to this by trying out various numbers for x. First try x = 1. Then try x = 2. Etc.]

. . . . C O M P L E T E S O L U T I O N S . . . .

1.

	sell houses	paint them
You	5	8
Him	3	6

	sell houses	paint them
You	$\frac{8}{5}$	$\frac{5}{8}$
Him	$\frac{6}{3}$	$\frac{3}{6}$

Since $\frac{8}{5} < \frac{6}{3}$ your opportunity costs for selling houses is less than his.

You should be the one selling houses.

Since $0.5 < 0.625$, he should be the one painting houses.

2A:

	✂	🗒
You	200	7
Her	100	x

	✂	🗒
You	$\frac{7}{200}$	$\frac{200}{7}$
Her	$\frac{x}{100}$	$\frac{100}{x}$

As long as x is less than seven, you will maintain an absolute advantage over your sister-in-law.

2B: For your sister-in-law to have a comparative advantage in designing houses, her opportunity cost, $\frac{100}{x}$, will have to be less than your opportunity cost, $\frac{200}{7}$.

For x = 1, it is *not* true that $\frac{100}{1}$ is less than $\frac{200}{7}$.

For x = 2, it is *not* true that $\frac{100}{2}$ is less than $\frac{200}{7}$.

For x = 3, it is *not* true that $\frac{100}{3}$ is less than $\frac{200}{7}$.

But for x = 4 (or more), it is true that $\frac{100}{x}$ is less than $\frac{200}{7}$.

Chapter Thirty-two
What Economics Is All About

F red couldn't do too many things at the same time. Thinking about zebras and toothpaste, he had put toothpaste on his dental floss. Listening to Shakespeare, he had dropped his toothbrush.*

Fred filled the basin with warm water so that he could wash his hands and face. He took a glass of water and rinsed out his mouth to get rid of the toothpaste. Oops. Fred looked down into the basin. It was a mess.

---

* It's time you learned about **dangling participles**. If I had written, "Listening to Shakespeare, his toothbrush dropped to the floor," that would have been silly. Whoever heard of a toothbrush listening to Shakespeare?

Dangling participles are fun to write.

While flying an airplane, my tooth hurt. Did you know that my tooth could fly an airplane?

While taking a shower, the phone rang. I know some phones can take pictures and access the Internet, but whoever heard of a phone that takes showers?

Fred looked down into that swirling mass and laughed. He thought to himself *That's what economics is all about. All those little individuals running around, bumping into other individuals. Thousands of little interactions. Ashley decides to buy a car. Jackie applies to work as assistant manager at Terry's Taffy & Taco. Morgan eats at home to save money. Jean buys books to learn how to repair computers.*

Nobody decides what the gross domestic product will be. Nobody decides what a nation's savings rate will be. All of economics is the result of human action—individual choices made one at a time.

One person has labor, things, or cash and trades with another person who has labor, things, or cash.

Fred has hot dogs—more than he could ever eat. Someone is hungry. They trade voluntarily—dollars for dogs. They are both happier than they were before.

Each of us has almost unlimited wants and desires. We could sit down and write a Christmas list a mile long.

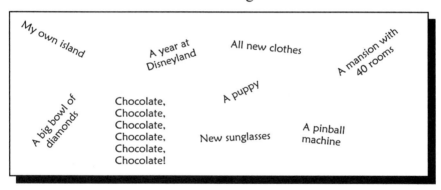

To get those things, we have to offer something that we have. We have $60 in the piggy bank, our skills and labor, or the stuff we have in our closet.

Unlimited wants. Limited money, labor, and things to offer.

That's why the **ordinal numbers** were invented. The ordinal numbers are used for making lists of things that we desire. We need to put our list in order. The ordinal numbers are: *first, second, third, fourth. . . .*

Fred once sat down to write a list of the things that he desired. He thought for a long time before he started writing his list.

My List of the Things That I Want
(using ordinal numbers)

First: I want students at *KITTENS* University to learn a lot of mathematics.

Second: I want students to <u>love</u> mathematics.

Third: I want books--lots of books--good books.

Fourth: I want to learn a lot of things so that I can become a better teacher.

Fifth: I want to get some new bow ties for my teaching.

Far down on Fred's list (32ⁿᵈ) was getting some yodeling lessons. Fred had seen a cowboy yodel in a movie, and he thought that would be fun.

Your Turn to Play

1. What is the cardinality of the set {first, second, third, fourth}?

2. Graph $y = x^2$ for values of x between 0 and 4.

3. Draw a Venn diagram showing two sets: the set of all people who like pizza and the set of all people who enjoy listening to J.S. Bach.

4. $\sqrt{100}$ = ?

5. Express $\frac{1}{6}$ as a percent.

6. Suppose the domain is the set of all students currently enrolled at KITTENS University. Suppose the codomain is { , }, and we assign each student to . Is this a function?

7. Using all his time and effort, the Tall Duck can either deliver 6 pieces of mail or repair 2 broken lamps. Using all her time and effort, Ima Happy can either deliver 16 pieces of mail or repair 4 broken lamps.

Make a production chart and an opportunity cost chart for these data.

Who should be delivering mail and who should be repairing broken lamps?

8. Solve $3x + 7 = 10x - 49$

........**COMPLETE SOLUTIONS**.......

1. This is somewhat strange. You use the cardinal numbers to count the number of ordinal numbers that are in this set. The cardinality of this set is equal to 4. **Cardinal numbers** are numbers used to count the number of elements in a set. The smallest cardinal number is zero, which corresponds to the set { }, which is known as the empty set.

2. First, we find some ordered pairs.

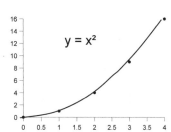

If x = 0, then y = 0² = 0.   (0, 0)
If x = 1, then y = 1² = 1.   (1, 1)
If x = 2, then y = 4.   (2, 4)
If x = 3, then y = 9.   (3, 9)
If x = 4, then y = 16.   (4, 16)

We plot those five points and sketch the curve.

3.

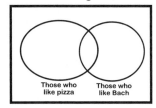

4. $\sqrt{100} = 10$

5. $\dfrac{1}{6} = 16\tfrac{2}{3}\%$

6. Yes, this is a function. Every element in the domain (each student) has been assigned to exactly one element of the codomain (⚞). There is no requirement that every element in the codomain be "hit" by some element in the domain.

7.

	Mail	Lamps
Tall Duck	6	2
Ima	16	4

	Mail	Lamps
Tall Duck	$\dfrac{2}{6}$	$\dfrac{6}{2}$
Ima	$\dfrac{4}{16}$	$\dfrac{16}{4}$

Since $\dfrac{1}{4} < \dfrac{1}{3}$ Ima should deliver the mail.

Since 3 < 4, the Tall Duck has a comparative advantage in repairing lamps.

8. $3x + 7 = 10x - 49$ ➥ $56 = 7x$ ➥ $8 = x$

Chapter Thirty-three
Dividing the Pudding

Fred took off his headphones and cleaned up everything. The words of Shakespeare were still going through his head: *There's place and means for every man alive.* In his head, he set those words to music:

Place and Means

Fred

Fred couldn't contain himself. He started to sing. In Sunday school he had learned that everyone has a place in God's heart, and David Ricardo had shown him that everyone has something to contribute in the economic world.

Sam Wistrom* came in and asked, "Is everything all right? I thought I heard someone in pain."

"It's okay, Mister Wistrom," Fred said. "I was just singing a happy song I made up."

"Well, you wouldn't feel so happy if you'd seen today's paper." Sam showed Fred the newspaper.

---

* Sam Wistrom is the janitor. His business card reads: Samuel P. Wistrom, Educational Facility Math Department Building, KITTENS University, Chief Inspector/Planner/Remediator for offices 225–324.

THE KITTEN Caboodle

The Official Campus Newspaper of KITTENS University   Wednesday 10¢

exclusive

State Donates to KITTENS

KANSAS: The Kansas legislature announced today that it was giving KITTENS University its historic flagship, the Mirabelle Lou. This ship has

a long history. It originally served as a supply ship in the War of 1812. It sat in dry dock until 1946, when it and 47 other ships were given away in the "Each State Gets One" program.

"Our university president declared today, "I am unsure . . .
(continued on p. 4)

Fate of the Mirabelle Lou Uncertain

The campus is in an uproar over the gift. Everyone is looking to our university president for guidance. The *KITTEN Caboodle* has asked various members of the university community for their reaction.

Sam, our custodian: "I guess I have to take care of it now."

Joe, student: "The Mirabelle Who?"

Alexander, graduate student: "It sounds like the results of another federal program."

FLASH UPDATE!

Minutes ago, our president announced that he was giving the Mirabelle Lou to the art department, the philosophy department, and the French department. It is to be shared equally by them.

DOUBLE FLASH UPDATE!!

Angry memos have been exchanged among the three departments regarding how they are going to share this gift.

"There's really no reason for those departments to fight about what they are going to do with the Mirabelle Lou," Fred said. "The courts have been dealing with this kind of situation for years. It's called a partition action. The court just appoints someone to sell the ship and divide the money equally among the parties."

Sam thought about that for a moment and asked, "But what if there's nobody to sell to? I remember when my mother gave my brother and me a big piece of chocolate cake to share. She was smart enough not to cut the cake herself, because she knew that we would fight over who got the biggest piece. Instead, she had me cut the cake into two pieces, and my brother could choose which piece he wanted.

"I couldn't complain that my brother got the bigger piece, because I did the dividing. My brother couldn't complain, because he got to choose." Sam said goodnight and left Fred alone in the restroom.

Fred wasn't singing anymore. He thought to himself *That's a cool idea that Sam's Mom had: one kid cuts the cake, and the other one chooses. Neither one could complain.*

Fred never had any brothers or sisters, so he had never heard of that divide-the-dessert-without-the-kids-complaining technique.

Fred imagined that someday he would get married and have six kids. He would make a big bowl of chocolate pudding and put it out on the table for his six kids to share. He would be smart, just like Sam's Mom, and not try to divide the pudding equally into six small bowls.

How to do it so that no one could complain?

☞ This is an economic question—"dividing the pie."

☞ This is a mathematics (logic) question.

☞ This is a practical question for anyone who has to arbitrate between conflicting parties.

☞ And this is a question that no other economics book (that we know of) talks about.

Some thoughts about the Pudding Problem . . .

#1: He wanted a method where the parents won't have to be involved.

#2: The method should involve only the big bowl, the six small bowls, and a spoon—no need for measuring cups, special scales, or other equipment.

#3: The method should be simple enough that a third-grader could understand it.

#4: There should be no way for some of the kids to act in collusion against the others. There should be no way, for example, for four of the kids to gang up against the other two and deny them their fair shares.

#5: The method must require that each kid say aloud, "I got a fair share." Then no one can complain.

#6: The number of kids should not be important. The method should work with two kids or twenty kids.

Is this possible? I'll have to give it some real thought. He turned off the light in the restroom and headed down the hallway toward his office.

That is a tough problem. Most adults don't know how to solve it. Let's do a little *Your Turn to Play* while we think about it. This *Your Turn to Play* will help you get ready for **The Final Bridge**, which is coming very soon.

Your Turn to Play

1. If the ship weighs 60 tons, how many kilograms is that? (One ton is approximately 907 kilograms.)

2. If the domain is the set {the Mirabelle Lou} and the codomain is the set consisting of the 27 departments at KITTENS University, and the university president assigns the Mirabelle Lou to the art department, the philosophy department, and the French department, is this a function?

3. One member of the French department found a treasure chest on the Mirabelle Lou. It contained $136 in silver coins and a whole bunch of gold coins that were each worth $52. Silver and gold coins were worth a total of $500. How many gold coins were there? Show your work, starting with Let x =. . . .

4. There were 230 rats on the ship. Twenty percent of them were gray. How many of them were *not* gray?

5. Express 83⅓% as a fraction.

6. $(\frac{7}{8})^2 = ?$

7. After the president announced that he was giving the Mirabelle Lou to the three departments, the art department started sending angry emails to the president at the rate of r emails per day. The philosophy department was sending angry emails to the president at the rate of r + 3 emails per day. In two days, they sent a total of 26 emails. What is the value of r?

·······COMPLETE SOLUTIONS·······

1. $\dfrac{60 \text{ tons}}{1} \times \dfrac{907 \text{ kilograms}}{1 \text{ ton}} = 54{,}420$ kilograms

2. The definition of function is a rule that associates to each element of the domain *exactly one* element in the codomain. Since the Mirabelle Lou was assigned to three elements in the codomain, it is not a function.

3. Let x = the number of gold coins.

Then 52x = the value of those gold coins.

Then 52x + 136 = the value of the silver and gold coins in the chest.

$$52x + 136 \ = \ 500$$
$$52x \ = \ 364 \qquad \text{Subtract 136 from both sides}$$
$$x \ = \ 7 \qquad \text{Divide both sides by 52}$$

There were 7 gold coins in the chest.

4. If 20% of the rats were gray, then 80% were not gray.

$\quad$ 80% of 230 $\qquad 0.8 \times 230 \ = \ 184 \qquad$ 184 rats were not gray.

5. $83\tfrac{1}{3}\% \ = \ \dfrac{5}{6}$

6. $(\dfrac{7}{8})^2 = \dfrac{7}{8} \times \dfrac{7}{8} \ = \ \dfrac{49}{64}$

7. Let r = the number of angry emails sent by the art department each day.

Let r + 3 = the number of angry emails sent by the philosophy department each day.

Then 2r = the number of angry emails sent by the art department in 2 days.

Then 2(r + 3) = the number of angry emails sent by the philosophy department in 2 days.

Then 2r + 2(r + 3) = the number of angry emails sent by both departments in 2 days.

$$2r + 2(r + 3) \ = \ 26$$
$$2r + 2r + 6 \ = \ 26 \qquad \text{Distributive law}$$
$$4r + 6 \ = \ 26 \qquad \text{Combine like terms}$$
$$4r \ = \ 20 \qquad \text{Subtract 6 from both sides}$$
$$r \ = \ 5 \qquad \text{Divide both sides by 4}$$

Chapter Thirty-four
Solution to the Pudding Problem

Fred gave some real thought to the pudding problem as he walked down the hallway. He stopped at the vending machines, but none of their goodies looked very appealing.

He headed into his office and sat at his desk. At first he thought of the case in which there are four kids. Maybe I can use something like Sam's mother used: one pair of kids divides, and the other pair chooses. Fred couldn't think of a way of having one pair of kids do the division. Besides, that method wouldn't work with six kids.

Maybe each kid in turn could take one spoonful out of the big bowl. But that wouldn't work, because when the bowl was almost empty, there might not be exactly 6 spoonfuls left.

Fred stood up and wandered around his office. Maybe I've thought of a problem that doesn't have a solution. Maybe, if I have six kids, I'll just have to do it the traditional way: dish out the six bowls as equally as I can and hope they don't fight.

Fred sat in the corner of his room and thought. He did some push-ups and thought some more. He ran around his desk clockwise six times and then ran around his desk counterclockwise six times. He put six erasers on his desk and pretended they were all attacking the stapler. Each eraser wanted a piece of the stapler.

Nine p.m. (his bedtime). 10 p.m., 11 p.m., 11:36 p.m., and then the solution came to him.

The Solution to the Pudding Problem
by Fred Gauss

One child spoons into his bowl what he declares to be a fair share of
the pudding.

If any other child says, "That's not a fair share. That's more than one-sixth of the pudding," the bowl is passed to that child who then has to put some of the pudding back into the big bowl. The second child now declares that this is a fair share of the pudding.

If any of the remaining four children says, "That's not a fair share," the bowl is passed to that child. He then puts some of the pudding back into the big bowl.

If any of the remaining three children says, "That's not a fair share," the bowl is passed to that child, etc.

At some point in this process, the child holding the bowl has declared that this is a fair share, and no other child objects.

That child and his bowl leave. Now we have five children and we repeat the process. One child spoons into his bowl what he considers to be a fair share of the pudding, and the four other children have the opportunity to object. Any person who objects receives the bowl and has to put some pudding back. At some point we have a child holding a bowl that he has declared to be a fair share, and none of the other four are objecting. That child and his bowl leave. We now have four children, and we continue the process.

This procedure will work starting with any number of kids.

One question that comes up is, "Could this process of objecting and passing the bowl go on forever? I'd hate to spend the whole evening watching the bowl being passed back and forth." That won't happen.

When the first child spoons the pudding into his bowl, he has declared that this is a fair share of the pudding. He can't later object to that same bowl with even less pudding in it.

Any other child who has objected, received the bowl, put some pudding back into the big bowl, and declared that it is now a fair share. That child can't later object.

In short, if we start with six people, there can be only at most five objections before a person and a bowl leave the table. With five people, there can be at most four objections before a person and a bowl leave the table.

This solution to the pudding problem will work with anything that is a **continuous** variable. Continuous variables are those that vary smoothly—can be infinitely subdivided into smaller pieces—like ounces of pudding, or time, or volume, or area, or lengths. **Discrete** variables, in contrast, are things that come in chunks that can't be subdivided. The number of sisters you have is a discrete variable. You can't have 3.7 sisters. The number of times you've flown on an airplane is a discrete variable.

❀   ❀   ❀

You and five other salesmen have to divide up the United States into six selling zones—one for each salesmen.

One salesman draws what he declares to be a fair one-sixth of the United States.

If any of the other five objects, he can "put some of the pudding back into the big bowl."
He can shrink the area, declaring the new boundaries to be a fair one-sixth.

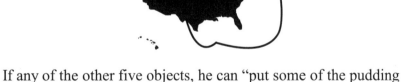

If any of the other four object, they can shrink the area even further.

❀   ❀   ❀

The pudding problem can be applied to situations that look more like discrete variables than continuous ones. Your grandfather dies and leaves to you and the five other grandchildren six houses on Euclid Court. In his will, he states that none of the six houses may be sold for the next 50 years. The problem is that the houses are not all alike.

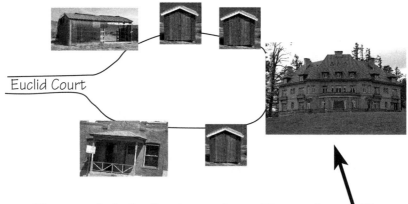

Euclid Court

Your cousin is the first to speak up. "I want that one!"

The question is, "How do you put some of the pudding back into the big bowl?"

Your sister says, "I'll take that big one, and I'll give $10,000 to be shared equally among you five. That will make it fair."

Another cousin says, "I'll take it and give $18,000 to be shared equally among you five."

After the ownership of the big house is settled, the remaining five grandchildren repeat the process with the remaining five houses. The owner of the big house is no longer involved in the process.

Fred felt so good. He had solved the pudding problem. He climbed into his sleeping bag underneath his desk. He said his prayers and was soon asleep.

1. Which of these are discrete variables?

   A) the number of cars your father owns

   B) the number of gallons of gasoline you put in your car

   C) the number of friends that came to your birthday party

   D) the number of computers your brother owns

2. Draw a Venn diagram showing two sets: the set of all people who are older than 18 and the set of all people who are older than 25.

3. If you put in all your time and effort, you can either write 10 postcards or you can compose 2 songs. If your uncle puts in all his time and effort, he can either write 50 postcards or he can compose 4 songs.

   Make a production chart and an opportunity cost chart for these data. Who should be writing postcards, and who should be composing songs?

4. Graph $y = x/2$ for the values of x between 0 and 20.

5. If you spent the afternoon napping, that would be worth 5 happiness points. If you spent the afternoon practicing the piano, that would be worth 8 happiness points. What is your opportunity cost if you choose to spend your afternoon talking on the telephone?

6. Let the domain be the set of all people now living in Kansas. Consider the function that assigns to each person now living in Kansas the number of coins that he is now carrying with him. Is this function 1-1?

7. Express $37\frac{1}{2}\%$ as a fraction.

8. Suppose your CD collection grows by 6% each year over the previous year. Roughly, how long will it take to double the number of CDs that you own?

9. Suppose you have a whole bunch of computer games that you could sell for $20 each. Suppose you have 20 more records than you have computer games, and you could sell those records for $3 each. Suppose you have twice as many CDs as computer games, and that you could sell each CD for $5. If you sold everything, you could make $258. How many computer games do you have?

10. What is the volume of a can of beans that is five inches tall and has a radius of two inches? Use 3 for π.

·······COMPLETE SOLUTIONS·······

1. The discrete variables are A) the number of cars your father owns, C) the number of friends that came to your birthday party, and D) the number of computers your brother owns.

2.   Note that those over 25 are a subset of those over the age of 18. Translation: Anyone who is over 25 is automatically a member of the set of those who are over 18.

3.

	Postcards	Songs
You	10	2
Uncle	50	4

production chart

	Postcards	Songs
You	2/10	10/2
Uncle	4/50	50/4

opportunity cost chart

From the opportunity cost chart, 2/10 = 0.2 and 4/50 = 8/100 = 0.08.

So your uncle should be writing postcards since 0.08 < 0.2.

For song writing, your opportunity cost is 10/2 = 5, which is less than his opportunity cost of 50/4 = 12.5. You should write the songs.

4. Graph y = x/2. First, we find some ordered pairs.

If x = 0, then y = 0/2 = 0.   (0, 0)

If x = 2, then y = 2/2 = 1.   (2, 1)

If x = 14, then y = 14/2 = 7. (14, 7)

If x = 20, then y = 20/2 = 10. (20, 10)

    Then sketch in the line.

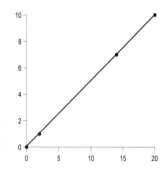

5. The opportunity cost is defined as the value of largest item that you give up. In this case, it is 8 happiness points.

6. A function is 1-1 if no two elements of the domain are assigned the same element in the codomain. At least two people in Kansas are not carrying any coins with them right now. (They are taking a shower.) So the function is not 1-1.

7. $37\frac{1}{2}\% = \frac{3}{8}$

8. By the rule of 72, a growth rate of 6% will double the size of your CD collection in approximately $\dfrac{72}{6}$ = 12 years.

9. In word problems, you let x equal the thing that you are trying to determine.

Let x = how many computer games you have.

Then x + 20 = the number of records you have (since we know that "you have 20 more records than you have computer games").

Then 2x = the number of CDs you have (since we know that "you have twice as many CDs as computer games").

Then 20x = how much the computer games could sell for (since they sold for $20 each, and you have x of them).

Then 3(x + 20) = how much the records could sell for (since you have x + 20 records, and they sell for $3 each).

Then 5(2x) = how much the CDs could sell for (since you have 2x CDs, and they sell for $5 each).

Total sales = $258, so

$$
\begin{aligned}
20x + 3(x + 20) + 5(2x) &= 258 \\
20x + 3x + 60 + 10x &= 258 \\
33x + 60 &= 258 \\
33x &= 198 \\
x &= 6
\end{aligned}
$$

You have 6 computer games.

   Notice that we cannot leap directly from reading the problem to the equation in one step.

10.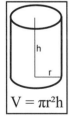

$V = \pi r^2 h$

If h = 5 inches, r = 2 inches, and we use 3 for π, then the volume of the cylinder = $\pi r^2 h$ = $3(2^2)(5)$ = $3(4)(5)$ = 60 cubic inches.

THE FINAL BRIDGE

There are 21 questions in your Final Bridge. Get 17 right and you pass. Write out all your answers before looking at the answers I give in the back of this book.

You *are* allowed to look back into the text. In the old days when you were memorizing $\frac{5}{6} = 83\frac{1}{3}\%$, things were different.

There is a trick to passing this Bridge on the first try. It is something that college students often do on their final examinations and that kindergarten students very rarely do. Look over your answers a second time—recheck your work. If you are human, you make silly errors.

I have worked each problem in this book at least twice. I use proofreaders who are <u>gud</u> in English.

Anything that is worth something requires effort.

 # The Final Bridge

first try

1. Joe and Darlene were sitting on the couch. He was watching television and she was reading her bridal magazines.

Watching the commercials, Joe would get ideas at the rate of four per hour. For example, he learned that radiators were on sale this week at Ralph's Radiators.

Reading her magazines, Darlene would get ideas at the rate of 80 per hour. For example, she learned that peanut butter could be used as a frosting on wedding cakes.

In one afternoon they had a total of 294 ideas. How long had they been sitting on the couch?

2. Joe saw this commercial with a whole pile of money in it. Joe liked to look at pictures of money. The man on the screen said that he had made all of this money investing in the Tippy Tap Typewriter company. He said that he had invested $984 and each year his investment grew by 24%.

How much would he have had at the end of seven years? You may express your answer in the form ■ × (■)■.

3. The commercial said that the results that this man had received might not be typical of the average investor. That was true. Of the 1300 people who invested in the Tippy Tap Typewriter company, only four percent of them ever made any money. How many of those people made money?

4. The man on the commercial showed a graph of the Tippy Tap Typewriter company's earnings during the first four years of its existence. It was a graph of $y = 1000x + 2000$ for x from 0 to 4. Draw the graph.

5. The commercial for the Tippy Tap Typewriter company lasted for 20 minutes. What fraction of an hour was that?

6. During the commercials, the man poured big gold coins into a large glass cylinder. The cylinder had a *diameter* of two feet and was three-feet tall. What was the volume of that cylinder? Use 3.1 for π.

7. The man poured the coins into the cylinder during the entire 20-minute commercial at the rate of 40 coins per minute. These big gold coins were heavy—10 of them weighed one kilogram. One kilogram is equal to 2.2 pounds. What was the weight in pounds of the coins that he poured into the cylinder?

8. The next commercial was offering Tippy Tap Typewriters for sale. In their special offer you could buy seven of those typewriters plus shipping for $623. The shipping charge for an order of any size was $14. How much did each typewriter cost?

9. Joe had nine cans of spray paint in his closet. Each of them was a different color. He imagined buying seven Tippy Tap Typewriters and painting each of them a different color. Joe quickly figured out—using his calculator—that he wouldn't be using two of the nine cans.

Let the domain be the seven Tippy Tap typewriters, and let the codomain be the nine cans of spray paint. Assign to each typewriter the color that it is painted. Is this a one-to-one function?

10. In an afternoon Joe could spray paint 4 typewriters, and Darlene could spray paint 6 typewriters. In an afternoon Joe could plant 2 roses in the garden. Darlene could plant 5.

Does Darlene have an absolute advantage over Joe?

11. Continuing the previous question, who has a comparative advantage in spray painting typewriters?

12. Draw a Venn diagram showing two sets: the set of all people in Kansas who have seen the movie "New Moon" (which starred Jeanette MacDonald and Nelson Eddy, 1940) and the set of all people in Kansas who own a typewriter.

13. Draw a Venn diagram showing two sets: the set of all dogs in Kansas and the set of all cats in Kansas.

14. One Saturday morning it was time to clean up Joe's apartment. Joe, Darlene, and Darlene's mom got together to pick up trash off of his floor. Joe could pick up three pieces of trash each minute. Darlene could pick up four pieces of trash each minute. And Darlene's mom, eight pieces of trash.

Joe worked for a little while and then quit. Darlene worked twice as long as Joe. And Darlene's mom worked 10 minutes longer than Darlene did.

Together they picked up 323 pieces of trash. How long did Joe work?

15. No one had the courage to clean up Joe's kitchen. There were dirty dishes in the sink, half-eaten sandwiches on the counter, and cookie crumbs everywhere.

Joe liked to count things. He noticed that the population of flies in his kitchen was increasing by 9% each day. Roughly, how long would it take for the population of flies to double?

16. $\dfrac{1}{3} + \dfrac{3}{5}$

17. $\dfrac{7}{8} - \dfrac{1}{5}$

18. Is the number of flies in Joe's kitchen a discrete variable or a continuous variable?

19. Solve $4x + 2(6x + 5) = 78$

20. If a function is one-to-one, what can you say about the cardinality of the domain versus the cardinality of the codomain?

21. $\dfrac{2}{21} \div \dfrac{3}{7}$ (Reduce your answer, if possible.)

1. When Darlene and her mom did venture into Joe's kitchen, a big surprise awaited them. It wasn't the dirty dishes in the sink or the half-eaten sandwiches on the counter. It was in Joe's pantry.

It was neat. It was filled to overflowing with jars and jars of every kind of delicacy. Draw a bar graph of:

> 20 jars of Greek olives
>
> 30 jars of British bumble berry jam
>
> 45 jars of Danish mayonnaise.

2. Darlene and her mother were speechless. They had known Joe for years and hadn't had any idea that this elegance was associated with the guy in the living room who was watching roller derby on television and munching on a bag of potato chips. They had always pictured a function like this:

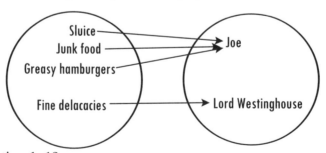

Is this function 1–1?

3. Darlene counted the number of jars of Turkish mustard. The jars were $4 apiece.

      Darlene's mother counted the number of jars of Bolivian relish. There were 30 more jars of relish than there were mustard. The jars of Bolivian relish were $3 apiece.

      The value of these two items was $216. How many jars of Turkish mustard did Joe have in his pantry?

4. Darlene was amazed at the number of jars of Peruvian pickles that he had. She thought, *If this were a math book, I would let z = the number of jars of Peruvian pickles that he had.*

      Is z a discrete or a continuous variable?

5. If each jar of Peruvian pickles was worth $8, how much would z jars be worth?

6. How many possible functions are there in which the domain is the set of all of the jars in Joe's pantry and the codomain is {Joe}?

7. Six percent of the jars in Joe's pantry were worth less than $5 apiece. Darlene's mother counted 84 jars in that category. How many jars were in Joe's pantry?

8. She picked up a 1-pound jar of Norwegian waffle bits. The label on the jar said that one serving (2 oz.) of the waffle bits contained 440 calories. How many calories were in the entire jar? (One pound = 16 ounces.)

9. The Norwegian waffle bits looked appetizing. Darlene's mom did two things: she opened the jar and she took out a waffle bit. Are these two things commutative?

10. Darlene found jars of cashews and jars of walnuts. She thought of her two uncles that she had not seen in years.

      Uncle Albert in Australia had 40 acres on which he could grow either 10 cases of cashews or 6 cases of walnuts.

      Uncle Philip in the Philippines also had 40 acres. On that land Uncle Philip could grow either 4 cases of cashews or 2 cases of walnuts. Create an opportunity cost chart and determine which uncle should be growing cashews.

The Final Bridge

11. There was a can of Russian whale oil that was 16 centimeters tall and had a diameter of 8 centimeters. What was its volume? Use 3 for π.

12. $(\frac{5}{8})^3$

13. Darlene couldn't figure out where Joe got all the money to buy these jars of food. She knew that he had $100 in a savings account that paid four percent per year (compounded annually). Roughly how long would it take for that $100 to turn into $200?

14. Solve $6(y - 2) = 60y - 138$

15. $2\frac{1}{4} - \frac{3}{8}$ —and—   16. $2\frac{1}{4} \div \frac{3}{8}$

17. What is the cardinality of this set: {pickle, olive, caper, sardine}?

18. Darlene knew that there were six happiness points associated with eating a jar of Peruvian pickles, four happiness points associated with eating a jar of Bolivian relish, and one happiness point associated with eating a jar of Turkish mustard. What she really liked was the jar of Swiss chocolate bites, which gave her 10 happiness points. She knew she could only eat one jar and chose the Swiss chocolate bites. What was the opportunity cost associated with that decision?

19. Graph $y = x^4$ from $x = 0$ to $x = 3$.

20. Darlene noticed that 20 of the jars contained cinnamon and that 15 of the jars contained turmeric. Draw a Venn diagram of the situation if you know that no jar contains both cinnamon and turmeric.

21. Darlene and her mom walked into the living room to talk to Joe about his pantry. When Darlene began to ask him, he said, "Wait a minute. This roller derby will soon be over." They waited. When it was over, Darlene started to ask again. Joe said, "Wait a minute. This is a cool commercial."

Darlene's mom turned off the television set. Darlene went and sat on Joe's lap to get his attention. "Honey, I have a question." Joe didn't respond, and so Darlene continued, "Where did you get all of those jars in the pantry?"

"Oh, they aren't all mine. One-twelfth of them are Uncle Milton's, one-twelfth of them are Uncle Dante's, and 83⅓% of them are Uncle Pete's. How many of the jars are Joe's?

# The Final Bridge

1. "Uncle Milton? Uncle Dante? Uncle Pete?" Darlene shouted. "You don't have any uncles. Your father didn't have any brothers since he was an only child, and your mother only had sisters who never married. How could you have uncles?"

Joe scratched his head. "I never thought of that. These three guys came to my door last week and asked if they could store some stuff in my pantry. I told them that it was okay because I wasn't using my pantry. After they filled my pantry with some stuff, they thanked me and began to leave. I said, 'You're welcome, Mr. ——.'"

One guy said to me, "Just call me Uncle Milton. This is Uncle Dante, and he's Uncle Pete." Then Uncle Milton told me, "And make sure that no one touches our stuff." I told him not to worry, because I never went into the pantry.

Darlene was relieved that she had not opened the jar of Swiss chocolate bites. She had just thought about opening it. But Darlene's mom had opened the $8 jar of Norwegian waffle bits and had taken out a waffle bit. She went back into the pantry and took the jar and put $8 on the shelf where the jar had been. Darlene's mom had an income of $400 a month. What percent of her monthly income had she just spent on Norwegian waffle bits?

2. She took the jar back into the living room and offered Darlene and Joe some of the waffle bits. Joe turned the TV back on, and they all began to eat waffle bits. Joe was eating 10 bits per minute. Darlene, 4 bits per minute. And Darlene's mom, who remembered how expensive these waffle bits were, was eating them at the rate of 2 bits per minute. How long would it be before the three of them had consumed 40 waffle bits?

3. "Ow!" Joe exclaimed. "I think there was a rock in one of these pieces." Joe continued, "Ow! Ow! Ow! Ow! Ow! It hurts. I either broke a tooth, or I got something jammed up into my gums."

Everyone agreed that they needed to get Joe to the dentist. Luckily, it was Saturday morning, and the dentist was available. It was 230 feet from the couch to Darlene's car. For the first 30 seconds, Joe walked toward her car. Then Darlene and her mom picked him up and carried him for 20 seconds to get to her car. They carried him 4 feet per second faster than Joe had been walking. How fast had Joe been walking?

4. In the car they turned on the radio to distract Joe from his pain. On the sports station, the announcer was giving a play-by-play description of the football game: They kicked the ball. They passed the ball. They passed the ball. They ran with the ball. They passed the ball. They kicked the ball. They ran with the ball. They passed the ball. Joe found this absolutely fascinating.

Darlene imagined that Joe had heard these descriptions a million times. If $10^x = 1,000,000$, then what is the value of x?

5. For every value of x that you can name, $y = 2x + 6$ gives you a value of y. For example, if you let x equal 7, then y would equal 20. If the domain and codomain are all numbers, is the assignment $y = 2x + 6$ a function?

6. Graph $y = 2x + 6$ for values of x between 0 and 10.

7. It was 10 a.m. and the radio interrupted the exciting football game for the news: Last night while Lord and Lady Westinghouse were at the ball, their mansion was burglarized. All of their paintings by Renoir were taken. Also missing are the six sets of silverware and Lord Westinghouse's large gem collection.

Just in . . . the giant water tower on the north side of town has just developed a serious leak. This famous water tower, which locals call the old tin can because of the shape, is 80-feet high, and has a diameter of 20 feet.

If we use 3 for π, what is the volume of that water tower?

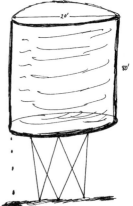

8. Luckily, as our engineers report, the tank only has 1000 cubic feet of water in it right now. Darlene's mom heard that and wondered how many gallons that was. Joe guessed that was about six gallons, and Darlene guessed it was about 1,000,000 gallons. They were both wrong. How many gallons was it? (One cubic foot is 29.92 quarts, and four quarts equals one gallon.)

9. We now take you back to the football game and resume the action: They passed the ball. They passed the ball. They ran with the ball. They passed the ball. They kicked the ball. They ran with the ball. Joe was

happy that they finished all that "newsy" stuff. If you get three points for making a field goal in football, how many points do you get for making x field goals?

10. Darlene told Joe, "We'll soon be at Dr. Quail's office." Joe always liked the name of his dentist. Draw a Venn diagram which shows two sets: the set of all birds and the set of all living things with two legs. (For this question, all birds have two legs.)

11. Dr. Quail both liked and hated his name. For patients, like Joe, who thought of cute little round birds, it was a perfect name for a dentist. But for adults who know the second meaning of *quail*, this was a terrible name for a dentist.[*]

   When they got to the front door of the dentist's office, Joe quailed. It would be 100 happiness points for him if he didn't have to go in to see the dentist. It would be 120 happiness points for him to go in and see the dentist and have the dentist stop his pain. What was his opportunity cost for going in and seeing the dentist?

12. Solve $3x + 220 = 5(x + 40)$.

13. $\frac{3}{4} \div \frac{3}{8}$

14. $\frac{3}{4} + \frac{3}{8}$

15. $\left(\frac{3}{4}\right)^3$

16. Each minute, Joe's gums and jaw would get six percent larger than they were in the previous minute. Roughly how long would it take for Joe's gums and jaw to double in size?

17. Darlene's mom makes $400 a month. The dentist makes $6000 a month. Illustrate this on a bar graph.

---

[*] To quail is to shrink with fear.

18. Joe, Darlene, and Darlene's mom sat in the waiting room for t minutes. Is t a continuous variable or a discrete variable?

19. They waited in the waiting room for 15 minutes. What fraction of an hour is that?

20. If anxiety could be expressed in points, Joe's anxiety level when he came into the waiting room was at 50 points. Each minute his anxiety increased by 7% over the previous minute. What was his anxiety level after 15 minutes? Express your answer in the form $\blacksquare \times (\blacksquare)^{\blacksquare}$.

21. In a working day, Dr. Quail could fill 10 cavities or pull 16 teeth. The dentist down the hall, Dr. Shakes, could fill 8 cavities or pull 10 teeth in a day. Create the production chart, the opportunity cost chart, and state which doctor should be filling cavities.

 # The Final Bridge

1. The receptionist announced, "The dentist will see you now." Joe walked slowly, very slowly, into the other room and sat down in the dentist's chair. Joe opened his mouth wide, and the dentist looked at his teeth. Are these two things commutative?

2. "Oh heavens!" The dentist exclaimed. "I think the hygienist will have to look at you first." The dentist headed to the bathroom and washed his hands and face. He tried to keep from trembling. He had just seen what they had called in dental school a Disaster Area—a perfect storm of poor dental hygiene. In dental school, Dr. Quail had been told to expect to see a Disaster Area maybe once or twice in his whole dental career. The sight was overwhelming.

   The hygienist came in and gave her usual lecture for new patients. She said, "You are supposed to floss your teeth regularly, and you are supposed to brush your teeth twice as often as you floss them. I'll give you five happy tooth points for every time you floss your teeth and three happy tooth points for every time you brush your teeth. By the next time I see you, I hope that you have earned 330 happy tooth points.

   How many times was the hygienist expecting Joe to floss his teeth before his next appointment?

3. The dentist had warned the hygienist that this was a Disaster Area patient, so she took the necessary precautions before she asked him to open his mouth. She put on a rubber cap, eye goggles, and a gas mask. When Joe opened his mouth, she also decided to put on rubber gloves and a rubber apron.

   ✓ Joe had never been to a dentist.

   ✓ Joe never brushed his teeth.

   ✓ He never flossed his teeth.

   ✓ His diet consisted almost entirely of things that come in plastic bags washed down by quarts of sugary Sluice.

The hygienist mixed together $1\frac{1}{3}$ cups of disinfectant with $2\frac{7}{8}$ cups of mouthwash. What was the volume of that mixture? (Do not leave your answer as an improper fraction.)

4. The hygienist irrigated Joe's oral cavity. (She flushed out his mouth with the solution.) She must have dislodged 10,000 food particles. Express 10,000 in the form 10^x.

5. Four of Joe's 32 teeth did *not* have cavities. What percent *did* have cavities?

6. Then the hygienist started cleaning each tooth individually. She could clean two teeth per minute. She worked on Joe's loose teeth for t minutes. For the rest of Joe's teeth, which were really loose, she spent t + 4 minutes. What is the value of t? (Recall that Joe has 32 teeth.)

7. Draw a Venn diagram for the two sets: Joe's loose teeth and Joe's really loose teeth. (Each tooth was either loose or really loose.)

8. Joe had never been to the dentist before and didn't realize that you are supposed to stop talking when the hygienist has her tools in your mouth. Is the number of words that Joe spoke a discrete variable or a continuous variable?

9. Joe was learning a lot about dentistry. He really liked the mirror, and each time he saw it, he always said, "Yes." However, when he saw the other two tools, he said, "No." This is a function. Is it one-to-one?

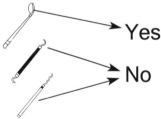

10. Suppose the domain was {Yes, No}, and the codomain was the set of the three dental tools. Is this a function?

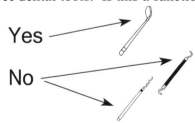

The Final Bridge

11. If the dentist, Dr. Quail, spent his time cleaning teeth he could make $20 an hour. If he spent his time filling cavities, he could make $100 an hour. If he spent his time doing the billing and making appointments, he could make $15 an hour. What would his opportunity cost be if he spent his time cleaning teeth?

12. Graph $y = 5x + 3$ from $x = 0$ to $x = 4$.

13. Solve $11x + 3 = 7(x + 2) + 5$.

14. When the hygienist had cleared out all the waffle bits, she discovered the "rock" that Joe had bitten. It shined like a star in the dark cave of Joe's mouth. With her dental tool, she pried out the biggest blue diamond that she had ever seen. She called in Dr. Quail, and he immediately recognized it from a picture he had seen in the *KITTEN Caboodle*. It was the famous cerulean diamond from the Lord Westinghouse gem collection. He put it on his scale. It weighed 0.1 pounds. How many carats is that?
(A carat is equal to 200 milligrams. 1000 milligrams is equal to a gram. There are 454 grams in a pound.)

15. $\dfrac{1}{7} + \dfrac{7}{8}$ 16. $\dfrac{1}{3} \div \dfrac{3}{4}$ 17. $37\frac{1}{2}\%$ of 24   18. $16\frac{2}{3}\%$ of ? is 60

19. While the hygienist entertained Joe with stories about using toothpaste to paint pictures on bathroom mirrors, Dr. Quail called the cops. They were there in three minutes. What fraction of an hour is that?

20. Officer Friday could handcuff people at the rate of two per minute and could ask questions at the rate of six per minute. Officer March could handcuff people at the rate of three per minute and ask questions at the rate of eight per minute. Create a production chart and an opportunity cost chart. Who should be asking the questions?

21. The first question was, "Where did you get the cerulean diamond that you stole from Lord Westinghouse?"

   Joe wasn't sure what *cerulean* meant, but he attempted an answer: "I got it in the waffle bits jar."

   "And who gave you the jar?"

   "That question is easier to answer," Joe said. "Darlene's mom. She's sitting out there in the waiting room." Running at 8 feet/second, how long did it take the cops to cover the 30 feet to Darlene's mom?

 # The Final Bridge

1. Joe, Darlene, and Darlene's mom were arrested. At the rate of 2 feet/second, the three of them walked to the police car. Then the car sped to the police station at the rate of 60 feet/second. They spent seven times as long in the police car as they did in walking to the car.

   They covered a total of 8440 feet. How long did they spend walking to the police car?

2. They first put handcuffs on Darlene and then on her mother. Were these two things commutative?

3. The set of things in the front of the police car consisted of Officer Friday, Officer March, a half-eaten donut, and a clipboard. What is the cardinality of this set?

4. Let the domain be the three suspects in the backseat. Let the codomain be the set of things in the front of the police car (see the previous question). Assign all three suspects to the clipboard. Is this a function?

5. When Darlene's mom had been in the waiting room, she had the chance to talk with her daughter, which gave her 100 happiness points. Riding in the back of a police car gave her 2 happiness points. What was her opportunity cost for riding in the back of a police car?

6. At the police station they had to wait three hours. What part of a 24-hour day is that? Express your answer as a percent.

7. While they were waiting for something to happen, they saw 20 men, 10 women, and 5 kids who had been arrested. Express this is as a bar graph.

8. By this time, 3 of Darlene's fake fingernails had fallen off. What percent of her fake fingernails had *not* fallen off?

9. When it came time to fingerprint Joe, he became very nervous until they explained to him that it was just like fingerpainting. He was disappointed that there was only one color ink—black. How many fingerprints could you get out of 2 ounces of ink? (One ounce = 31 grams. 1 gram = 1000 milligrams. Seven fingerprints takes 50 milligrams of ink.)

10. The fingerprint ink came in a can that had a radius of two inches and a height of six inches. What was its volume? Use 3 for π.

11. The trial was short. The police officer reported Joe's confession:
Question from police officer: Where did you get the cerulean diamond that you stole from Lord Westinghouse? Joe's answer: I got it in the waffle bits jar. The court's finding: Joe admitted he stole it. Second question from police officer: And who gave you the jar? Joe's answer: Darlene's mom. The court's finding: Darlene's mom furnished Joe with stolen goods. Since Darlene had been there and had eaten from the waffle bits jar, she would be sentenced as an accomplice.

Every word that Joe spoke at the trial seemed to increase the length of their jail sentences by about 8 percent over the previous word. Using the Rule of 72, how many words would Joe have to speak in order to double his sentence?

12. The lawyer turned to Darlene and said, "It looks like you're going to get a nickel." (A "nickel" means a five-year prison sentence.) If Joe was going to be sentenced to x nickels, how many years would he get?

13. "Look! It's Uncle Milton," Joe almost shouted to Darlene. "And Uncle Dante and Uncle Pete are there." Joe waved to them. They were wearing orange jumpsuits . . . and handcuffs. Darlene talked to her lawyer. The lawyer talked to the judge. The judge dismissed the case. Draw the graph of Darlene's happiness, $y = x^3$ for x = 0 to x = 4.

(x represents the number of minutes after Darlene talked to her lawyer, and y represents her happiness.)

14. $\frac{7}{8} - \frac{1}{5}$ 15. $\frac{7}{8} \div \frac{1}{5}$ 16. 4 is what percent of 32?

17. Solve $7(x + 8) = 9x + 48$ 18. Find x if $2^x = 32$.

19. In prison Milton could either wash 100 dishes or launder 20 pants. Dante could wash 50 dishes or launder 2 pants. Create the opportunity cost chart. Which of the two should be doing the laundry?

20. When they got back to Joe's apartment, Joe and Darlene sat on the couch, and Darlene's mom went into the kitchen. She peeked into the pantry. Uncle Leonardo had gotten there first and had stolen all the jars. What percent of the jars were not stolen?

21. $\frac{1}{3} + \frac{1}{4} + \frac{1}{5}$

The Bridge
answers

from p. 45—*first try*

1. It is not a function. Some words have more than one meaning. The word *go* has 84 definitions in my dictionary.

2. 7% of $16 = 0.07 \times 16 = $1.12

3. $\dfrac{1500 \text{ pages}}{1} \times \dfrac{1 \text{ day}}{1 \text{ page}} \times \dfrac{1 \text{ month}}{30 \text{ days}} = 50$ months

4.
$$3x + 5x + 23 = 4x + 375$$
Combine like terms $\qquad 8x + 23 = 4x + 375$
Subtract 4x from both sides $\quad 4x + 23 = 375$
Subtract 23 from both sides $\qquad 4x = 352$
Divide both sides by 4 $\qquad\qquad x = 88$

5. x dictionaries would cost $16x.

6. Let x = the number of German–English dictionaries that Joe bought. Then 11x = the value of those dictionaries. Then 11x + 14 = value of the dictionaries plus the candy.
$$11x + 14 = 487$$
$$11x = 473 \qquad \text{Subtract 14 from both sides}$$
$$x = 43 \qquad \text{Divide both sides by 11}$$
Joe bought 43 German–English dictionaries.

7. $\dfrac{3}{7} \times \dfrac{3}{8} = \dfrac{9}{56}$

8. $\dfrac{1}{5} + \dfrac{2}{3} = \dfrac{1(3)}{5(3)} + \dfrac{2(5)}{3(5)} = \dfrac{3 + 10}{15} = \dfrac{13}{15}$

9. Every element in the domain is assigned exactly one element in the codomain, so this is a function. (It isn't 1-1.)

10. Since more than one woman in Kansas has given birth to four children, this function is not one-to-one.

from p. 47—*second try*

1. $\dfrac{2.1 \text{ kilograms}}{1} \times \dfrac{1000 \text{ grams}}{1 \text{ kilogram}} \times \dfrac{0.012 \text{ cups}}{1 \text{ gram}} \times \dfrac{1 \text{ quart}}{4 \text{ cups}} = 6.3$ quarts

2. Not 1-1 since, e.g., both Ruby red and Blood red are assigned to her bathroom

3. The Eleven Conversions turn
$$\dfrac{3}{4} < 72\% \qquad \dfrac{7}{8} > 0.8 \qquad \dfrac{1}{8} = 0.125 \qquad \dfrac{5}{6} > 82\%$$
into $\quad 0.75 < 72\% \quad 0.875 > 0.8 \quad 0.125 = 0.125 \quad 83\frac{1}{3}\% > 82\%$
$\qquad\qquad$ false $\qquad\qquad$ true $\qquad\qquad$ true $\qquad\qquad$ true

4. Three-fourths of $\dfrac{2}{3}$ is $\quad \dfrac{3}{4} \times \dfrac{2}{3} = \dfrac{1}{2}$ ounce of Sky pink.

254

5. 3 is what percent of 8?   3 = ?% of 8. We don't know both sides of the *of* so we divide the number closest to the *of* into the other number.

$\frac{3}{8}$ which is 37½% by the Eleven Conversions you memorized.

In the southeast part of France there is a resort seaport called Nice. It's pronounced NIECE.

6. Let x = the price of a bottle.

Then 27x = the value of all the bottles.

Then 27x + 16 = the value of the bottles plus the value of the nail files.

$$27x + 16 = 124$$
$$27x = 108 \qquad \text{Subtract 16 from both sides.}$$
$$x = 4 \qquad \text{Divide both sides by 27.}$$

Darlene's bottles cost $4 each.

7. In this case there is only one possible function. Assign each whole number to Joe.

8. $\frac{1}{3} + \frac{1}{4} + \frac{1}{6} = \frac{1(4)}{3(4)} + \frac{1(3)}{4(3)} + \frac{1(2)}{6(2)} = \frac{4+3+2}{12} = \frac{9}{12} = \frac{3}{4}$

9. Since each element in the domain is assigned exactly one element in the codomain, this is a function. (Not every element in the codomain has to have an element assigned to it.)

10.

$$18 + 5y + 17 = 90$$

Combine like terms	$35 + 5y = 90$
Subtract 35 from both sides	$5y = 55$
Divide both sides by 5	$y = 11$

from p. 49—*third try*

1. $\frac{1}{3} - \frac{1}{4} = \frac{1(4)}{3(4)} - \frac{1(3)}{4(3)} = \frac{4-3}{12} = \frac{1}{12}$ It works.

2. $\frac{1}{2} - \frac{1}{3} = \frac{1(3)}{2(3)} - \frac{1(2)}{3(2)} = \frac{3-2}{6} = \frac{1}{6}$

or (using problem 1) create $\frac{1}{12}$ twice and that will give you $\frac{1}{6}$ cup.

3. $\frac{1}{12} + \frac{1}{6} = \frac{1}{12} + \frac{1(2)}{6(2)} = \frac{1+2}{12} = \frac{3}{12} = \frac{1}{4}$ cup

4. If we discard 15%, we keep 85%.

85% of 160 = 0.85 × 160 = 136 perfectly shaped marshmallows

5. Let x = the weight of a Smash.

Then 24x = the weight of all the Smashes.

Then 24x + 18 = the weight of the whole thing.

$$24x + 18 = 78$$
$$24x = 60 \qquad \text{Subtract 18 from both sides}$$
$$x = 2.5 \ \ (\text{or } x = 2\tfrac{1}{2}) \qquad \text{Divide both sides by 24}$$

Each Smash weighs two and a half ounces.

6. They started with 24 Smashes. They ate 22 of them. There were 2 left for Joe. 2 is ?% of 24. Since we don't know both sides of the *of*, we divide the number closest to the *of* into the other number. $\dfrac{2}{24} = \dfrac{1}{12}$

$$12\overline{)1.00}^{\,0.08\tfrac{1}{3}} \qquad 0.08\tfrac{1}{3} = 8\tfrac{1}{3}\%$$

Or, if you remembered the Eleven Conversions, you knew that $\dfrac{1}{6} = 16\tfrac{2}{3}\%$, so $\dfrac{1}{12}$ would be half of that, or $8\tfrac{1}{3}\%$.

7. Since each Smash is assigned to exactly one stomach, this is a function. Since two Smashes were assigned to the cat, it is not 1-1.

8. $\dfrac{2 \text{ liters}}{1} \times \dfrac{1.06 \text{ quarts}}{1 \text{ liter}} \times \dfrac{32 \text{ ounces}}{1 \text{ quart}} = 67.84$ ounces

9.
$$2x = 9x - 119$$
Subtract 2x from both sides $\qquad 0 = 7x - 119$
Add 119 to both sides $\qquad 119 = 7x$
Divide both sides by 7 $\qquad 17 = x$

10. $\dfrac{1}{1000}$

from p. 51—*fourth try*

1. $\dfrac{5/8 \text{ cup whipping cream}}{1} \times \dfrac{3 \text{ cups whipped cream}}{3/8 \text{ cup whipping cream}} = \dfrac{5}{8} \times 3 \div \dfrac{3}{8}$
$= \dfrac{5}{8} \times \dfrac{3}{1} \times \dfrac{8}{3} = 5$ cups of whipped cream

2. $20\% + 40\% + 37\tfrac{1}{2}\% = 97\tfrac{1}{2}\%$. That leaves $2\tfrac{1}{2}\%$. $(100\% - 97\tfrac{1}{2}\%)$

3. $2\tfrac{1}{2}\%$ of $\$500 = 0.025 \times 500 = \$12.50$

4. 16 is what percent of 20? $16 = ?\%$ of 20 Since we don't know both sides of the *of*, we divide the number closest to the *of* into the other

number. $\frac{16}{20}$ The hard way to change $\frac{16}{20}$ into a percent would be to first convert it into a decimal $20\overline{)16}$ and then into a percent.

An easier way would be to multiply the top and bottom of $\frac{16}{20}$ by 5 and get $\frac{80}{100}$ which is 80%.

5. Let x = the number of dollars the manicurist charges for a nail.
Then 10x = the cost of doing all the fingernails.
Then 10x + 3 = the total bill.

$$10x + 3 = 16.50$$
$$10x = 13.50 \qquad \text{Subtract 3 from both sides}$$
$$x = 1.35 \qquad \text{Divide both sides by 10}$$

Each nail cost $1.35.

6. Suppose we assigned ☎ → π. In order to keep the function from being 1-1, we would then have to assign ✈ → θ. But then, no matter where we assigned ✆ (either to π or to θ), the function would not be 1-1.

   Another way of saying this is: *If three bees sting two people, then someone is going to be stung at least twice.*

7. $\frac{3}{5} + \frac{1}{3} = \frac{3(3)}{5(3)} + \frac{1(5)}{3(5)} = \frac{9+5}{15} = \frac{14}{15}$ cups

8.
$$100 - 2x = 18x$$
Add 2x to both sides $\qquad 100 = 20x$
Divide both sides by 20 $\qquad 5 = x$

9. Using the Eleven Conversions

$\frac{1}{4} > 22\%$ $\qquad$ $\frac{3}{8} < 0.37$ $\qquad$ $\frac{5}{6} = 83\frac{1}{3}\%$ $\qquad$ become

$25\% > 22\%$ $\qquad$ $37\frac{1}{2}\% < 0.37$ $\qquad$ $83\frac{1}{3}\% = 83\frac{1}{3}\%$
true $\qquad\qquad$ false $\qquad\qquad\qquad$ true

10. $\frac{5}{7} \times \frac{3}{8} = \frac{15}{56}$

from p. 53—*fifth try*

1. $\frac{14}{15} - \frac{2}{3} = \frac{14}{15} - \frac{2(5)}{3(5)} = \frac{14-10}{15} = \frac{4}{15}$

2. Since each element in the domain is assigned *exactly one* element in the codomain, this is a function.

3. Here is one assignment that would make the function not 1-1:

The Bridge

answers

A → L and B → L.   (A → M and B → M would also work.)

4. $\dfrac{7 \text{ weeks}}{1} \times \dfrac{6 \text{ servings}}{1 \text{ week}} \times \dfrac{400 \text{ grams}}{1 \text{ serving}} = 16{,}800 \text{ grams}$

5. If she spent 20% less, then she spent 80% of her normal amount.
80% of $90 = 0.8 × 90 = $72.

6. Using the Eleven Conversions:

$$12\% > \dfrac{1}{8} \qquad 62\tfrac{1}{2}\% < \dfrac{5}{8} \qquad \dfrac{1}{6} > 0.16 \quad \text{become}$$

$$12\% > 12\tfrac{1}{2}\% \quad 62\tfrac{1}{2}\% < 62\tfrac{1}{2}\% \quad 16\tfrac{2}{3}\% > 16\%$$

          false   false   true

7. Let x = the cost of one straw.
Then 10x = the cost of ten straws.
Then 10x + 40 = the cost of the straws and the cheese.

          10x + 40 = 200   (Keep everything in cents)
          10x = 160   Subtract 40 from both sides
          x = 16   Divide both sides by 10

Each straw cost 16¢.

8. $\dfrac{3 \text{ hours of football}}{1} \times \dfrac{60 \text{ minutes}}{1 \text{ hour}} \times \dfrac{4 \text{ cents}}{1 \text{ minute}} = 720¢ \text{ (or } \$7.20)$

9. 3 hours = 180 minutes.

          54 is ?% of 180   Since we don't know both sides of the *of*, we
divide the number closest to the *of* into the other number.

$$\dfrac{54}{180} = 0.3 = 30\%$$

10. If it takes her x minutes to clean off one nail, it will take her 10x
minutes to clean off ten nails.

from p. 94—*first try*

1. None of these functions is one-to-one. A function is not 1-1 if two
elements of the domain have the same image in the codomain.

2. $\$1{,}000{,}000{,}000 = 10 \times 10 \times 10 \times 10 \times 10 \times 10 \times 10 \times 10 \times 10 = 10^9$.

3. Let x = the cost of a ticket.
Then 20x = the cost of 20 tickets.
Then 20x + 55 = the cost of 20 tickets and the $55 administrative fee.

          20x + 55 = 1235
          20x = 1180   Subtract 55 from both sides
          x = 59   Divide both sides by 20

$59 is the cost of a ticket.

The Bridge
answers

4. $-100 + 1000 = 900$ His new balance would be $900.

5. $30 \times 1.09 \times 1.09 = 35.643$ kilograms

6. $43\% + 10\% + 3\% = 56\%$
    56% of $1,000,000,000 = $0.56 \times 1,000,000,000 = 560,000,000$.
    Joe would pay $560,000,000 in taxes.

7. The conversion factor is either $\dfrac{7 \text{ pieces of gum}}{18 \text{ minutes}}$ or $\dfrac{18 \text{ minutes}}{7 \text{ pieces of gum}}$
depending on which one will make the units cancel.

$$\frac{200 \text{ pieces of gum}}{1} \times \frac{18 \text{ minutes}}{7 \text{ pieces of gum}} \doteq 514.29 \text{ minutes}$$

which is closer to 514 minutes than it is to 515 minutes.

8. $21x

9. Yes, it must be one-to-one. A function is not one-to-one if two
elements of the domain have the same image. Since there is only one
element in the domain, {☎}, it would be impossible for two elements of the
domain to have the same image.

10. 9% of $21 = $0.09 \times 21 = 1.89$
    The sales tax would be $1.89.

from p. 96—*second try*

1. Let x = the price of one park ranger hat.
Then 12x = the cost of 12 hats.
Then 12x + 49 = the cost of 12 hats plus sales tax.

$$12x + 49 = 613$$
$$12x = 564 \qquad \text{Subtract 49 from both sides}$$
$$x = 47 \qquad \text{Divide both sides by 12}$$

Each park ranger hat cost $47.

2. The codomain = {suitcase, paper bag, pocket, crate}.

3. It is 1-1 since no two elements in the domain have the same image in
the codomain.

4. Use a conversion factor.

$$\frac{13 \text{ letters}}{1} \times \frac{11 \text{ minutes}}{3 \text{ letters}} \approx 47.66 \text{ minutes.}$$

   47.66 is closer to 48 minutes than it is to 47 minutes.

5. $47 \times 1.09 \approx 51.23$ pounds.   (See #2 on page 87 for explanation.)
    51.23 is closer to 51 pounds than it is to 52 pounds.

6. $4 \times 0.94 = 3.76$ kilograms

7. 82, 84, 86, and 88.

8. Since $2 \times 2 \times 2 \times 2 \times 2 \times 2 \times 2 \times 2 \times 2 \times 2 = 1024$, $2^{10} = 1024$. $x = 10$

9. $\dfrac{1}{3} + \dfrac{3}{4} = \dfrac{1(4)}{3(4)} + \dfrac{3(3)}{4(3)} = \dfrac{4+9}{12} = \dfrac{13}{12} = 1\dfrac{1}{12}$

10.

$$7x - 6 = 2x + 54$$

$5x - 6 = 54$	Subtract 2x from both sides
$5x = 60$	Add 6 to both sides
$x = 12$	Divide both sides by 5

from p. 98—*third try*

1. $\dfrac{\$1,000,000,000}{1} \times \dfrac{1 \text{ hour}}{\$80} = 12,500,000 \text{ hours}$

2. Twenty sheets is 40% of what? 20 is 40% of ? We don't know both sides of the *of*, so we divide the number closest to the *of* into the other number. $0.4\overline{)20.0} \;\rightarrow\; 4\overline{)200.}$ gives 50. 50 sheets of binder paper

3. $\dfrac{3}{5} - \dfrac{1}{2} = \dfrac{3(2)}{5(2)} - \dfrac{1(5)}{2(5)} = \dfrac{6-5}{10} = \dfrac{1}{10}$

He had a tenth of a gallon left.

4. $80 \times 1.02 = 81.6$ It weighed 81.6 pounds after being painted. (See #2 on page 87 for explanation.)

5. 72, 73, 74, 75, 76

6. Let x = the price of a gallon of pink paint.

Then 6x = the price of six gallons.

Then 6x + 8 = the price of six gallons plus sales tax.

$6x + 8 = 110$	
$6x = 102$	Subtract 8 from both sides
$x = 17$	Divide both sides by 6

Each gallon of pink paint cost $17.

7. It is a function since each element of the domain is assigned exactly one element of the codomain.

  1-1? No. A function is 1-1 if no two elements of the domain are assigned the same image. So in this case it is not one-to-one since, for example, lamp $\rightarrow$ pink, and dog $\rightarrow$ pink.

8. $500x

9. $16\frac{2}{3}\% = \dfrac{1}{6}$ One of the Eleven Conversions you memorized (page 43).

The Bridge
answers

10.
$$3x + 7 = 4x - 32$$
$$7 = x - 32 \quad \text{Subtract 3x from both sides}$$
$$39 = x \quad \text{Add 32 to both sides}$$

from p. 100—*fourth try*

1. $\dfrac{1 \text{ week}}{1} \times \dfrac{7 \text{ days}}{1 \text{week}} \times \dfrac{24 \text{ hours}}{1 \text{ day}} \times \dfrac{60 \text{ minutes}}{1 \text{ hour}}$

   $\times \dfrac{60 \text{ seconds}}{1 \text{ minute}} \times \dfrac{8 \text{ drips}}{5 \text{ seconds}} = 967{,}680 \text{ drips}$

2. $\dfrac{1}{7}$ $7\overline{)1.000}^{\,0.142}$ 14.2% which is closer to 14% than to 15%.

3. It is 1-1. No house gets two papers.

4. 600x¢ (or $6x)

5. $600 \times 1.06 \times 1.06 \times 1.06 \times 1.06 \approx 757.48$ which is closer to 757 than to 758. He would have 757 subscribers after four months.

6. $\dfrac{1}{6} + \dfrac{1}{3} + \dfrac{1}{2} = \dfrac{1}{6} + \dfrac{1(2)}{3(2)} + \dfrac{1(3)}{2(3)} = \dfrac{1+2+3}{6} = \dfrac{6}{6} = 1 \text{ hour}$

7. $2^3 > 3^2$ means $8 > 9$ which is false.

   $(0.1)^2$ means 0.1×0.1 which is 0.01 which is $\dfrac{1}{100}$ so $(0.1)^2 = \dfrac{1}{100}$ is true.

   $0 < 7$ is true

8. Let x = the number of dimes he would receive.

Then 10x = the worth of those dimes.

Then 10x + 50 = his total income.

$$10x + 50 = 1240$$
$$10x = 1190 \quad \text{Subtract 50 from both sides}$$
$$x = 119 \quad \text{Divide both sides by 10}$$

He would have received 119 dimes.

9.
$$40x - 7 = 263 + 10x$$
$$30x - 7 = 263 \quad \text{Subtract 10x from both sides}$$
$$30x = 270 \quad \text{Add 7 to both sides}$$
$$x = 9 \quad \text{Divide both sides by 30}$$

10. $-17 + 27 = 10$

The Bridge

answers

from p. 102—*fifth try*

1. $\dfrac{1 \text{ hour}}{1} \times \dfrac{60 \text{ min}}{1 \text{ hour}} \times \dfrac{60 \text{ secs}}{1 \text{ min}} \times \dfrac{\$7}{1/60 \text{ sec}} = 25{,}200 \div \dfrac{1}{60} =$

$25200 \times \dfrac{60}{1} = 1{,}512{,}000$ \$1,512,000 isn't bad for an hour's wages.

2. $6 = ?\%$ of 300 $300\overline{)6.000}^{\,0.020}$ $0.020 = 2.\% = 2\%$

3. $10 \times (1.06)^{20}$

4. Answers will vary. My answer is Joe's plane $\to$ Reno. Your answer might have been Joe's plane $\to$ San Francisco or it might have been Joe's plane $\to$ Zutphen (which is in the Netherlands).

5. $6^3 = 6 \times 6 \times 6 = 216$

6. $(\dfrac{1}{2})^3 = \dfrac{1}{2} \times \dfrac{1}{2} \times \dfrac{1}{2} = \dfrac{1}{8}$

7.

$$2x - 7 = 3x - 15$$
$$-7 = x - 15 \qquad \text{Subtract 2x from both sides}$$
$$8 = x \qquad \text{Add 15 to both sides}$$

8. 80% of $70 = 0.8 \times 70 = 56$ letters that Joe read.

9. $\dfrac{1}{2} + \dfrac{1}{3} + \dfrac{1}{4} = \dfrac{1(6)}{2(6)} + \dfrac{1(4)}{3(4)} + \dfrac{1(3)}{4(3)} = \dfrac{6 + 4 + 3}{12} = \dfrac{13}{12} = 1\dfrac{1}{12}$

10.
```
   38.20
   10.58
    7.77
  ------
   56.55
```

from p. 138—*first try*

1. There are six quantities involved: the number of helmets and footballs, their prices, and the total costs.

	total cost	cost per item	number bought
Helmets	$60x$	60	x
Footballs	$200(x+10)$	200	$x+10$

$$60x + 200(x + 10) = 9800$$
$$60x + 200x + 2000 = 9800$$
$$260x + 2000 = 9800$$
$$260x = 7800$$
$$x = 30 \qquad \text{Joe purchased 30 helmets.}$$

2. The cardinality of a set is the number of elements in the set. Since this set contains three elements, the cardinality is 3.

3. 20% more than 4 feet → $1.2 \times 4 = 4.8$ feet (or 4 4/5 feet) *(See #2 on page 87 for explanation.)* By the way, 4.8 feet does not equal 4 feet 8 inches. 0.8 feet equals $\dfrac{0.8 \text{ feet}}{1} \times \dfrac{12 \text{ inches}}{1 \text{ foot}} = 9.6$ inches, so 4.8' equals 4' 9.6")

4. Yes. Every function that has only one element in the domain must be 1-1. A function is not 1-1 if two different elements in the domain have the same image. If there is only one element in the domain, it is pretty tough to have two elements in the domain have the same image.

5. Using a conversion factor,
$$\dfrac{60 \text{ minutes}}{1} \times \dfrac{12 \text{ injuries}}{16 \text{ minutes}} = 45 \text{ injuries}$$

6.
$$
\begin{aligned}
15w + 7 + 2w &= 5(w + 8) + 27 & \\
15w + 7 + 2w &= 5w + 40 + 27 & \text{Distributive law} \\
17w + 7 &= 5w + 67 & \text{Combine like terms} \\
12w + 7 &= 67 & \text{Subtract 5w from both sides} \\
12w &= 60 & \text{Subtract 7 from both sides} \\
w &= 5 & \text{Divide both sides by 12}
\end{aligned}
$$

7. $7 \times 2\dfrac{3}{8} = \dfrac{7}{1} \times \dfrac{19}{8} = \dfrac{133}{8} = 16\dfrac{5}{8}$

8. $400 \times (1.05)^5$

9. Let x = the weight of one book.
Then 3x = the weight of all three books.
Then 3x + 2 = the weight of the books plus the bag.
$$
\begin{aligned}
3x + 2 &= 6 \\
3x &= 4 \\
x &= \dfrac{4}{3} = 1\dfrac{1}{3} \quad \text{Each book weighed } 1\dfrac{1}{3} \text{ pounds.}
\end{aligned}
$$

10. $(1.8)^2 = 1.8 \times 1.8 = 3.24$

from p. 140—*second try*
1. Let t = hours walking in commercial area.
Then t + 1 = hours walking in residential area.
Then 3t = miles walked in commercial area.
Then 4(t + 1) = miles walked in residential area.
Since the total distance that Darlene walked was $6\dfrac{1}{3}$ miles,

The Bridge
answers

$$3t + 4(t + 1) = 6\frac{1}{3}$$

$$3t + 4t + 4 = 6\frac{1}{3} \qquad \text{Distributive law}$$

$$7t + 4 = 6\frac{1}{3} \qquad \text{Combine like terms}$$

$$7t = 2\frac{1}{3} \qquad \text{Subtract 4 from both sides}$$

$$t = 2\frac{1}{3} \div 7 \qquad \text{Divide both sides by 7}$$

$$t = \frac{7}{3} \div \frac{7}{1} = \frac{7}{3} \times \frac{1}{7} = \frac{1}{3}$$ Darlene walked for $\frac{1}{3}$ hour in the commercial area.

2. Darlene might have assigned all the houses to *yes*. ("Any house would be good if I were married to Joe.") She might have assigned all the houses to *no*. ("None of these are fancy enough for us.") Or she might have assigned the pink houses to *yes* and the other houses to *no*. In any event, no matter how she assigned the houses, either *yes* or *no* (or both) will be the image of more than one house. If two elements of the domain (two houses) are assigned to the same element of the codomain, then the function can't be 1-1. So, no matter how Darlene made her assignment, the function could not be 1-1.

3. Start with 30 helmets. "20% more" translates to 30×1.2, which is 36. (See #2 on page 87 for explanation.)

4. He had 30 helmets (according to the previous problem), and he increased his collection by 20%. Twenty percent of 30 is $0.2 \times 30 = 6$. He increased his collection by 6 helmets. (This could also have been done by noticing in the previous problem that he went from 30 to 36 helmets—an increase of 6.)

5.

	$90(z - 4) = 42z - 240$
Distributive law	$90z - 360 = 42z - 240$
Subtract 42z from both sides	$48z - 360 = -240$
Add 360 to both sides	$48z = 120$
Divide both sides by 48	$z = \dfrac{120}{48}$
Reduce the fraction	$z = 2.5 \ \ (\text{or } 2\frac{1}{2})$

6. $\dfrac{1}{3} + \dfrac{2}{7} + \dfrac{1}{2} = \dfrac{1(14)}{3(14)} + \dfrac{2(6)}{7(6)} + \dfrac{1(21)}{2(21)} = \dfrac{14 + 12 + 21}{42}$

$= \dfrac{47}{42} = 1\dfrac{5}{42}$

7. $(1/3)^3 = \dfrac{1}{3} \times \dfrac{1}{3} \times \dfrac{1}{3} = \dfrac{1}{27}$

264

8. $\dfrac{\text{9 Sluice Dolls}}{1} \times \dfrac{\text{120 Sluice Points}}{\text{1 Sluice Doll}} \times \dfrac{\text{6 bottle caps}}{\text{80 Sluice Points}} = 81 \text{ bottle caps}$

9. $7\dfrac{1}{6} \div \dfrac{1}{3} = \dfrac{43}{6} \div \dfrac{1}{3} = \dfrac{43}{6} \times \dfrac{3}{1} = \dfrac{43}{\underset{2}{6}} \times \dfrac{\overset{}{3}}{1} = \dfrac{43}{2} = 21\dfrac{1}{2}$

10. x + 24 verses

from p. 142—*third try*

1. $\dfrac{\text{1 Sluice Doll}}{1} \times \dfrac{\text{0.4 kilograms}}{\text{1 Sluice Doll}} \times \dfrac{\text{2.2 pounds}}{\text{1 kilogram}} \times \dfrac{\text{1 ounce}}{\text{0.0625 pounds}}$

 = 14.08 ounces, which is closer to 14 ounces than it is to 15 ounces.

2. {setting the date, dieting, picking a cake, choosing a dress} is a set with four elements in it, so its cardinality is 4.

3. $10^6 = 10 \times 10 \times 10 \times 10 \times 10 \times 10 = 1,000,000$ which is one million.

4. Joe's choice was not in the codomain. In order for it to be a function, he would have had to have selected one of the flavors in the codomain.

(If he had said, "Carrot, lemon, and pumpkin," it also would not have been a function, since each element of the domain has to be assigned to *exactly one* element of the codomain.)

5. $\$24 \times 1.15 = \$27.60$ (See #2 on page 87 for explanation.)

6. If she lost one-tenth of her weight, she retained $\dfrac{9}{10}$ of her weight.

$\dfrac{9}{10} \times 9 \text{ ounces} = \dfrac{81}{10} \text{ ounces} = 8\dfrac{1}{10}$ (or 8.1) ounces.

	Touchdowns	rate	time
First game	3t	3	t
Second game	4(t + 1)	4	t+1

7. Let t = the length of the first game.
Then t + 1 = the length of the second game.
Then 3t = number of touchdowns during the first game.
Then 4(t + 1) = number of touchdowns during the second game.

$$3t + 4(t + 1) = 25$$

Distributive law	3t + 4t + 4 = 25
Combine like terms	7t + 4 = 25
Subtract 4 from both sides	7t = 21
Divide both sides by 7	t = 3 hours

8. 9, 11, 13, 15, 17

9. x + 2

10. One-fifth of $21\dfrac{1}{2} = \dfrac{1}{5} \times 21\dfrac{1}{2} = \dfrac{1}{5} \times \dfrac{43}{2} = \dfrac{43}{10} = 4\dfrac{3}{10}$ (or 4.3)

from p. 144—*fourth try*

1. Whenever you multiply something by zero, the answer is always zero.
2. If it loses 70% of its value, it would retain 30% of its value.

$$30\% \text{ of } \$600 = 0.3 \times 600 = \$180$$

3. $\dfrac{80 \text{ ounces}}{1} \times \dfrac{1.29 \text{ pounds}}{4.3 \text{ ounces}} = 24 \text{ pounds}$

(Sluice weighs so much because of all the sugar it contains.)

4. We are told that the total number of drops was 240.

$$20r + 20(r - 2) = 240$$
$$20r + 20r - 40 = 240$$
$$40r - 40 = 240$$
$$40r = 280$$
$$r = 7$$

	drops	rate	time
During 1st 20 minutes	$20r$	r	20
During 2nd 20 minutes	$20(r-2)$	$r-2$	20

The rate of dripping during the first 20 minutes was 7 drops/minute.

5. $2^6 = 2 \times 2 \times 2 \times 2 \times 2 \times 2 = 64$

6.
$$4(x + 5) = 7(x + 2)$$

$4x + 20 = 7x + 14$	Distributive law
$20 = 3x + 14$	Subtract 4x from both sides
$6 = 3x$	Subtract 14 from both sides
$2 = x$	Divide both sides by 3

7. $83\frac{1}{3}\% = \dfrac{5}{6}$ Here are the **Eleven Conversions** that you memorized:

$\dfrac{1}{2} = 50\%$ $\dfrac{1}{4} = 25\%$ $\dfrac{3}{8} = 37\frac{1}{2}\%$ $\dfrac{1}{6} = 16\frac{2}{3}\%$

$\dfrac{1}{3} = 33\frac{1}{3}\%$ $\dfrac{3}{4} = 75\%$ $\dfrac{5}{8} = 62\frac{1}{2}\%$ $\dfrac{5}{6} = 83\frac{1}{3}\%$

$\dfrac{2}{3} = 66\frac{2}{3}\%$ $\dfrac{1}{8} = 12\frac{1}{2}\%$ $\dfrac{7}{8} = 87\frac{1}{2}\%$

8. Let x = the smallest of the three.
Then x + 2 = the second consecutive even number.
Then x + 4 = the third consecutive even number.
Since the sum of those three numbers is 630,

$$x + x + 2 + x + 4 = 630$$

$3x + 6 = 630$	Combine like terms
$3x = 624$	Subtract 6 from both sides
$x = 208$	Divide both sides by 3

9. $2\frac{1}{3}$ $\qquad$ $1\frac{3}{3}+\frac{1}{3}$ $\qquad$ $1\frac{4}{3}$

$\quad -\frac{2}{3}$ $\qquad\quad -\frac{2}{3}$ $\qquad\quad -\frac{2}{3}$

$\qquad\qquad\qquad\qquad\qquad\qquad 1\frac{2}{3}$

10. $-13 + 7 = -6$

from p. 146—*fifth try*

1. {solitary, parallel, associative, cooperative} is a set with four elements in it. The cardinality of the set is 4.

2. $V = \pi r^2 h = (3)(2^2)(4) = (3)(4)(4) = 48$ cubic inches

3. Let t = the time to heat up the can at the 8°-per-minute rate. Since the temperature rise is the same in both cases,

$$8t = 12(t - 2)$$
$$8t = 12t - 24$$
$$8t + 24 = 12t$$
$$24 = 4t$$
$$6 = t$$

	rise in temparture	rate	time
Heating at the slow rate	$8t$	$8°/min$	t
Heating at the fast rate	$12(t-2)$	$12°/min$	$t-2$

It took 6 minutes to heat up the can of spaghetti.

4. 2% of 250 grams $= 0.02 \times 250 = 5$ grams

5. Dividing 8 inches into 15 equal pieces is simply $\frac{8}{15}$ or you might have done it by arithmetic: $8 \div 15 = \frac{8}{1} \div \frac{15}{1} = \frac{8}{1} \times \frac{1}{15} = \frac{8}{15}$

6. 18 seconds $\times 1.2 = 21.6$ seconds   (See #2 on page 87 for explanation.)

7. $4\frac{1}{4} \div 5\frac{1}{5} = \frac{17}{4} \div \frac{26}{5} = \frac{17}{4} \times \frac{5}{26} = \frac{85}{104}$

8. $(\frac{1}{5})^3 = \frac{1}{5} \times \frac{1}{5} \times \frac{1}{5} = \frac{1}{125}$

9.
$$20x + 4(x + 3) = 18$$
$$20x + 4x + 12 = 18 \qquad \text{Distributive law}$$
$$24x + 12 = 18 \qquad \text{Combine like terms}$$
$$24x = 6 \qquad \text{Subtract 12 from both sides}$$
$$x = \frac{6}{24} \qquad \text{Divide both sides by 24}$$
$$x = \frac{1}{4} \qquad \text{Reduce the fraction}$$

10. Joe had not eaten any spaghetti. He had eaten 0%.

The Bridge
answers

from p. 186—*first try*

1. 42 minutes is what part of 60 minutes. $\frac{42}{60}$ which equals $\frac{7}{10}$.

2. 36 minutes. There are two ways to do this problem. The longer way is to take 20% of 30 minutes ($0.2 \times 30 = 6$) and then add it on to the 30 and get 36 minutes. The shorter way is 1.2×30 which is 36. (1.2 is 120%.)

3. Let t = the time it took Joe to get to the kitchen.
Then t + 2 = the time it took him to get from the kitchen to the TV.
Then 4t = the distance from the TV to the kitchen.
Then 3(t + 2) = the distance from the kitchen to the TV.
Since those two distances are equal, we have $\quad$ 4t = 3(t + 2)
$$\qquad\qquad\qquad \text{Distributive law} \qquad\qquad 4t = 3t + 6$$
$$\qquad\qquad \text{Subtract 3t from both sides} \qquad t = 6$$
It took Joe 6 seconds to get to the kitchen.

4. Let x = the number of cookies in the bag.
Then 70x = the number of Calories in a whole bag of cookies.
Then 70x + 600 = the total Calories he ate.
$$70x + 600 = 2000$$
$$70x = 1400$$
$$x = 20$$
There were 20 cookies in the bag.

5. Using conversion factors:
$$\frac{1 \text{ bag}}{1} \times \frac{100 \text{ batteries}}{1 \text{ bag}} \times \frac{65 \text{ grams}}{1 \text{ battery}} \times \frac{0.002 \text{ lbs.}}{1 \text{ gram}} = 13 \text{ lbs.}$$

6. $\dfrac{2}{3} + \dfrac{2}{5} = \dfrac{2(5)}{3(5)} + \dfrac{2(3)}{5(3)} = \dfrac{10 + 6}{15} = \dfrac{16}{15} = 1\dfrac{1}{15}$ cups

7. 2n batteries required for n changes.

8. $2^5 = 2 \times 2 \times 2 \times 2 \times 2 = 32$

9. $V = \pi r^2 h = 3(2^2)8 = 3(4)(8) = 96$ cubic inches

10. There are many possible answers. Your answer may be different than mine. One possible function would be to map A to 398 and B to 503979273.

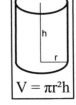

$$V = \pi r^2 h$$

Another possible function would be to map A to 7 and map B to 7.

It wouldn't be correct to map A to the even numbers and B to the odd numbers, since every element in the domain is to be assigned to *exactly one* element in the codomain.

The Bridge

answers

from p. 188—*second try*

1. $\frac{1}{2} = 50\%$ $\frac{2}{3} = 66\frac{2}{3}\%$ $\frac{3}{8} = 37\frac{1}{2}\%$ $\frac{7}{8} = 87\frac{1}{2}\%$ $\frac{1}{6} = 16\frac{2}{3}\%$

2. If he consumed 40% of the food, he left 60%.
60% of 8 lbs. = 0.6 × 8 = 4.8 lbs.

3. Since it doesn't make any difference whether you put your shoe or your sweater on first, the two operations are commutative.

4. His time is increasing at 4% per month. By the Rule of 72, it will take $\frac{72}{4}$ = 18 months for Joe's time to double from 10 minutes to 20.

5.
We want to find out how long it takes if Darlene carries the food.

	distance	rate	time
Darlene carries the food			t
Joe carries the food			

Filling in the boxes we know:

	distance	rate	time
Darlene carries the food		5	t
Joe carries the food		4	$t+3$

Since distance = rate times time
  d = rt

	distance	rate	time
Darlene carries the food	$5t$	5	t
Joe carries the food	$4(t+3)$	4	$t+3$

The distance from his front door to the car is the same regardless of who is carrying the food.
$$5t = 4(t + 3)$$
t = 12 seconds for the trip when Darlene is carrying the food.

6. 2 is ?% of 25. We divide the number closest to the *of* into the other number. $\frac{2}{25}$ There are two ways you could change this into a percent.

First way: $25\overline{)2.00}^{\,0.08}$ = 8%   Second way: $\frac{2}{25} = \frac{2(4)}{25(4)} = \frac{8}{100}$ = 8%

The Bridge
answers

7. Using conversion factors:

$$\frac{3 \text{ blocks}}{1} \times \frac{110 \text{ meters}}{1 \text{ block}} \times \frac{1 \text{ foot}}{0.3 \text{ meters}} = 1100 \text{ feet}$$

8. The domain is {left foot, right foot}.

9. The function is one-to-one since no two elements of the domain are mapped onto the same element in the codomain.

10. $\frac{1}{2} + \frac{1}{3} + \frac{1}{5} = \frac{1(\mathbf{15})}{2(\mathbf{15})} + \frac{1(\mathbf{10})}{3(\mathbf{10})} + \frac{1(\mathbf{6})}{5(\mathbf{6})}$

$= \frac{15 + 10 + 6}{30} = \frac{31}{30} = 1\frac{1}{30}$

from p. 190—*third try*

1. 3 dimes are worth 30¢.

   8 dimes are worth 80¢.

   n dimes are worth 10*n*¢.

2. It does make a difference whether you cook the pizza before or after you eat it. Actually, cooking the pizza after you eat it could be very painful. These two operations are not commutative.

   Always put on your socks before you put on your shoes. Doing it in the other order makes a big difference. These two operations are not commuative.

   It doesn't matter whether you brush your teeth before or after you read your mail. These are commutative.

3. $\frac{50 \text{ batteries}}{1} \times \frac{3.2 \text{ lbs.}}{20 \text{ batteries}} \times \frac{\$1.10}{1 \text{ lb.}} = \$8.80$

4. There are two ways to compute the total bill after taxes.

First way: Find the tax. 7% of $8.80 = 0.07 × 8.8 = 0.616 and add it on to the $8.80 to get $9.416 which rounds to $9.42.

Second (shorter) way: 1.07 × $8.80 = $9.416 ≐ $9.42.

5. Let x = the number of ounces of Sluice that Joe drank.

Then 40x = the cost of x ounces of Sluice.

Then 40x + 14 = the cost of the Sluice and the 14¢ napkin.

$$40x + 14 = 614$$

Subtract 14 from both sides	40x = 600
Divide both sides by 40	x = 15

Joe drank 15 ounces of Sluice.

The Bridge

answers

6. $10,000 = 10 \times 10 \times 10 \times 10 = 10^4$. $n = 4$

7. Question 7A: even. The sum of three consecutive even numbers is always even. For example: $98 + 100 + 102$.

Question 7B: odd. The sum of three consecutive odd numbers is always odd. For example: $7 + 9 + 11$.

Question 7C: even. The sum of four consecutive odd numbers is always even. For example: $3 + 5 + 7 + 9$.

In fact, you may have figured out that the sum of an even number of odd numbers is always even, and the sum of an odd number of odd numbers is always odd.

8. The definition of a function is a rule which assigns to each element of the domain *exactly one* element of the codomain. Since aisle 12 was assigned to two different elements of the codomain, this is not a function.

9. $2\frac{3}{4} \div 1\frac{2}{3} = \frac{11}{4} \div \frac{5}{3} = \frac{11}{4} \times \frac{3}{5} = \frac{33}{20} = 1\frac{13}{20}$

10.
$$
\begin{array}{r}
2\frac{3}{4} \\
+\ 1\frac{2}{3} \\
\hline
\end{array}
\qquad
\begin{array}{r}
2\frac{9}{12} \\
+\ 1\frac{8}{12} \\
\hline
3\frac{17}{12}
\end{array}
= 3 + 1\frac{5}{12} = 4\frac{5}{12}
$$

from p. 192—*fourth try*

1. 14 minutes.   If he could handle one new concept every $4\frac{2}{3}$ minutes, it would take him three times as long to handle three concepts.
$3 \times 4\frac{2}{3} = \frac{3}{1} \times \frac{14}{3} = \frac{42}{3} = 14$ minutes to handle three concepts.

2. Let t = how long it took Joe to eat a piece of taffy.

Then 6t = how long it took him to eat 6 pieces of taffy.

Then 6t + 16 = how long to eat the taffy and drink the Sluice.

$$6t + 16 = 160$$
$$6t = 144$$
$$t = 24 \qquad \text{It took him 24 seconds to eat each piece.}$$

3. 4 The cardinality of a set is the number of elements in that set.

4.

Since the distance in each direction is the same:

	distance	rate	time
Going to the store	$3(t+80)$	3	$t+80$
Going to Joe's	$6t$	6	t

$$6t = 3(t + 80)$$
$$6t = 3t + 240$$
$$3t = 240$$
$$t = 80 \quad \text{It took 80 seconds to get from the hardware store to Joe's.}$$

5. $\qquad\qquad\qquad\qquad\qquad 5(x - 12) = 3(x + 2)$

Distributive law $\qquad\qquad\quad 5x - 60 = 3x + 6$

Subtract 3x from both sides $\quad 2x - 60 = 6$

Add 60 to both sides $\qquad\qquad\qquad 2x = 66$

Divide both sides by 2 $\qquad\qquad\qquad x = 33$

6. $\dfrac{88 \text{ flowers}}{1} \times \dfrac{\$16}{5 \text{ flowers}} = \$281.60$

7. $\dfrac{2}{3} = 66\tfrac{2}{3}\% \qquad \dfrac{3}{4} = 75\% \qquad \dfrac{7}{8} = 87\tfrac{1}{2}\% \qquad \dfrac{5}{6} = 83\tfrac{1}{3}\%$

8. $9^5 \times 9^7 = 9 \times 9 \times 9 \times 9 \times 9 \ \times \ 9 \times 9 \times 9 \times 9 \times 9 \times 9 \times 9 = 9^{12}$

(In algebra, the general rule is: $x^a x^b = x^{a+b}$)

9. $\dfrac{1}{6} + \dfrac{1}{8} = \dfrac{1(4)}{6(4)} + \dfrac{1(3)}{8(3)} = \dfrac{4 + 3}{24} = \dfrac{7}{24}$

(Note: You could have used 48 as a common denominator, but that takes a little more work. 24 is the *least* common denominator.)

10. $\dfrac{1}{6} \div \dfrac{1}{8} = \dfrac{1}{6} \times \dfrac{8}{1} = \dfrac{8}{6} = 1\dfrac{2}{6} = 1\dfrac{1}{3}$

from p. 194—*fifth try*

1. $\dfrac{1}{2} = 50\% \qquad \dfrac{1}{3} = 33\tfrac{1}{3}\% \qquad \dfrac{2}{3} = 66\tfrac{2}{3}\% \qquad \dfrac{1}{4} = 25\% \qquad \dfrac{5}{6} = 83\tfrac{1}{3}\%$

2. Any function with only one element in the domain has to be 1-1. A function is 1-1 if two different elements in the domain never have the same image in the codomain.

3. Using the Rule of 72: $\dfrac{72}{6} = 12$. It would take approximately 12 minutes for her blood pressure to double.

4. If her heart rate dropped by 20%, it was beating at 80% of the previous rate. 80% of 160 $= 0.8 \times 160 = 128$ beats per minute.

5. $\dfrac{2000 \text{ tears}}{1} \times \dfrac{0.3 \text{ grams}}{1 \text{ tear}} \times \dfrac{0.035 \text{ ounces}}{1 \text{ gram}} = 21 \text{ ounces}$

6. $\dfrac{3}{4} \div \dfrac{7}{8} = \dfrac{3}{4} \times \dfrac{8}{7} = \dfrac{3}{\cancel{4}} \times \dfrac{\cancel{8}^{2}}{7} = \dfrac{6}{7}$

7. 44^{13} (See #8 on previous page for explanation.)

8. $\dfrac{1}{6} + \dfrac{4}{9} = \dfrac{1(\mathbf{3})}{6(\mathbf{3})} + \dfrac{4(\mathbf{2})}{9(\mathbf{2})} = \dfrac{3+8}{18} = \dfrac{11}{18}$

9. $(\tfrac{1}{7})^{2} = \dfrac{1}{7} \times \dfrac{1}{7} = \dfrac{1}{49}$

10. 5 divided equally into 8 parts is $5 \div 8$, which is $\dfrac{5}{8}$ years.

from p. 239—*first try*

1. Let t = the number of hours they had been sitting on the couch.
Then 4t = the number of ideas that Joe got during those hours.
Then 80t = the number of ideas that Darlene got during those hours.
They got a total of 294 ideas.

$$4t + 80t = 294$$
$$84t = 294$$
$$t = 3.5$$

They had been sitting on the couch for three and a half hours.

2. $984 \times (1.24)^{7}$

3. 4% of 1300 = 52. Only fifty-two people made any money at all.

4. If x = 1, then y = 1000(1) + 2000 = 3000
If x = 2, then y = 1000(2) + 2000 = 4000
If x = 4, then y = 1000(4) + 2000 = 6000
It's a straight line, which we sketch in.

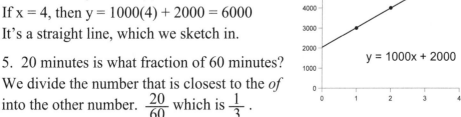

y = 1000x + 2000

5. 20 minutes is what fraction of 60 minutes?
We divide the number that is closest to the *of*
into the other number. $\dfrac{20}{60}$ which is $\dfrac{1}{3}$.

6. If the diameter is 2 feet, then the radius is 1 foot.
$V = \pi r^{2}h = 3.1(1^{2})(3) = 9.3$ cubic feet.

7. $\dfrac{20\text{ minutes}}{1} \times \dfrac{40\text{ coins}}{1\text{ minute}} \times \dfrac{1\text{ kg}}{10\text{ coins}} \times \dfrac{2.2\text{ lbs}}{1\text{ kg}} = 176$ pounds

8. Let x = the price of one typewriter.

Then 7x = the price of seven typewriters.

Then 7x + 14 = the price seven typewriters plus shipping cost.

$$7x + 14 = 623$$
$$7x = 609$$
$$x = 87$$

Each typewriter costs $87.

9. Since no two typewriters are assigned the same color of paint, this function is one-to-one.

10. Here is the production chart:

	Spraying	Planting
Joe	4	2
Darlene	6	5

Since Darlene can spray more typewriters than Joe and can plant more roses than Joe, she has an absolute advantage over Joe.

11. Here is the opportunity cost chart:

	Spraying	Planting
Joe	2/4	4/2
Darlene	5/6	6/5

When it comes to spraying, Joe's opportunity cost (0.5) is less than Darlene's (0.83⅓), so Joe has a comparative advantage in spray painting typewriters.

12.

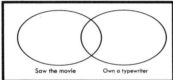

Note that there are people that have both seen the movie and own a typewriter.

13. The set of dogs and the set of cats are disjoint. In the Venn diagram the regions do not overlap.

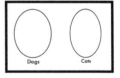

14.

	Total number of pieces each picked up	How fast each picked up trash	Minutes worked
Joe	3t	3	t
Darlene	4(2t)	4	2t
Darlene's mom	8(2t+10)	8	2t+10

Together, they picked up a total of 323 pieces.

$$3t + 4(2t) + 8(2t + 10) = 323$$ So t = 9. Joe worked for 9 minutes.

 **The Bridge**
answers

15. Using the Rule of 72, $\frac{72}{9} = 8$. It would take approximately 8 days for the population to double.

16. $\frac{1}{3} + \frac{3}{5} = \frac{1(5)}{3(5)} + \frac{3(3)}{5(3)} = \frac{5+9}{15} = \frac{14}{15}$

17. $\frac{7}{8} - \frac{1}{5} = \frac{7(5)}{8(5)} - \frac{1(8)}{5(8)} = \frac{35-8}{40} = \frac{27}{40}$

18. Since the number of flies couldn't be 73⅓ or 82.9, it is a discrete variable.

19. $\quad 4x + 2(6x + 5) = 78$

$\qquad 4x + 12x + 10 = 78 \qquad\qquad$ Distributive law

$\qquad\qquad 16x + 10 = 78 \qquad\qquad$ Combine like terms

$\qquad\qquad\qquad 16x = 68 \qquad\qquad$ Subtract 10 from both sides

$\qquad\qquad\qquad x = \frac{68}{16} = 4\frac{4}{16} = 4\frac{1}{4} \quad$ Divide both sides by 16

20. If a function is one-to-one, then no two elements of the domain may have the same image. There must be at least as many elements in the codomain as in the domain.

The cardinality of the domain ≤ the cardinality of the codomain.

21. $\frac{2}{21} \div \frac{3}{7} = \frac{2}{21} \times \frac{7}{3} = \frac{2}{\cancel{21}_{3}} \times \frac{\cancel{7}}{3} = \frac{2}{9}$

from p. 242—*second try*

1.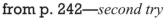

2. If a function is 1-1, then no two elements of the domain are mapped onto the same element of the codomain. Since, for example, Sluice and Junk food are mapped to Joe, this is not a 1-1 function.

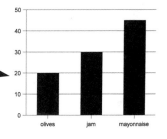

3. Let x = the number of jars of mustard (since this is what we are trying to find out).

Then x + 30 = the number of jars of relish (since we are told that there are 30 more jars of relish than there were of mustard).

Then 4x = the value of the mustard (since each jar is worth $4 and there are x jars).

Then 3(x + 30) = the value of the jars of relish (since each jar is worth $3 and there are x + 30 jars).

Then 4x + 3(x + 30) = the value of the mustard and the relish.

$$4x + 3(x + 30) = 216$$

Distributive law	4x + 3x + 90 = 216
Combine like terms	7x + 90 = 216
Subtract 90 from both sides	7x = 126
Divide both sides by 7	x = 18

There were 18 jars of Turkish mustard.

4. The number of jars of pickles is a discrete variable. You can't have 32.17 jars.

5. 8z (or $8z)

6. The only possibility is mapping each jar to Joe. There is only one possible function.

7. Six percent of all the jars equals 84.

    6% of ? = 84

    Since we don't know both sides of the *of*, we divide the number closest to the *of* into the other number. 84 ÷ 0.06 which is $\frac{84}{0.06}$ which is 1400. There are 1400 jars in Joe's pantry.

8. Using conversion factors and the fact that one pound = 16 ounces and the fact that 2 ounces = one serving and that one serving = 440 calories,

$$\frac{\text{the entire jar}}{1} \times \frac{1 \text{ pound}}{\text{entire jar}} \times \frac{16 \text{ oz.}}{1 \text{ lb.}} \times \frac{1 \text{ serving}}{2 \text{ oz.}} \times \frac{440 \text{ calories}}{1 \text{ serving}}$$

= 3520 calories.

Note: We started with one entire jar. We converted it to pounds. Then to ounces. Then to servings. Then to calories.

9. These two acts are not commutative. It's easy to open a jar and take out a waffle bit. It's impossible to take out a waffle bit and then open the jar.

10.

	Cashews	Walnuts
Albert	10	6
Philip	4	2

Production chart

	Cashews	Walnuts
Albert	6/10	10/6
Philip	2/4	4/2

Opportunity cost chart

Since the opportunity cost for Philip (0.5) is less than the opportunity cost for Albert (0.6), Philip should grow cashews.

11. $V = \pi r^2 h = 3(4^2)(16) = 768$ cubic centimeters.

12. $\left(\dfrac{5}{8}\right)^3 = \dfrac{5}{8} \times \dfrac{5}{8} \times \dfrac{5}{8} = \dfrac{125}{512}$

13. Using the Rule of 72, it should take $\dfrac{72}{4} = 18$ years to double his money.

14.
$$6(y-2) = 60y - 138$$

$6y - 12 = 60y - 138$	Distributive law
$6y + 126 = 60y$	Add 138 to both sides
$126 = 54y$	Subtract $6y$ from both sides
$\dfrac{126}{54} = y$	Divide both sides by 54

Simplifying $\quad \dfrac{126}{54} = 54\overline{)126}\;^{2\ R\ 18} = 2\dfrac{18}{54} = 2\dfrac{1}{3}$
$$\begin{array}{r} -108 \\ \hline 18 \end{array}$$

15. $2\dfrac{1}{4} - \dfrac{3}{8} = 2\dfrac{2}{8} - \dfrac{3}{8} = 1\dfrac{10}{8} - \dfrac{3}{8} = 1\dfrac{7}{8}$

16. $2\dfrac{1}{4} \div \dfrac{3}{8} = \dfrac{9}{4} \div \dfrac{3}{8} = \dfrac{9}{4} \times \dfrac{8}{3} = \dfrac{\cancel{9}^3}{\cancel{4}} \times \dfrac{\cancel{8}^2}{\cancel{3}} = 6$

17. The cardinality is 4.

18. The opportunity cost is defined as the value of the most valuable thing you give up. In this case, it is 6 happiness points.

19. If $x = 0$, then $y = 0^4 = 0$. $\quad$ (0, 0)
If $x = 1$, then $y = 1^4 = 1$. $\quad$ (1, 1)
If $x = 2$, then $y = 2^4 = 16$. $\quad$ (2, 16)
If $x = 3$, then $y = 3^4 = 81$. $\quad$ (3, 81)
Then sketch the curve.

20. The two sets are disjoint. The regions will not overlap.

21. $83\frac{1}{3}\% = \dfrac{5}{6}$ is one of the Eleven Conversions you have memorized.

$\dfrac{1}{12} + \dfrac{1}{12} + \dfrac{5}{6} = 1$, so none of the jars are Joe's.

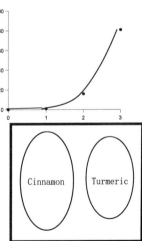

from p. 245—*third try*

1. 8 is ?% of 400 $\quad \dfrac{8}{400} = \dfrac{2}{100} = 2\%$

The Bridge
answers

2. Let t = the number of minutes that each of them ate waffle bits.

Then 10t = the number of waffle bits that Joe ate.

Then 4t = the number of waffle bits that Darlene ate.

Then 2t = the number of waffle bits that Darlene's mother ate.

   Then 10t + 4t + 2t = total number of waffle bits that they ate.

$$10t + 4t + 2t = 40$$
$$16t = 40$$
$$t = \frac{40}{16} = 2\frac{8}{16} = 2\frac{1}{2}$$

They ate waffle bits for $2\frac{1}{2}$ minutes.

3.

	distance	rate	time
Joe walked	30r	r	30
Joe was carried	20(r+4)	r + 4	20

Since they went a total of 230 feet, we have

$$30r + 20(r + 4) = 230$$
$$30r + 20r + 80 = 230$$
$$50r + 80 = 230$$
$$50r = 150$$
$$r = 3$$

Joe walked at the rate of 3 feet/second.

4. x = 6 since 10^6 = 1,000,000

5. For each number you substitute in place of x, you only get exactly one value for y. Each x gives you one y. This is the definition of a function.

6. If we let x = 0, then y = 2(0) + 6 = 6   (0, 6)

If we let x = 1, then y = 2(1) + 6 = 8   (1, 8)

If we let x = 2, then y = 2(2) + 6 = 10   (2, 10)

If we let x = 10, then y = 2(10) + 6 = 26 (10, 26)

Then we sketch the curve (which in this case is a line).

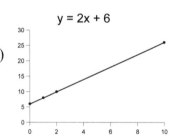

7. V = $\pi r^2 h$ = 3(10^2)(80) = 24,000 cubic feet

8. Using conversion factors,

$$\frac{1000 \text{ cubic feet}}{1} \times \frac{29.92 \text{ quarts}}{1 \text{ cubic foot}} \times \frac{1 \text{ gallon}}{4 \text{ quarts}} = 7,480 \text{ gallons}$$

9. 3x points

10. The set of all birds is a subset of the set of living things with two legs.

11. The opportunity cost is the value of the most valuable thing that you give up.
In this case the most valuable thing for Joe would be his 100 happiness points
if he did not go in and see his dentist.

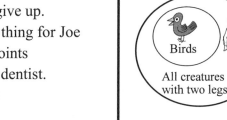

Birds

All creatures with two legs

12.

$$3x + 220 = 5(x + 40)$$
$$3x + 220 = 5x + 200$$
$$220 = 2x + 200$$
$$20 = 2x$$
$$10 = x$$

13. $\frac{3}{4} \div \frac{3}{8} = \frac{3}{4} \times \frac{8}{3} = 2$

14. $\frac{3}{4} + \frac{3}{8} = \frac{3(2)}{4(2)} + \frac{3}{8} = \frac{6+3}{8} = \frac{9}{8} = 1\frac{1}{8}$

15. $\left(\frac{3}{4}\right)^3 = \frac{3}{4} \times \frac{3}{4} \times \frac{3}{4} = \frac{27}{64}$

16. Using the Rule of 72, $\frac{72}{6} = 12$ minutes to double in size.

17.

18. Time is a continuous variable. It doesn't come in "chunks" like the number of teeth you have. You can have any amount of time, such as 920.8927⅔ seconds.

19. 15 minutes is $\frac{1}{4}$ of an hour.

20. $50 \times (1.07)^{15}$

21.

	Fill	Pull
Quail	10	16
Shakes	8	10

Production chart

	Fill	Pull
Quail	16/10	10/16
Shakes	10/8	8/10

Opportunity cost chart

Dr. Shakes should be filling cavities since $\frac{10}{8} < \frac{16}{10}$

279

The Bridge
answers

from p. 249—*fourth try*

1. It is not commutative. It would be very difficult for the dentist to look at Joe's teeth before he opened his mouth.

2. Let x = the number of times Joe is expected to floss.

Then 2x = the number of times Joe will brush, since he is brushing twice as often as flossing.

Then 5x = number of happy tooth points from flossing.

Then 3(2x) = number of happy tooth points from brushing.

5x + 6x = 330 $\rightarrow$ 11x = 330 $\rightarrow$ x = 30   Joe should floss 30 times.

3. $\begin{aligned} & 1\frac{1}{3} & 1\frac{8}{24} \\ +\ & 2\frac{7}{8} & +\ 2\frac{21}{24} \\ \hline & & 3\frac{29}{24} = 4\frac{5}{24} \quad \text{cups of the mixture} \end{aligned}$

4. $10^4 = 10,000$

5. 28 is ?% of 32.

Dividing by the number closest to the *of*: $\frac{28}{32} = \frac{7}{8} = 87\frac{1}{2}\%$

6. Let t = time spent working on the loose teeth.

Let t + 4 = time spent working on the really loose teeth.

Then 2t = number of loose teeth worked on.

Then 2(t + 4) = number of really loose teeth worked on.

2t + 2(t + 4) = 32 $\rightarrow$ 2t + 2t + 8 = 32 $\rightarrow$ . . . $\rightarrow$ t = 6 minutes

7.

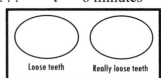

8. Discrete. You can't say 3.83 words.

9. Not 1-1. Two elements of the domain were mapped onto the same element of the codoman.

10. Each element of the domain must be mapped to *exactly one* element of the codomain. This is not a function.

11. His opportunity cost is the $100 that he forgoes by cleaning teeth.

12. If x = 0, then y = 5(0) + 3 = 3.   (0, 3)

If x = 1, then y = 5(1) + 3 = 8.   (1, 8)

If x = 4, then y = 5(4) + 3 = 23.   (4, 23)

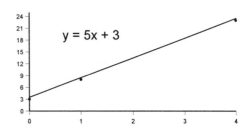

y = 5x + 3

13. $11x + 3 = 7(x + 2) + 5 \rightarrow 11x + 3 = 7x + 14 + 5 \rightarrow 11x + 3 = 7x + 19$
$\rightarrow 4x + 3 = 19 \rightarrow 4x = 16 \rightarrow x = 4$

14. $\dfrac{0.1 \text{ lbs}}{1} \times \dfrac{454 \text{ g}}{1 \text{ lb}} \times \dfrac{1000 \text{ mg}}{1 \text{ g}} \times \dfrac{1 \text{ carat}}{200 \text{ mg}} = 227$ carats.

15. $\dfrac{1}{7} + \dfrac{7}{8} = \dfrac{1(\mathbf{8})}{7(\mathbf{8})} + \dfrac{7(\mathbf{7})}{8(\mathbf{7})} = \dfrac{8 + 49}{56} = \dfrac{57}{56} = 1\dfrac{1}{56}$

16. $\dfrac{1}{3} \div \dfrac{3}{4} = \dfrac{1}{3} \times \dfrac{4}{3} = \dfrac{4}{9}$

17. You have memorized that 37½% is $\dfrac{3}{8}$. $\quad \dfrac{3}{\cancel{8}} \times \dfrac{\cancel{24}^{3}}{1} = 9$

18. 16⅔% is $\dfrac{1}{6}$ $\quad \dfrac{1}{6}$ of ? is 60 $\quad 60 \div \dfrac{1}{6}$ $\quad 60 \times 6 = 360$

19. $\dfrac{1}{20}$ $\quad$ 3 minutes is what part of 60 minutes?
Divide by the number closest to the *of*.

20.

	Handcuff	Question
Friday	2	6
March	3	8

Production chart

	Handcuff	Question
Friday	6/2	2/6
March	8/3	3/8

Opportunity cost chart

Since $\dfrac{1}{3} < \dfrac{3}{8}$ Friday should do the questioning.

21. $d = rt$ $\quad 30 = 8t$ $\quad \dfrac{30}{8} = t$ $\quad \dfrac{30}{8} = 3\dfrac{6}{8} = 3\dfrac{3}{4}$ seconds

from p. 252—*fifth try*

1. Let t = time walking to police car. That's what we're looking for.
Then 7t = time in police car.
Then 2t = distance walked.
Then 60(7t) = distance traveled in police car.
$\quad 2t + 60(7t) = 8440$ $\quad$ So t = 20 seconds walking.

2. They can be done in either order. It is commutative.

3. There are 4 elements in this set. Its cardinality is 4.

4. It satisfies the definition of function: Each element of the domain is assigned exactly one element in the codomain. (The fact that it is not 1-1 doesn't stop it from being a function.)

5. 100 happiness points. The opportunity cost of some choice is the value of the most valuable thing you are giving up to make that choice.

6. 12½% 3 hours is what part of 24 hours. Divide by the number closest to the *of*. $\quad \dfrac{3}{24} = \dfrac{1}{8} = 12\frac{1}{2}\%$

7.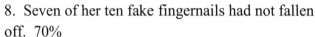

8. Seven of her ten fake fingernails had not fallen off. 70%

9. $\dfrac{2 \text{ oz}}{1} \times \dfrac{31\text{g}}{1 \text{ oz}} \times \dfrac{1000 \text{ mg}}{1 \text{ g}} \times \dfrac{7 \text{ fingerprints}}{50 \text{ mg}}$ = 8680 fingerprints

10. $V = \pi r^2 h = 3(2^2)(6) = 72$ cubic inches

11. Using the Rule of 72: $72/8 = 9$ words spoken by Joe

12. 5x years

13. If $x = 0$, then $y = 0^3 = 0$. $(0, 0)$
If $x = 1$, then $y = 1^3 = 1$. $(1, 1)$
If $x = 2$, then $y = 2^3 = 8$. $(2, 8)$
If $x = 3$, then $y = 3^3 = 27$. $(3, 27)$
If $x = 4$, then $y = 4^3 = 64$. $(4, 64)$

$y = x^3$

14. $\dfrac{7}{8} - \dfrac{1}{5} = \dfrac{35}{40} - \dfrac{8}{40} = \dfrac{27}{40}$

15. $\dfrac{7}{8} \div \dfrac{1}{5} = \dfrac{7}{8} \times \dfrac{5}{1} = \dfrac{35}{8} = 4\dfrac{3}{8}$

16. You divide by the number closest to the *of*. $\dfrac{4}{32}$ which is $\dfrac{1}{8} = 12\frac{1}{2}\%$

17. $7(x + 8) = 9x + 48$
    $7x + 56 = 9x + 48$ Distributive law
    $56 = 2x + 48$ Subtract 7x from both sides
    $8 = 2x$ Subtract 48 from both sides
    $4 = x$ Divide both sides by 2

18. $x = 5$, since $2^5 = 2 \times 2 \times 2 \times 2 \times 2 = 32$

19.

	Dishes	Laundry
Milton	100	20
Dante	50	2

Production chart

	Dishes	Laundry
Milton	20/100	100/20
Dante	2/50	50/2

Opportunity cost chart

Since $100/20 < 50/2$, Milton should do the laundry.

20. Since 100% were stolen, 0% were not stolen.

21. $\dfrac{1}{3} + \dfrac{1}{4} + \dfrac{1}{5} = \dfrac{20}{60} + \dfrac{15}{60} + \dfrac{12}{60} = \dfrac{47}{60}$

Index

If you would like to learn more about the books written about Fred . . .

FredGauss.com

285

The Key Points of Economics

1. *Your labor is something you sell. It has a price.*
2. *Consumers are concerned about both the price and the quality of the product.*
3. *Our goal is not to have everybody working 60 hours a week, but to have abundant, cheap things.*
4. *You have to look at the whole picture—especially the consequences that are not immediately obvious.*
5. *Everyone is in business.*
6. *If you want a successful business, you need to find a significant need that others don't see.*
7. *Ownership = Control. If you don't control something, you don't own it.*
8. *If you separate the rewards from the work, very little work will be done.*
9. *The division of labor dies as you lose people you can trade with.*
10. *If you and the other guy are selling identical products, the one with the lower opportunity cost is the one who makes the sale.*

High School Mathematics

You have just finished *Life of Fred: Pre-Algebra 2 with Economics.* You are now ready for high school mathematics.

FOUR COURSES
BEGINNING ALGEBRA, ADVANCED ALGEBRA, GEOMETRY, AND TRIG

Every college asks, "How much math have you had?"

If you have had these four courses, you can answer, "I've had all of high school math."

In the government school system, each of these courses takes a year. It takes that long because they have football days, sick days, fire alarm days, teacher-training days, and holidays to "celebrate" things that most people aren't really celebrating.

Life of Fred: Beginning Algebra Expanded Edition presents more material than is usually taught in high school beginning algebra classes—and takes only 104 daily lessons.

For many students, the hardest part of beginning algebra is the word problems. You have already started working on word problems in the book you have just finished. Back in Chapter 24, you solved:

In one 20-minute quiet time, he first prepared his Gourmet Gauss Dogs. He could do that at the rate of 22/minute. Then for the rest of the 20 minutes he prepared his Hot Hot Dogs.

He could prepare his Hot Hot Dogs at the rate of 18/minute.

In that 20-minute period, he made as many Hot Hot Dogs as Gourmet Gauss Dogs. How long did he spend making the Gourmet Gauss Dogs?

That's not an easy word problem. If you don't believe me, show this problem to a friend of yours who is studying beginning algebra (also known as algebra 1) in a government school. You were doing this problem, and you are not even in algebra yet.

Next comes *Life of Fred: Advanced Algebra Expanded Edition.* 105 daily lessons. If you started in September, could you be done by Valentine's day? This book is a complete second course in algebra. Many other courses skip math induction proofs, linear programming, sigma notation, permutations, and the difference between the range and the codomain of a function.

Third is *Life of Fred: Geometry*. If you do three pages/day, you will finish the entire book in about 172 days. This book contains 13 regular chapters and 6 honors chapters (chapters 5½, 7½, 8½, 11½, 12½, and 13½). A standard high school geometry course omits these six honors chapters.

Even in the remaining 13 chapters, we will see a lot more geometry that most high school classrooms offer. For example, in *Life of Fred: Geometry* we'll do 46 ruler-and-compass constructions. Other courses may offer a dozen.

Fourth is *Life of Fred: Trigonometry Expanded Edition*. ("Expanded Edition" means that I work out in detail the answers to *every* problem in the book.) 94 daily lessons. And 15 of those lessons are *not* trigonometry but a looking ahead to what will be coming in calculus.

Trig deals with angles in triangles.

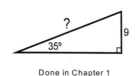

Done in Chapter 1

Done in Chapter 7